Psychological Recovery

Psychological Recovery

Beyond Mental Illness

Retta Andresen
Lindsay G. Oades
Peter Caputi

A John Wiley & Sons, Ltd., Publication

This edition first published 2011
© 2011 John Wiley & Sons, Ltd

Wiley-Blackwell is an imprint of John Wiley & Sons, formed by the merger of Wiley's global Scientific, Technical and Medical business with Blackwell Publishing.

Registered Office
John Wiley & Sons Ltd, The Atrium, Southern Gate, Chichester, West Sussex, PO19 8SQ, UK

Editorial Offices
The Atrium, Southern Gate, Chichester, West Sussex, PO19 8SQ, UK
350 Main Street, Malden, MA 02148-5020, USA
9600 Garsington Road, Oxford, OX4 2DQ, UK

For details of our global editorial offices, for customer services, and for information about how to apply for permission to reuse the copyright material in this book please see our website at www.wiley.com/wiley-blackwell.

The right of Retta Andresen, Lindsay G. Oades and Peter Caputi to be identified as the authors of this work has been asserted in accordance with the UK Copyright, Designs and Patents Act 1988.

Library of Congress Cataloging-in-Publication Data

Andresen, Retta.
  Psychological recovery : beyond mental illness / Retta Andresen, Lindsay G. Oades, Peter Caputi.
    p. ; cm.
  Includes bibliographical references and index.
  ISBN 978-0-470-71143-9 (hardback : alk. paper) – ISBN 978-0-470-71142-2 (pbk. : alk. paper)
  1. Mentally ill–Rehabilitation. 2. Psychotherapy. I. Oades, Lindsay G. II. Caputi, Peter. III. Title.
  [DNLM: 1. Mental Disorders–rehabilitation. 2. Mental Disorders–psychology. 3. Models, Psychological. 4. Outcome Assessment (Health Care) 5. Recovery of Function. WM 400]
  RC439.5A53 2011
  616.89'14–dc22

                                                                                            2011006418

A catalogue record for this book is available from the British Library.

This book is published in the following electronic formats: ePDFs 9781119975151; Wiley Online Library 9781119975182; ePub 9781119975168

Set in 10.5/13pt Minion by Thomson Digital, Noida, India
Printed in Singapore by Ho Printing Singapore Pte Ltd

1 2011

Dedication

This book is dedicated to all those people who have experienced mental illness and have generously shared their stories in print or taken part in research in order to further the understanding of mental illness and recovery.

Contents

Part II Elaboration of the Model: From Hopelessness to Flourishing

Part III Measuring Recovery

Part IV Towards a Positive Future

About the Authors

Retta Andresen
Dr Retta Andresen is a Research Fellow at the University of Wollongong, Australia. Her research interests were inspired by personal accounts of the experience of schizophrenia, which led to the development of the stage model of psychological recovery. She is committed to the use of the recovery model in mental health services. To that end, she has developed outcome measures to reflect the consumer recovery experience that have received international attention. Retta is a strong believer in positive psychological approaches in mental health, and worked to develop *Flourish*, a self-development programme of recovery. She is currently working on a project which trains mental health practitioners in the use of a recovery model that focuses on the identification of core values as the basis for a meaningful life.

Lindsay Oades
Dr Lindsay Oades is a Clinical and Health Psychologist and Director of the Australian Institute of Business Wellbeing, Sydney Business School, University of Wollongong, Australia. Lindsay works to combine principles of mental health recovery with positive psychology and positive organizational scholarship in order to develop approaches to recovery oriented services, including measurement of psychological recovery, the development of the Collaborative Recovery Model (CRM) and the *Flourish* self-development programme. During his career Lindsay has worked as a practitioner, manager, researcher, trainer and coach in the service of mental health. Lindsay currently chairs the Serious Mental Disorders Panel at the Illawarra Health and Medical Research Institute, and is on the Board of Directors of Neami, a major Australian mental health non-government organization.

Peter Caputi
Associate Professor Caputi's expertise is in the area of measurement, with particular interest in outcome measurement. His innovative work on measuring recovery from serious mental illness, in collaboration with Drs Retta Andresen and Lindsay Oades, has received national and international recognition. Peter is an active reviewer for *The Journal of Psychology: Interdisciplinary and Applied, Journal of Constructivist Psychology, Personal Construct Theory and Practice, Personality and Individual Differences, Australian Journal of Psychology, Clinical Schizophrenia & Related Psychoses*. He is also a consulting editor for the *Journal of Constructivist*

Psychology and *The Journal of Psychology: Interdisciplinary and Applied.* Since 2000, he has published over 100 peer-reviewed conference papers, journal articles, and book chapters and is currently teaching several statistics based subjects at the University of Wollongong.

Foreword

This book is written in the context of the consumer movement dating back to the 1960s. Alongside that movement, an evolving recovery movement specifically emphasised the empowerment of consumers to get on with their lives and to achieve the goals they choose to pursue and that they value. Some observers of history say that themes and principles of the recovery movement are more than 160 years old but have come to the fore only relatively recently.

My credentials are that I have experienced three mental illnesses since 1984 – paranoid schizophrenia, anxiety attacks and major depression – and have been involved with a modern day mental health service since 1988. I have lived in group homes, being case managed and encouraged to work on my recovery journey since then. My last hospital admission was in 1990. I have developed my role with the mental health service, initially as a Consumer Representative (both unpaid and paid), then as Coordinator of Consumer Initiatives, as a Community Development Officer and now as a Consumer Advocate working in hospital and community settings. I became aware of and exposed to recovery philosophy in the late 1990s.

Consumer workers can be great role models, and I had a good positive group of people around me who encouraged me in the early days after diagnosis. None of them told me I could not recover (unlike the experience of some of my friends). This gave me immense hope. But, like many people, after my diagnosis I reassessed my life and lowered my expectations of and for myself – in a very big way. My identity had taken a huge beating, and only after a long struggle (recovery is hard work) did I rebuild it. The core of this is a very strong world view based on our place in the universe and caring for our planet and all living things on it (live in harmony with the universe).

My job – I have the best job in the world – is now a big part of my identity and gives me a huge sense of meaning; but it is my interest and active participation in philosophy, science, astronomy, scrabble, my housing community and my local mental health fellowship that give me the greatest meaning. I have accepted that I have a mental illness and am moving on with my life and working on my recovery journey. I give back to my local community by doing a range of voluntary community development activities, and this is one way in which I have taken responsibility for my life. Working on my spiritual development (not to be confused with religious beliefs) by taking an interest in everything around me, and respecting and appreciating it, I try to be the best human being I can be in a rapidly changing technological world.

I first met and worked with Lindsay Oades on the Consumer Evaluation of Mental Health Services Project between 1999 and 2004. I soon learnt that Lindsay has immense understanding of and sensitivity to consumer needs, and his accuracy and meticulous attention to detail make him stand out against other researchers. I have also participated in the Collaborative Recovery Model Training with Lindsay. I met and worked with Retta Andresen on '*Flourish – A Recovery-Based Self Development Program*' in the late 2000s. Retta demonstrated great patience and tolerance for participants and facilitators, and showed significant insight into and understanding of those living with mental illness.

In my profession, as a consumer worker and as a mental health professional, we talk about treating each other (human being to human being) with respect and dignity as a foundation to working in a modern mental health setting. We expect all mental health professionals to treat their clients with this in mind. In working with the authors I have seen that they show the utmost care and consideration to their work colleagues and the people with whom they interact, and this is reflected in their understanding of recovery philosophy and the human condition.

The book opens with an examination and historical record of recovery from schizophrenia, showing that recovery from any mental illness is not only possible but highly likely. As schizophrenia has been seen as the most disabling and stigmatised mental illness, if recovery from schizophrenia is possible, recovery from other mental illnesses is perhaps even more attainable. The notion that recovery requires 'returning to a former state' (or a period in your life) is well examined as a myth and misunderstanding of recovery philosophy, and it is very important to see this highlighted here. The outstanding feature of the book is that the model of psychological recovery is based on thematic analysis of many 'real' personal recovery stories; and from these also emerged the major themes: finding and maintaining hope; taking responsibility for life and wellbeing; rebuilding a positive identity, and finding meaning and purpose in life. The stages of recovery - Moratorium, Awareness, Preparation, Rebuilding and Growth – are examined in detail with a separate chapter for each, and this forms the bulk of the text. The ideas therein are supported by many meticulously researched references.

I know the authors believe in life-long learning and have left no stone unturned to adapt, update and find new ways of incorporating new developments, initiatives and insights in philosophy, psychology and spirituality into their work. Chapter 8 explains how the ideas being developed in positive psychology are relevant to, and complement, recovery philosophy. These ideas can be especially useful in helping someone to get back on track and live the life that they want and value. Psychological recovery is clearly not just absence of symptoms, or about preventing symptoms, but something much bigger, a human growth process, promoting strengths and increasing wellbeing. This is explained clearly and developed in this chapter and I hope interested persons take note, for this is a major step forward in thinking about these issues.

The content of this book will be helpful to students of psychology and mental health, mental health staff, service providers, consumers and carers who want to further understand the recovery process as examined herein, how it relates to their life and how we can all better support persons living with mental health issues. I believe that this text will be a landmark in the development, understanding and uptake of personal psychological recovery in our communities.

On a wealthy planet like Earth, I think we are all entitled to, and deserve, a happy and rewarding life that encourages us to reach our growth potential; a life that we appreciate and respect. This book shows that this is possible, and an increased understanding of recovery philosophy, as demonstrated in the stage model of psychological recovery, may facilitate this for all human beings.

Jon R. Strang
Consumer Advocate
December, 2010

Preface

The moving stories that people with a mental illness have published were the inspiration for this work, and we are deeply indebted to all those people who have shared their experiences with others in order to enhance our understanding. We have written this book to share a model of psychological recovery from mental illness which was derived from many personal accounts. There is a large and growing scholarly literature on recovery, most of which is in broad agreement about the elements of recovery and the many influences on the course of mental illness and its impact on the individual. Our model focuses on the intrapersonal psychological aspects, and does not include external factors such as employment, housing or other social factors. Although these are all extremely important to recovery, they are not the focus of the model. The simplicity of the model brings structure to a very complex field, and has proven to be a useful heuristic in clinical work, education and research. The book elaborates on the model, which was originally published in a journal article (Andresen *et al.*, 2003), and presents our ongoing work, in the hope of furthering understanding of recovery and contributing towards the scientific endeavour of advancing recovery-oriented practice. Although aimed primarily at mental health professionals and students, we hope a wider audience will find the book interesting and informative, particularly people with a mental illness and their loved ones, who may find hope within these pages.

Throughout the book, we have used the term 'consumer' – synonymous with 'service user' or 'user' in the UK – to describe a person who has experienced mental illness. We acknowledge that not all people with a mental illness use mental health services, and are therefore not consumers in this context. We are also aware of, and deeply respect, the preference for other terminology, including 'survivor' and 'ex-patient'. However, even these terms do not apply to all. Since there is broad consensus on the term 'consumer' in the literature, and the book is aimed primarily at professionals, we have adopted this word for simplicity's sake.

In Part I we look at the concept of recovery. Schizophrenia may be considered an exemplar of mental illness, having historically had the worst prognosis. Due to the severity of the illness, there is a large body of literature on the course and outcome of schizophrenia, which provided us with the empirical evidence for recovery. Chapter 1 sets the scene for the book with a historical background of the concept of schizophrenia. It covers how recovery from schizophrenia came to be considered impossible, how this notion was disproved by empirical research, and the reasons for its persistence. The chapter also introduces the consumer recovery movement, and the difference between clinical definitions of recovery and the consumer definition. In Chapter 2 we describe our exploration of what consumers say about recovery, and the psychological processes that they describe. Because this research used earlier consumer accounts, these were less likely to have been influenced by the then burgeoning recovery literature and thus imbued with the language of recovery. This enhances the authenticity of the consumers' voices. These stories led us to a definition of psychological recovery. We also reviewed qualitative studies, and found that a number of researchers had described similar phases of recovery, although they identified varying numbers of phases or stages. From the experiential accounts and qualitative studies, we gleaned the elements of the stage model of psychological recovery, consisting of four psychological processes that develop across five stages.

Part II elaborates on the model, stage by stage. Chapters 3 to 7 each examine the four processes of recovery within one of the five stages. The discussion is structured around quotes from the consumer stories, and for this we have included some more recent consumer literature. We draw parallels between aspects of recovery and concepts in the broader psychology literature, culminating with the Growth stage, in which we expand on the themes of resilience and wisdom. Chapter 8 addresses some issues and criticisms relating to the model, such as the assertion that recovery is a highly individual and non-linear process, and therefore cannot be 'modelled'. In order to apply the recovery model to the advancement of research and the enhancement of mental health services, it is necessary to develop measures of recovery, and in Part III we describe our empirical work. Chapter 9 covers our work on developing and testing three approaches to recovery measurement based on the model. These measures have received international attention. The chapter under-lines the complexity of this task and the need for more empirical research into the process of recovery and its measurement.

Part IV presents the implications of the model and directions for future research. The recovery literature has clear parallels with that of the positive psychology movement, and these are highlighted in Chapter 10. We explore ways in which the tenets of positive psychology can combine with the recovery literature in developing programmes for promoting recovery. Examples of such programmes, which have been developed with colleagues at the University of Wollongong, are described.

In conclusion, Chapter 11 serves to reflect on our findings, describe some current applications of the model and measures and propose directions for future research. We hope this book will be an inspiration for service providers, researchers, people with a mental illness and their families.

Retta Andresen
Lindsay G. Oades
Peter Caputi
University of Wollongong
November, 2010

Acknowledgements

The authors wish to thank all the people who have contributed to the publication of this book. Most importantly, we wish to thank the people living with a mental illness who published stories of their experiences and recovery. These have provided the foundations of our research, and enriched the text of the book. We also thank the mental health practitioners who participated in collecting data for our research, and their clients who consented to the use of their data for publication.

We would also like to thank our families. Retta especially thanks her husband John, children Mandy, Tony, Paul and Kat, Dave and Jess, parents Martin and Janet, and her brothers and sisters for their love, encouragement and support. Lindsay would like to thank his wife Alison and two sons Bodhi and Jai. Peter wishes to thank Elayne, James and Jack for their support and encouragement. We also wish to thank editor Karen Shield for her assistance, publisher Andy Peart and the team at John Wiley & Sons for their work in bringing this book to publication.

Part I
Recovery in Historical Context

1

Introduction: Recovery from Schizophrenia

Overview

In this chapter, schizophrenia serves as an exemplar of a most serious form of mental illness, which historically has been difficult to understand, classify or treat. As such, it has been widely researched over many years, generating a large body of empirical research into recovery. Much of the consumer-oriented qualitative research into recovery, however, includes other mental illnesses Therefore, we have utilized the empirical research into schizophrenia to provide 'hard evidence' for recovery from mental illness before expanding our work to incorporate the consumer-oriented literature.

Here we put into historical perspective how the idea that there was no hope of recovery from schizophrenia became entrenched within the mental health profession. First we present an historical overview of concepts of schizophrenia, and how these influenced diagnostic systems and prognosis. Next, we present findings from longitudinal and cross-cultural research that show that recovery, in the medical sense – that is, freedom from signs and symptoms of mental illness – occurs more frequently than once believed, and discuss why the rate of recovery went unrecognized for most of the twentieth century.

We then look at how the consumer recovery movement grew from diverse ideological standpoints, and how the consumer movement describes a form of recovery in addition to the traditional medical meaning of the term. Finally we conclude that there is a need for consensus on the consumer definition of recovery, which can be operationalized, in order to meet demands for evidence-based practice with a recovery orientation.

Psychological Recovery: Beyond Mental Illness, First Edition.
Retta Andresen, Lindsay G. Oades and Peter Caputi.
© 2011 John Wiley & Sons, Ltd. Published 2011 by John Wiley & Sons, Ltd.

Early Conceptualizations of Schizophrenia

A diagnosis of schizophrenia has traditionally been considered tantamount to a 'prognosis of doom' (Deegan, 1997, p.16), which denied all hope of recovery or even of a reasonably satisfying life. Mental health professionals, in particular medical professionals, have a pessimistic outlook regarding the prognosis for schizophrenia (Hugo, 2001; Jorm *et al.*, 1999). The idea that schizophrenia had an inevitable deteriorating course culminating in a life which revolved around stabilization, medication management and survival, has its roots in early descriptions, in which chronicity was considered a criterion for schizophrenia. The earliest description of schizophrenia was that of Emil Kraepelin, who, over many years of clinical observation, asserted that the diseases then known as hebephrenia, catatonia, and paranoia were all characterized by commencement in adolescence followed by a progressively deteriorating course culminating in dementia (1913, cited in Weiner, 1966/1997; Turner, 1999). Kraepelin believed that these diseases all had a common aetiology, course and outcome, and should be identified as forms of a single disorder, *dementia praecox*, the fundamental criterion for which was its outcome, dementia (Turner, 1999; Pull, 2002). Kraepelin considered the illness to be an irreversible disease of the brain, probably caused by autointoxication – toxicity due to metabolic or other bodily processes (Turner, 1999) – and was not open to the idea that any symptoms of the illness could have psychological underpinnings (Weiner, 1966/1997). Although 12% of Kraepelin's patients made a complete, or almost-complete, recovery (Warner, 2004), he felt that those who recovered had been incorrectly diagnosed, as an outcome of dementia was fundamental to the disease (Weiner, 1966/1997; Read, Mosher and Bentall, 2004).

Eugen Bleuler, on the other hand, did not think that dementia was an essential aspect of the disease, and he noted that the illness did not always commence in adolescence (E. Bleuler, 1911/1950). He asserted that the fundamental symptom of schizophrenia was a 'splitting' of the various psychic functions – a loosening of associations between ideas and incongruous emotional responses. Bleuler coined the term *schizophrenia*, which comes from the Greek for 'to split' (schizin) and 'mind' (phren), and advocated the use of this term to replace *dementia praecox* (E. Bleuler, 1911/1950). Bleuler elaborated on Kraepelin's formulation of *dementia praecox* with a number of new concepts. First, he argued that symptoms could range over a continuum from the almost unnoticeable to the most florid; second, he claimed that the label schizophrenia could apply to people who are making reasonable life adjustments in the community, with no psychotic symptoms; and third, he asserted that, although a person may be socially reinstated after an acute episode, residual symptoms were always present (Weiner, 1966/1997). Bleuler also argued that schizophrenia was not one single illness, but rather a group of several diseases with different aetiologies, courses and outcomes (Pull, 2002). He added two new subgroups: *simple schizophrenia*, which broadened the concept of schizophrenia considerably (to apparently include those who hold menial jobs and bad housewives who are nagging shrews); and *latent schizophrenia*, which parallels later concepts of schizoid and schizotypal personality (Wing, 1999). Bleuler's conceptualization of schizophrenia was much more psychodynamic than was Kraepelin's, and he believed that there was a link between symptoms of schizophrenia and psychological processes (Weiner, 1966/1997). Bleuler posited that the symptoms of schizophrenia may be the result of psychological factors, but was unsure as to the underlying cause of the disease. He concluded that schizophrenia was a group of disorders, some endogenous (and therefore organic), and some reactive (and therefore psychological) (E. Bleuler, 1911/1950; Clare, 1980). The organic form carried a worse prognosis than the reactive form.

In contrast to those of Kraepelin, 60% of Bleuler's patients recovered well enough to work and support themselves outside hospital. There are a number of possible explanations for this difference in outcome. First, Bleuler broadened the definition of schizophrenia to include those with a better prognosis; and second, Kraepelin would have defined recovery as freedom from symptoms, rather than social functioning (Warner, 2004). However, we cannot overlook the effects of Bleuler's more psychodynamic perspective, and his belief that there were psychogenic causes for much of the observed symptomatology (Warner, 2004). This point of view resulted in a more therapeutic approach to treatment, in which great importance was placed on minimizing hospital-based care, on the quality of the person's environment, and on providing opportunities for work (Warner, 2004). Although Bleuler did not agree that schizophrenia necessarily resulted in dementia, neither did he believe that people ever fully recovered: 'Personally I have never treated a patient who has proved on close examination to be entirely free from signs of the illness' (E. Bleuler, 1911/1950, p. 256).

These early formulations of Kraepelin and Bleuler have had long-reaching effects. With no firm evidence of its aetiology, schizophrenia has continued to be conceptualized and classified in terms of its clinical manifestations. Theorists have classified the symptoms of schizophrenia on a number of dimensions, in attempts to improve diagnosis and prognosis. In terms of diagnosing schizophrenia, the formulations of Bleuler (1911/1950) and Schneider (cited in Pull, 2002) have been widely influential. Bleuler differentiated *fundamental* symptoms from *accessory* symptoms. The fundamental symptoms – disturbances in association and affect, ambivalence and autism – were always present in schizophrenia, while the accessory symptoms – including hallucinations and delusions – may or may not be present, and may also be present in other illnesses. The fundamental symptoms were direct manifestations of the disorder, and therefore necessary for a diagnosis of schizophrenia, whereas the accessory symptoms were psychological reactions to the illness, and were not required for a diagnosis (E. Bleuler, 1911/1950; Pull, 2002). In contrast to Bleuler, Schneider (1950, cited in Pull, 2002) held that such symptoms as hallucinations and delusions were pathognomonic of schizophrenia. That is, these symptoms alone were sufficient to give a diagnosis of schizophrenia. Schneider differentiated between abnormal *experiences* and abnormal *expressions* (1950, cited in Pull, 2002). He identified 11 first-rank symptoms, which can be grouped into three categories: passivity experiences, in which thoughts, emotions and actions are felt to be externally controlled; auditory hallucinations in the third person; and primary delusions, which arise suddenly and without explanation from a normal perception (Clare, 1980). These abnormal experiences he called 'first-rank' symptoms, and the presence of any one of these was sufficient for a diagnosis of schizophrenia. 'Second-rank' symptoms included disturbances in language, writing and movement, affective symptoms and emotional blunting, all of which could occur in other illnesses (Clare, 1980). A diagnosis of schizophrenia could also be given when only second-rank symptoms were present (Schneider, 1950, cited in Pull, 2002).

Whereas Kraepelin's definition of schizophrenia was based on onset, course and prognosis, Bleuler focused on the dissociative symptoms and Schneider emphasized the importance of the psychotic symptoms such as hallucinations and delusions. All three formulations have been influential to varying degrees in different diagnostic systems until the present day, including the *Diagnostic and Statistical Manual of Mental Disorders* (4th Edition) (DSM-IV; American Psychiatric Association, 1994), the tenth revision of the *International Classification of Diseases and Related Health Problems* (ICD-10; World Health Organization, 1992) and Present State Examination (PSE; Wing, Cooper and Sartorius, 1974).

Diagnostic Systems and Prognostic Pessimism

For the first half of the twentieth century, there was no universal or even widespread definition of schizophrenia. In the United States, the strong psychoanalytic tradition led to a leaning towards Bleuler's broader definition, while in the United Kingdom, Schneider's first-rank symptoms were dominant, and in Europe diagnosis was largely based on Kraepelin's prognostic approach (Clare, 1980). Different countries, even different schools within a country, had widely differing conceptualizations of schizophrenia (Leff, 1988). The first classification systems for mental disorders were published in the mid-twentieth century. The World Health Organization (WHO) included mental disorders in the sixth edition of the *International Classification of Diseases, Injuries and Causes of Death* (ICD-6; WHO, 1948) and the American Psychiatric Association (APA) published the first edition of the *Diagnostic and Statistical Manual* in 1952 (DSM I; APA, 1952). However, diagnosis of schizophrenia was much more frequent in the United States than it was in the United Kingdom or Europe. Two major research programmes highlighted this problem. The United States–United Kingdom Diagnostic Project (Cooper *et al.*, 1972) found that there were almost twice as many people admitted to hospital with a diagnosis of schizophrenia in the USA than in the UK. In addition, when UK psychiatrists diagnosed the USA schizophrenia patients, only approximately 50% were given the same diagnosis (Cooper *et al.*, 1972). The WHO then conducted the International Pilot Study of Schizophrenia (IPSS), a transcultural research project that compared diagnostic practices across nine countries (WHO, 1973). Again it was found that many patients diagnosed with schizophrenia in the United States would have been given a diagnosis of neurosis in other centres.

Following from these studies, the DSM-III (APA, 1980) represented a major change in official diagnostic procedures, advocating the use of operationally defined phenomenological criteria based on Schneider's (1957, cited in Leff, 1988) first-rank symptoms, and specifying a minimum duration of illness of six months (Leff, 1988). As a consequence, the DSM-III diagnostic criteria were much narrower than those of its predecessors, or even the ICD criteria (Leff, 1988), which still retains simple schizophrenia, a diagnosis not requiring any psychotic symptoms (Bertelsen, 2002). The DSM-III took an atheoretical approach to classification which avoided descriptions based on an assumed aetiology, although a chronic course was still emphasized (Carpenter and Buchanan, 1994). It was not until work began on the tenth edition of the ICD (ICD-10; WHO, 1992) that international efforts were made to coordinate diagnostic criteria, mainly for the purposes of research. As a result, diagnostic criteria for schizophrenia in the fourth edition of the DSM (DSM-IV; APA, 1994) and the ICD-10 are much more closely aligned than previous systems. The ICD-10 continues to give diagnostic importance to Schneider's first-rank symptoms, and, although the DSM-IV states that no single symptom is pathognomonic for schizophrenia, the presence of 'bizarre' delusions, or auditory hallucinations consisting of a voice giving a running commentary on the person's behaviour, or two voices conversing, are sufficient to meet the psychosis criterion for schizophrenia.

Kraepelin's belief that all mental illnesses arise from biological causes has tended to dominate psychiatric classification systems. It was not until the DSM-IV that any remaining distinction between organic and psychological disorders was eliminated (Barlow and Durand, 1995). In practice, Bleuler's broad definitions of 'simple' and 'latent' schizophrenia became coupled to Kraepelin's organic formulation, giving a wide range of disagreeable behaviour the weight of a medical diagnosis (Wing, 1999). Thus the pessimistic prognosis inherent in Kraepelin's early formulation became incorporated into the expectations of those professionals who were using Bleuler's more inclusive definition, with the result that people who were diagnosed with schizophrenia on even the most loosely-defined criteria were not expected to recover.

Empirical Evidence for Recovery

Despite the pessimistic culture within psychiatry which flowed on to inform societal expectations and ultimately those of the afflicted individual and his or her family, there is a growing literature surrounding the notion of recovery from schizophrenia. The concept of recovery started gaining momentum in the 1980s, when people with schizophrenia began publishing accounts of their recovery. These accounts revealed that many had managed to overcome the problems imposed by the illness and went on to enjoy a full and meaningful life. Influential consumer advocates have been working towards breaking down the notion that schizophrenia necessarily has a long-term deteriorating course, for example, Curtis (2000), Deegan (1997), Fisher (1994), Frese (2000) and Schmook (1996). Autobiographical evidence of a more positive outlook for schizophrenia is supported by a number of quantitative studies, including longitudinal and cross-cultural studies of outcome.

Longitudinal studies of outcome

The Vermont longitudinal study was a landmark study of long-term outcomes of schizophrenia (Harding *et al.*,1987a, 1987b). This research involved 269 of the most disabled, long-stay patients who had been ill for an average of 16 years, had been totally disabled for 10 years and hospitalized continuously for six years. During the era of deinstitutionalization in the mid-1950s, these patients, who had not responded well to modern drug therapy, took part in a comprehensive rehabilitation programme. Ten years after their release from hospital, 70% remained out of hospital. The study used blind raters and comprehensive, reliable, structured protocols, including the Global Assessment Scale (Endicott, Spitzer and Fliess, 1976), the Strauss–Carpenter Levels of Functioning Scale (Hawk, Carpenter and Strauss, 1975) and 13 other well-established measures. It was found at follow-up 20 to 25 years later, that 68% were functioning at a level most people would consider 'normal' (Harding *et al.*, 1987a). When restricting the cohort to those who retrospectively met the DSM-III criteria for schizophrenia, 34% were found to have achieved full recovery, and a further 34% to have achieved significant improvement in both psychiatric status and social functioning. The criteria were strict and included: living in the community, being employed, not using psychiatric medications, being free of symptoms, not having behaviours that would be considered those of a 'mental patient', and having good relationships with others (Harding *et al.*, 1987b). Harding and colleagues have championed the cause of heterogeneous outcome expectations for schizophrenia. In a review of longitudinal studies, Harding, Zubin and Strauss (1987) noted a number of methodological problems with earlier studies that had produced contradictory results. They therefore proceeded to review the more recent, methodologically sound studies of the time and found that poor outcomes were much less common than had been previously assumed.

The Harding, Zubin and Strauss, (1987) review included the Vermont study and four other long-term studies: M. Bleuler (1972/1978), Tsuang, Woolson and Fleming (1979), Huber *et al.* (1980) and Ciompi and Muller (1976). Combining the results of the five studies, Harding, Zubin and Strauss (1987) found that, of over 1300 ex-patients, one-half to two-thirds had recovered or significantly improved. A number of more recent studies have lent further support to these findings. For example, in a five-year follow up study of a cohort of 70 schizophrenia patients, good social functioning was recorded in 62% of the entire cohort, and a good outcome in terms of combined symptoms and hospital admissions for 58% of the first-admission cohort (Shepherd *et al.*, 1989). Harrison *et al.* (1993) explored 15- and 25-year follow-up outcomes of 644 subjects from the WHO International Study of Schizophrenia (ISoS; Sartorius *et al.*, 1996). Using Bleuler's (1972/1978) scale, 48% of the 15-year incidence cohort and 54% of the 25-year prevalence cohort were rated as recovered, meaning 'he could be fully employed in meaningful work and resume his former role in society' (Bleuler, 1972/1978, p. 191). Furthermore, 42% of the total cohort had not experienced a psychotic episode in the past two years. Mason *et al.* (1995) conducted a 13-year follow-up study on an incidence cohort of 67 patients. Using measures including positive and negative symptoms, social disability, functioning and treatment status, they found that 44% achieved a 'mild' or 'recovered-treated' outcome. Using a definition of 'complete recovery' as no symptoms, no disability and no treatment, 17% of the sample were completely recovered at follow-up, while using Bleuler's criteria, approximately 57% were recovered. Harrow *et al.* (2005) conducted a prospective 15-year follow-up study. Recovery was defined as status over the follow-up year based on the following criteria: absence of psychotic or negative symptoms, adequate psychosocial functioning including at least half-time employment (not necessarily paid), absence of poor social activity level, and no psychiatric hospitalizations. Harrow *et al.* found that at 15 years, 19% of the schizophrenia cohort were in recovery. In addition, they found that, over the course of 15 years, 41% of patients had been in recovery at some point, demonstrating that schizophrenia was not necessarily chronic and continuous, but episodic in nature. It is worth noting that the criteria for recovery in some of these studies perhaps describe a higher level of functioning than would be met by many people who do not have a mental illness or other disability.

Cross-cultural studies

In addition to the longitudinal studies conducted in the United States, United Kingdom and Europe, cross-cultural studies have found sociocultural differences in outcome. A number of studies have found that outcome from schizophrenia is better in developing than in developed countries.[1] Warner (2004) reviewed follow-up studies conducted in Third World countries. Warner's review included a number of studies from India, as well as studies in China, Mauritius, Sri Lanka, Hong Kong, Singapore, Nigeria and Bali that were published between 1971 and 2001. The follow-up intervals for these studies varied from one to 15 years. The majority of the studies found better outcomes than would be expected in Western countries, with two exceptions: Chandigargh, India and Sichuan, China. These two centres did not return substantially better outcomes than achieved in Western countries. However,

---

[1] There has been some criticism of the dichotomy 'developed/developing', as some centres, although non-Western, are nonetheless developed (e.g. Hong Kong). Other terminology used is 'industrialized/ non-industrialized', 'Western/Non-Western' and 'Third World'. We use terminology consistent with that of the author cited.

the Indian study can be faulted by the high percentage of subjects lost to follow-up. Only 57% of the original Indian sample could be traced for follow-up, a group that included those who had remained in hospital, but did not include those who had moved on (Warner, 2004). The Sichuan results can perhaps be explained by the fact that the sample was a point prevalence cohort, which, since it includes those who have already demonstrated a long-term course, will be biased towards poorer outcomes (Warner, 2004).

Comparing findings of studies conducted in various countries may be limited by the method of identification of subjects, differences in diagnostic practices and in measurement of outcome. To address these issues, the WHO conducted two standardized international follow-up studies into schizophrenia (WHO, 1979; Jablensky *et al.*, 1992). The IPSS research project, described earlier, compared outcomes from nine centres: Aarhus, Denmark; Agra, India; Cali, Colombia; Ibadan, Nigeria; London, Moscow, Prague, Taipei and Washington, DC; representing both developed and developing centres (WHO, 1973). Patients were evaluated using a standardized system, the PSE, enabling comparison of similar subjects across developed and developing centres. Five outcome categories were devised from the results of a two-year follow-up. The best outcome was described as full symptom remission, no social impairment and less than four months of psychosis during the two-year follow-up period (WHO, 1979). An unexpected finding from this study was that 35% of patients from developing countries fell in the best recovery category, compared with only 15% of patients from the developed centres.

One possible explanation for these results is that of selection bias in developing countries. Leff (1988) posited that those people who are violent or disruptive to the community may be more likely to be referred for treatment in developing countries, and at the same time, may have a better prognosis than others (Leff, 1988). However, in a review, Leff (1988), found that these characteristics were not associated with better prognosis, nor were they a source of selection bias. The possibility of selection bias was minimized in a second international WHO study, the Determinants of Outcome of Severe Mental Disorders (DOSMeD; Jablensky *et al.*, 1992). In this study, care was taken – including contacting traditional healers – to locate all patients at centres in 10 countries who had made their initial contact with help services during the study period. The study encompassed 12 centres across 10 countries: Aarhus, Denmark; Agra and Chandigarh, India; Cali, Colombia; Dublin, Ireland; Honolulu and Rochester, United States; Ibadan, Nigeria; Moscow, Russia; Nagasaki, Japan; Nottingham, United Kingdom; and Prague, Czechoslovakia (Jablensky *et al.*, 1992).

One- and two-year follow-up data confirmed the findings of earlier studies, with a more benign course and better outcome in developing countries. Sixty-three per cent of cases in developing countries were in the best outcome group, compared with 37% of those in developed countries. In contrast, 16% of patients in developing countries were in the worst outcome group – impairment in functioning throughout the follow-up period – compared with 42% of cases in developed countries (Jablensky *et al.*, 1992). Interestingly, the two strongest predictors of two-year course and outcome were found to be type of onset and setting (developed versus developing country; Jablensky *et al.*, 1992). Using an alternative analytic procedure on the data, Craig *et al.* (1997) found that the strongest predictor of course was 'centre', but with two developed centres grouping with the developing centres, and one developing centre grouping with the developed centres. Hopper and Wanderling (Hopper, 2004; Hopper and Wanderling, 2000) further explored these outcome differences in a 15-year follow-up study of only the incidence cohort of the WHO ISoS studies. They found that a more favourable outcome for developing centres was consistent on all outcome measures, even when different diagnostic groupings were used (ICD-10 schizophrenia, broad-spectrum schizophrenia and all psychoses). As well, a 15-year follow-up study of the DOSMeD incidence cohort also found that 'centre' was the second strongest predictor of outcome after 'short-term course' (Harrison *et al.*, 2001).

Why should it be that developing countries, which often lack the facilities and resources of the West, consistently show better outcomes for schizophrenia? These studies suggested that environmental factors had a profound impact on the course and outcome of schizophrenia, although some researchers have questioned the validity of this conclusion.

Explanations for cross-cultural differences

Some explanations for the observed cross-cultural differences in outcomes for schizophrenia question the methodology of the studies, while others describe cultural factors that may affect outcome. If the differences can be explained by poor methodology, then we can retain the assumption that the natural course of schizophrenia ends in a poor outcome. However, if methodological problems can be ruled out, we need to examine cultural factors that may explain the better outcomes in non-Western countries, in an effort to understand the processes of recovery.

Methodological sources of bias. The WHO studies were designed to minimize diagnostic artefact, with clinicians undergoing training in the use of the PSE, and having to demonstrate reliability during the study both within and across centres. In addition, in the DOSMeD study, diagnoses were reviewed by WHO experts. Nonetheless, Hopper and colleagues discussed several sources of potential bias and offered evidence to counter each of these issues (Hopper and Wanderling, 2000; Hopper, 2004).

- *Attrition pattern.* Although efforts were made to reduce selection bias, Hopper and Wanderling (2000) explored the possibility of systematic bias in attrition rates. They found that the rates of loss to follow-up were comparable across centres. Furthermore, it was found that in developed countries, the subjects with a more favourable early course of illness were more likely to be traced for follow-up. Therefore the data would more likely be skewed in favour of developed countries (Hopper and Wanderling, 2000).

- *Arbitrary grouping.* The 'developing/developed' dichotomy used in the WHO studies has been criticized. One centre that stands out is Hong Kong, which was categorized as 'developing' (Hopper, 2004). However, when reanalysed with Hong Kong in the 'developed' group, differences in symptoms were reduced, but differences in functioning became greater. The overall change in results was small. So although the terminology may be inappropriate, there are unidentified differences between the groups that affect outcome (Hopper and Wanderling, 2000).
- *Diagnostic ambiguities.* Although the WHO studies were designed to minimize potential differences in diagnostic practices, there was a possibility that a higher percentage of 'non-acute remitting psychosis' (NARP) in the developing countries may bias the results. When the results were reanalysed excluding these subjects, recovery rates remained significantly better in developing countries (Hopper and Wanderling, 2000). Even when all single-episode cases were excluded from the analysis, recovery rates favoured developing countries (Hopper, 2004).
- *Gender or age bias.* Since female gender has been found to predict better outcome, Hopper and Wanderling (2000) compared gender differences in the initial cohort, the follow-up group, and in recovery rates. No significant differences were found. Older subjects also had better prospects of recovery. However, the developing centres had proportionally more young subjects, so age was not a source of bias favouring developing countries.

If the results of the cross-cultural studies are indeed veritable, then we must consider the properties of non-Western cultures that distinguish them from Western cultures and may be conducive to better outcomes.

Sociocultural factors. Leff (1988) identified two main classes of social factors that may influence the differences in outcomes: the attitude of the patient's family, and the ease with which the person can be reintegrated into society. However, both these factors are likely to be influenced by community attitudes towards mental illness generally, as demonstrated by the degree of stigma attached to the illness.

- *Labelling and stigma.* There are differences between industrialized and traditional cultures in labelling and in opportunities to integrate into the community. Warner (2004) provides many examples of Third World countries in which mental illness is considered the work of spirits. The afflicted person bears no blame for their condition, as the cause is from outside the person. Furthermore, in some cultures a person may actually gain increased status from treatment rituals (Warner, 2004). In contrast, in Western nations, the label 'schizophrenia' comes with a constellation of blame, fear and discrimination, affecting every aspect of life (e.g. Kruger, 2000; Warner, 2004).
- *Family relationships.* Relapse rates have been found to be higher for people who live with family who are very critical or emotionally overinvolved compared with

those who live with less emotional relatives (Leff, 1988). The typical Western family is nuclear, with more emotional investment between individual family members, whereas people in developing countries tend to live in extended families. Leff suggests that the resultant lower emotional involvement may be a positive factor in recovery. The degree of emotional involvement across countries has been found to be related to the degree of Westernization, and one of the factors posited for this was the degree to which a person was held responsible for his or her symptoms (Leff, 1988).

- *Care within the community.* In developing countries there is less likelihood of the hospitalization and segregation from the family and community typical of Western styles of treatment (Bresnahan *et al.*, 2003). In some countries, such as India, the person stays within the home, and the family is closely involved in treatment and support (Bresnahan *et al.*, 2003). As well, communities themselves in developing countries may be more cohesive and conducive to recovery than industrialized centres (Bresnahan *et al.*, 2003), and community involvement in care can reduce family tensions (Warner, 2004).
- *Informal economies.* It has been shown that employment is beneficial to recovery (e.g. Bell, Lysaker and Milstein, 1996). Warner (2004) argues that there may be greater opportunity to carry out meaningful work roles in developing countries. Non-competitive subsistence economies provide a natural gradation of work (Kruger, 2000). The person can work at his or her current ability levels and their contribution is valued, whereas in a wage-based economy, the mentally ill are the lowest on the employment hierarchy, often considered less employable than ex-convicts (Warner, 2004).

These features of non-Western cultures may promote recovery from mental illnesses. With so much evidence for the possibility of recovery from schizophrenia, the reason for the pervasiveness of pessimistic expectations and the prevalence of poor outcomes in the West must be explored.

The Persistence of a Pessimistic Prognosis

Although there is a body of literature describing and attempting to explain a more benign course of schizophrenia in the latter half of the twentieth century (e.g. Harrison and Mason, 1993; Zubin, Magaziner and Steinhauer, 1983), this notion has been disputed by a number of researchers. Meta-analyses conducted by Hegarty *et al.* (1994) and Warner (2004) failed to find unequivocal improvements in outcome between early and late twentieth century studies. Although there was an improvement in outcomes around mid-twentieth century, this was followed by a decline from the 1970s, with the percentage of good outcomes at the end of the century comparable to that at the beginning (Hegarty *et al.*, 1994). The most surprising finding was from Warner's (2004) meta-analysis, which focused solely on developed countries. No improvement in outcomes was found in Western countries in the periods before and after the introduction of antipsychotic medications (Warner, 2004). Moreover, although a decrease in hospital use between 1945 and 1955 was associated with an improvement in recovery rates, the later introduction of antipsychotics brought no further improvement in symptoms or social functioning (Warner, 2004). Why do poor outcomes persist in the West? A number of explanations have been put forward.

Sampling bias and the 'clinician's illusion'

Kraepelin's conviction that schizophrenia had a deteriorating course culminating in dementia was most likely a result of sampling bias. Kraepelin's patients may well have been ill for some time before entering hospital and, once admitted, were likely to remain in hospital for custodial care (Harding, Zubin and Strauss, 1987). The effects of institutionalization are discussed below. M. Bleuler (1972/1978) pointed out that his father's (E. Bleuler) initially quite optimistic prognosis for schizophrenia gradually became more pessimistic during his yearly visits to his former clinic after the First World War. He found that most of the patients seemed to have deteriorated. However, in E. Bleuler's facility, there was an emphasis on early release and finding patients placements in the community (Warner, 2004). E. Bleuler was therefore seeing only the more unwell patients (M. Bleuler, 1972/1978). Therefore, both of these early psychiatrists were observing only the most severely ill patients (Harding, Zubin and Strauss, 1992).

In the day-to-day work of the clinician, a similar effect is known as the 'clinician's illusion' (Harding, Zubin and Strauss, 1987). The clinician sees only a cross-section of people who have been diagnosed with schizophrenia, which is biased towards those who need long-term care (Harding, Zubin and Strauss, 1987). They are denied feedback from clients who never used the service, or who no longer need the service, and therefore gain a distorted impression of the course and outcome of the illness, leading to an expectation amongst professionals of poor outcome (Harding, Zubin and Strauss, 1987; Kruger, 2000).

Circularity in diagnosis

Kraepelin's original prognosis, which was influenced by the clinician's illusion and sampling bias, became intertwined with the diagnosis of schizophrenia. When one of Kraepelin's patients improved, he assumed that there had been an error in diagnosis (Harding, Zubin and Strauss, 1987). In attempting to increase reliability of diagnosis internationally, the DSM-III introduced a narrower definition of schizophrenia, which incorporated prognosis in the diagnosis, with the criterion that the symptoms should have been present for at least six months (APA, 1980). Therefore, people who otherwise meet all the criteria for schizophrenia are diagnosed differently if they improve. Thus, the classification of schizophrenia *excludes* people who recover (Kruger, 2000).

The DSM-III (APA, 1980), which was current until 1994, included the statements: 'The most common course is one of acute exacerbation with increasing residual impairments between episodes' (p. 185), and 'A complete return to premorbid functioning is ... so rare ... that some clinicians would question the diagnosis' (p. 185). The current DSM-IV (APA, 1994) continues to encourage pessimism, stating that a return to premorbid functioning is 'probably not common' (p. 282).

Sensitive to the stigma and negative prognosis attached to schizophrenia, some clinicians may withhold diagnosis of schizophrenia until a chronic course has been established (Weiner, 1966/1997). A paradoxical consequence of this is that the belief in a poor outcome for schizophrenia is reinforced. In addition, treatment may not be timely, further jeopardizing optimal outcome (Weiner, 1966/1997).

Treatment effects

Medication effects. First, conventional medications have been shown to cause some of the 'negative symptoms' and cognitive deficits that are attributed to the illness itself (Gerlach and Larsen, 1999; Velligan and Miller, 1999). The neuroleptic-induced deficit syndrome (NIDS), which includes anhedonia, apathy, feelings of emptiness and slowing of thought processes, can be misinterpreted as disease symptoms. In addition, the benefits of antipsychotics are equivocal (Warner, 2004). Long-term use can cause a dependency in which withdrawal could exacerbate symptoms. This effect has been interpreted by some researchers as a demonstration of the success of the medication in controlling symptoms. However, a number of studies have demonstrated that, for patients who enter treatment with a good prognosis, antipsychotics can, by this action, bring about a poorer course of illness (Warner, 2004). Ironically, this may be one reason for the more benign course in developing countries, where there is likely to be less access to medications than in the West.

The newer 'atypical' antipsychotics have been shown to have fewer extrapyramidal side-effects, reduce secondary negative symptoms (Kopelowicz *et al.*, 2000) and improve cognitive functioning (Manschreck *et al.*, 1999; McGurk, 1999), thereby increasing the possibility of successful rehabilitation (Noordsy and O'Keefe, 1999). Whether or not the newer antipsychotics will have the same detrimental effects on outcome as the conventional medications has yet to be shown (Warner, 2004).

Institutionalization. Findings of earlier studies, and research that included patients who experienced long-term hospitalization before the deinstitutionalization period which began in the mid-twentieth century, would have been confounded by the effects of institutionalization. Goffman (1968) described the processes by which patients in asylums were denied their personal history and encouraged to take on the life of a mental patient. If a person resisted the patient identity, 'Consequently he may avoid talking to anyone . . . so as to avoid ratifying any interaction that presses a politely reciprocal role upon him and opens him up to what he has become in the eyes of others' (Goffman, 1968, p. 146). Of course this would only serve to 'confirm' his or her illness to others. First-person experience of the dehumanizing and depersonalizing effects of institutionalization, the 'breaking of the spirit' and helplessness have been described eloquently by Deegan (1990). Long-term patients later released into the community have difficulty overcoming the helplessness and dependence that they have learned (Chovil, 2005).

Psychological effects of the diagnosis

The pessimistic expectations brought on by the factors discussed in the foregoing sections lead to a self-fulfilling prophecy of poor outcome. As a result, psychological responses to the diagnosis itself, which are not an essential part of the illness, can lead to poor outcomes.

- *The patient role.* Even without long-term institutionalization, chronicity may be exacerbated by engulfment in the 'patient role', in which the person becomes resigned to being a passive recipient of care (Lally, 1989). Estroff (1989) asserts that 'becoming a schizophrenic' (p. 194) is essentially a social and interpersonal process, not an inevitable consequence of primary symptoms and neurochemical abnormality. The patient role is one of the few remaining open to the person, and although negative, it serves to organize the person's experience better than no identity at all (Rosenberg, 1993).
- *Self-stigma.* The label of schizophrenia carries with it status loss and discrimination (Link and Phelan, 2001), and delivers 'a judgment on that person's whole history, prospects, and indeed basic worth as a citizen' (Summerfield, 2001, p. 148). Self-stigma occurs when the expectation of social rejection by people with a mental illness brings about self-defeating styles of coping, such as social withdrawal and helplessness (Gray, 2002; Fekete, 2004), affecting their self-esteem, social relationships and employment prospects, thus leading to depressive symptoms and poor quality of life (Link and Phelan, 2001). A consequence of stigma is that people who have received a diagnosis of schizophrenia, but go on to lead a normal life, do not wish their diagnosis to be known, ironically increasing the pessimistic expectations for others with the diagnosis (Leete, 1989; Frese, 1997).
- *Motivated withdrawal.* Consumers have described withdrawal as a strategy for self-protection from the 'numerous . . . psychological assaults inflicted by the disorder, by society and even by oneself' (Strauss, 1989, p. 184). In a first-person account of recovery, Deegan described apathy and indifference to others as 'a strategy that desperate people, who are at the brink of losing hope, adopt in order to remain alive' (Deegan, 1996b, p. 93). Therefore, rather than resulting from a lack of volition, withdrawal can be very much goal-directed (Strauss, 1989). Indeed, early last century, E. Bleuler (1911/1950) showed insight into this

response: 'Of course, *conscious withdrawal* from the surroundings may easily be mistaken for lack of interest' (p. 332; italics added).

These secondary bases for apparent negative symptoms and poor course and outcome stand in contrast to the purported cultural benefits to outcome offered in developing nations. Warner (2004) pointed out that many features of chronic schizophrenia – for example, apathy, negativity, social withdrawal, isolation and loneliness – are mirrored in the psychological sequelae of long-term unemployment in otherwise mentally healthy people. It is clear that the iatrogenic effects of treatment as well as the psychological consequences of the label could easily be misinterpreted as signs of the illness itself. That these same psychological reactions would be exceptionally detrimental to recovery serves to highlight the self-fulfilling prophecy that is inherent in the diagnosis of schizophrenia. When the diagnosis of schizophrenia is '. . . synonymous with "chronically mentally ill" . . . this pessimistic outlook pervades verbal and nonverbal clinical interaction as well as programs and policies that aim only for stabilization and maintenance' (Harding, 1987, p. 1227).

The Real Possibility of Recovery

We have reviewed research that shows recovery from schizophrenia is more prevalent than traditionally recognized, and that the course and outcome of schizophrenia is more benign in developing countries, with fewer financial resources, than Western countries. Then we looked at some possible sources of bias that may account for the differential outcomes found in research, and found them unsupported. We have also considered cultural differences that may have some bearing on the superior outcomes observed in developing countries, including less stigma and better integration into society. And finally, we have discussed some iatrogenic effects of treatment and the psychological sequelae of the diagnosis which may contribute to poor outcomes, and that stand in contrast to treatment in some developing countries.

That environmental factors favourable to recovery can improve outcomes in the West was made evident in the differential outcomes obtained in a comparison study involving the patients of the Vermont longitudinal study (Harding *et al.*, 1987a). DeSisto *et al.* (1995a, 1995b) compared long-term outcomes for matched groups of patients from Maine and Vermont. Patients in Maine received traditional services, consisting of drug treatment and aftercare, while those from Vermont took part in a comprehensive rehabilitation programme. The Vermont programme had as its overarching goal the self-sufficiency of the patients. In hospital, the rehabilitation programme strengthened relationships between staff and patients, and included home-like wards, group therapy, vocational therapy and counselling, and self-help groups. After discharge, community care included halfway houses, community clinics, job placements and the establishment of links to natural support networks (Harding *et al.*, 1987a). Even though the Vermont subjects were those patients who had not responded well to drug treatment, they had a better course and long-term outcome than the Maine cohort. This study demonstrated the importance of environment in the outcomes of schizophrenia and the role social and psychological factors play in the chronic course prevalent in the West (DeSisto *et al.*, 1995a, 1995b).

> [The Vermont] legacy is the values and principles that guided it. Perhaps the most important value was that the program has a pervasive attitude of hope and optimism about human potential. ... (DeSisto *et al.*, 1995b, p. 340)

Kleinmann (1988) has stated that 'the forms and functions of mental illness are not "givens" in the natural world. They emerge from a dialectic connecting – and changing – social structure and personal experience' (p. 3). The importance of social consensus as a factor in recovery has been highlighted by Warner (2004), who maintained that the beliefs of society as a whole can be a powerful factor in the outcomes of treatment.

> It is accepted that people with schizophrenia have no hope of recovery and always deteriorate, and so the subjective experience of a catastrophic illness is worsened by the very psychiatric establishment that should be involved in the succour and healing of people. (Kruger, 2000, p. 30)

The discussion thus far has illuminated the real possibility of better outcomes for people in Western cultures by the adoption of practices more conducive to recovery, beginning with optimism among mental health professionals. The consumer recovery movement has now thrown down the gauntlet to clinicians, researchers and policy makers, demanding that services and systems become recovery-oriented.

The Emergence of the 'Recovery' Movement

In response to the mounting evidence that people with schizophrenia could go on to live a normal and meaningful life, the recovery movement emerged. The recovery movement grew out of the mental health consumer movement. The contemporary consumer movement began as the 'ex-patients' movement, which arose in the 1970s as a result of deinstitutionalization policies that led to many ex-patients being released from hospitals to no viable alternative care (Everett, 1994). Initially, the ex-patients' movement was focused on the human and legal rights of people with psychiatric disabilities (Chamberlin, 1990), and worked to improve conditions in hospitals and community treatment centres (Kaufmann, 1999). By the 1980s the consumer movement was largely an advocacy and self-help movement, focusing on fighting for the legal and human rights of patients, and forming mutual support and self-help groups in the community (Chamberlin, 1990). However, the consumer movement is not a single unified organization, but a diverse collection of groups

(Epstein and Olsen, 1998). Following the publication of the abuses and degradation of hospital patients and the iatrogenic effects of hospitalization, the anti-psychiatry movement arose, which rejects the concept of mental illness as a disease, and coined the term 'psychiatric survivors' (Kaufmann, 1999). A guiding principle of the 'ex-patients' movement is the exclusion of non-patients from their organizations (Chamberlin, 1990). However, many people accept a medical model of mental illness, while supporting the need for social change and the importance of psychological factors to recovery. Therefore, the major thrust of the consumer movement was towards a more coherent community health system for people with a mental illness (Kaufmann, 1999). Reflecting this direction, the term 'consumer' has become the preferred term for most mental health advocates, signifying a degree of power and freedom of choice, while accepting the existence of mental illness (Kaufmann, 1999). It is recognized that this is not the preferred term for everybody, as not all agree that they have choice or power, preferring 'ex-patients' (Chamberlin and Rogers, 1990), or, more militantly, 'psychiatric survivors' (Kaufmann, 1999). In addition, not all people with mental illness use mental health services.

Notwithstanding these differences, the consumer movement can be conceptualized as a movement with common aims (Epstein and Olsen, 1998). Epstein and Olsen listed these aims as: (i) the right to be recognized as human beings, rather than diagnoses; (ii) the right to accurate information and input regarding their treatment; (iii) the need for changes in community attitudes; and (iv) the need for consumer-run support and advocacy groups. More recently, consumer advocates have fought for consumer involvement in all aspects of personal treatment, service provision and policy-making (e.g. Chamberlin, 1990; Fisher, 1994; McLean, 1995; Epstein and Olsen, 1998; Deegan, 1997; Tenney, 2000; Frese *et al.*, 2001).

In parallel with the mounting evidence for recovery provided by longitudinal studies, people had begun writing and publishing first-person accounts of their own recovery experiences (e.g. Deegan, 1988; Leete, 1989; Armstrong, 1994; John, 1994; Koehler, 1994; Mary, 1994; McDermott, 1994; Roman, 1994; Schmook, 1994; Unzicker, 1994; Watson, 1994; Wentworth, 1994). With the networking occurring in the consumer movement, awareness of recovery from mental illnesses became more widespread and became the goal of self-help and community organizations (Schmook, 1996; Chadwick, 1997; Bassman, 2000; Tenney, 2000), although the term recovery may not always have been used (Turner-Crowson and Wallcraft, 2002). Thus the recovery movement emerged to advocate for public mental health and rehabilitation services to become recovery-oriented: operating on the assumption of the possibility of recovery, rather than on the entrenched objectives of medication management and coping (e.g. Anthony, 1993; Crowley, 1997; Frese, 1997; Acuff, 2000; Glass and Arnkoff, 2000; Jacobson and Curtis, 2000; Curtis, 2001). 'Recovery is no longer the exception. Recovery is the expectation' (Tenney, 2000, p. 1439). Consequently, recovery has been adopted in policy as the goal of mental health services in many English-speaking countries, for example, Australia (Australian Health Ministers, 2003), Canada (Pape and Galipeault, 2002), Ireland (Mental Health Commission, 2009), Israel (see Roe *et al.*, 2007), the United Kingdom

(Department of Health, 2001), New Zealand (Mental Health Commission, 1998) the United States (New Freedom Commission on Mental Health, 2003b) and Scotland (Scottish Government, 2009). The non-English-speaking world is also becoming aware of and researching the concept, for example, Japan (Chiba *et al.*, 2009), Taiwan (Song and Shih, 2009) and continental Europe (see Slade, Amering and Oades, 2008). However, the meaning of 'recovery' is not always clear (Davidson *et al.*, 2006; Meehan *et al.*, 2008; Onken *et al.*, 2007; Silverstein and Bellack, 2008; Slade and Hayward, 2007).

What Do We Mean by 'Recovery'?

Consensus on a definition and a way of measuring, recovery is a prerequisite for the development of recovery-oriented services. Davidson and McGlashan (1997) and Harrison *et al.* (2001) pointed out the lack of consensus of a definition of recovery across longitudinal studies of outcome, and called for careful operationalization of the concept.

An even more fundamental problem is that the word 'recovery' has been used in the literature with different meanings. The traditional meaning is based on the medical model of illness. There are two main medical definitions of recovery: the first describes complete cure, the second refers to recovery from a discrete episode. The medical meaning of recovery from schizophrenia is synonymous with 'cure'. In studies of the course and outcomes of schizophrenia, recovery has traditionally been assessed with objective measures such as symptomatology, hospitalization history and functioning (Harrison *et al.*, 2001). That is, all signs and symptoms of the illness have disappeared, and the person returns to his or her former level of functioning. These measures of outcome, based on the medical model, have been the most frequently used definition of recovery.

Another use of the term recovery is in describing the end of a discrete episode of schizophrenia. This meaning is also based on the medical model, and refers to the end of the psychotic phase of an episode. Phases of an episode have been outlined by Keshavan (2005) as:

> [A] premorbid phase (characterized by subtle cognitive and social difficulties), a prodromal phase (gradual beginning of subtle psychotic-like symptoms, social withdrawal and functional decline), the psychotic phase (with florid symptoms such as hallucinations and delusions), the transitional or recovery phase (a return to functioning but with increased proneness to relapses and comorbid difficulties), and the stable or residual phase (with persistent cognitive and social deficits) (p. 22).

This description seems to beg the question of whether full recovery is even possible, implying that one is never completely free of the illness. Recovery from an episode is usually operationalized in terms of the abatement of symptoms. In proposing consensus criteria for assessing clinical outcomes, Andreasen *et al.* (2005)

distinguished symptom abatement from complete recovery by adopting the term 'remission' to describe a level of symptomatic recovery in which symptoms do not influence behaviour. In their formulation, remission is necessary, but not sufficient for recovery (Andreasen *et al.*, 2005), which should also be assessed in terms of cognitive or psychosocial functioning. Liberman and Kopelowicz (2005) suggest that recovery from an episode for a prerequisite period is equivalent to recovery from schizophrenia itself. They agree that, although remission of symptoms is a key dimension, it is inadequate as a definition of recovery, and improvements in psychosocial functioning must also be taken into account.

Given that schizophrenia is characterized by an episodic course, with recurrent exacerbations of symptoms followed by periods of remission, neither of these medical definitions describe recovery as it is described by consumers. Consumers do not see psychiatric symptoms as incompatible with recovery (e.g. Anthony, 1993; Fekete, 2004) even if these require hospitalization (Deegan, 1997). This claim is supported by the finding of a discrepancy between outcomes assessed by clinical measures and outcomes in social functioning (Shepherd *et al.*, 1989). Shepherd *et al.* pointed out that, as long ago as early last century, E. Bleuler discriminated between a medical definition of recovery based on symptoms, and social recovery, where a person can support him- or herself outside hospital. Shepherd *et al.* (1989) assessed both clinical and social outcomes, and found that a high level of social functioning was often achieved despite persistent clinical symptoms. Conversely, Liberman and Kopelowicz (2005) argue that even with complete symptom remission, psychosocial functioning may still be impaired in psychiatric disorders. Liberman and Kopelowicz (2005) assert that a definition of recovery should also include participation in work or study, and social, family and recreational activities. So, for the purpose of studying the course and outcomes of schizophrenia, there is a need for consensus on a comprehensive measurement protocol that is broader than typical clinical measures. Regrettably, over the years, the drive towards objective measures of pathology and physiology led researchers to neglect the measurement of psychological and social aspects of mental health (Anthony, 2001). Nevertheless, most of the longitudinal studies supporting the notion of recovery described earlier used strict definitions that included both symptomatic and psychosocial dimensions.

However, with empirical evidence for recovery over the long term well documented, the main concern for consumers is not with demonstrating that recovery is possible, but with the adoption of the recovery vision in mental health services. Moreover, people who have experienced serious mental illness speak of recovery in terms that are at odds with traditional measures, even the more comprehensive definitions that include psychosocial functioning as well as symptoms. Consumers have argued that the medical model is not appropriate to recovery from mental illness (Fisher, 1994; Crowley, 1997; Bassman, 2000; Tenney, 2000). Rather, the recovery vision is one of attaining a productive and fulfilling life regardless of the presence of recurring symptoms (Crowley, 1997). The person recovers from the 'psychological catastrophe' of the illness (Anthony, 1993). Consumers urge us to abandon the 'pathology model' which binds us to pessimism and denies hope

(Frese, 2000; Tenney, 2000) and instead to look at a person's strengths and abilities and to explore the possibilities for transformation and growth (Fisher, 1994; Bassman, 2000). As Schmook (1996) asserts, 'The process of recovery then moves from survival to realizing individual potential with its transforming power of personal growth' (p. 13). The consequence of this alternative view of recovery is that, in addition to the underestimation of the recovery rate using conventional definitions, many more people consider themselves recovered, or recovering, by their *own* definitions.

Conclusion

In an era calling for evidence-based best practice internationally, for example, in Australia (Australian Health Ministers, 2003), New Zealand (Mental Health Commission, 1998), the United Kingdom (Department of Health, 1999), Ireland (Mental Health Commission, 2009), Scotland (Scottish Government, 2009), Canada (Clarke Institute of Psychiatry, 1998) and the United States (New Freedom Commission on Mental Health, 2003a), there is no universally accepted criterion for defining and operationalizing the concept of recovery (Silverstein and Bellack, 2008; Warner, 2009). Therefore, in view of the large and growing consumer literature on recovery, we should strive to conceptualize recovery in the terms of those who have experienced it (Lehman, 2000; Frese *et al.*, 2001; Fisher and Ahern, 2002; Anthony, Rogers and Farkas, 2003; Solomon and Stanhope, 2004; Farkas *et al.*, 2005). A model of recovery that honours consumers' experience can be the only valid basis on which to advance research into the processes of recovery, and to develop and evaluate recovery-oriented programmes. In the following chapter we describe a conceptual model and definition of recovery based on consumers' accounts of their experiences.

Summary

- Historical diagnostic practices led to pessimism regarding the outcome of schizophrenia.
- Longitudinal and cross-cultural studies provide evidence of clinical recovery from schizophrenia.
- Sources of continued pessimism include the 'clinician's illusion' and circularity in diagnosis.
- Some 'negative symptoms' of schizophrenia can be attributed to the effects of medication and treatment.
- Social and psychological repercussions of the diagnosis also play a role in course and outcome.
- Consumers claim that clinical definitions of recovery are too narrow, and that recovery can occur in the presence of recurring symptoms.
- Consumer-oriented models and measures are needed for the development and evaluation of programmes.

2

Conceptualizing Recovery:
A Consumer-oriented Approach*

Overview

There is much consumer-authored literature criticizing the medical, or pathology, model of mental illness and recovery. However, even within the consumer literature, there are many different ways of understanding recovery. In examining consumers' accounts of the experience of recovery, we broadened the scope of our exploration to include other serious and enduring mental illnesses besides schizophrenia. We also examined the findings of extant qualitative studies. We were able to find common ground within this literature, which we used to formulate a conceptual model of recovery. Although each person's recovery is a highly individual experience, we identified four overarching psychological processes: (i) finding and maintaining hope; (ii) taking responsibility for health and wellbeing; (iii) establishing a positive identity; and (iv) finding meaning in life. In addition, a number of the qualitative studies described stages or phases of recovery, and from these we identified five stages to the recovery process: (1) Moratorium, (2) Awareness, (3) Preparation, (4) Rebuilding and (5) Growth. These four processes and five stages make up the stage model of psychological recovery.

---

* The research presented in this chapter was originally published in a journal article: Andresen, R., Oades, L. and Caputi, P. (2003). The experience of recovery from schizophrenia: Towards an empirically-validated stage model. *Australian and New Zealand Journal of Psychiatry*, 37, 586–594.

Developing a Consumer-oriented Model of Recovery

While mental health policies are embracing consumers' demand for recovery-oriented services, there is at the same time a widespread push for the use of only evidence-based best practices. Both in the development of new programmes and treatment, and in the evaluation of services, the demand is that outcomes be measurable and measured. The challenge is to identify measurable outcomes while at the same time ensuring that those outcomes match consumers' personal experience of recovery. In Chapter 1 we explored the traditional meanings of the term recovery, and recognized that consumers are not talking of recovery as defined in the pathology model of mental illness. Therefore, measures based on the medical model often do not resonate with consumers. Consumers do not always gauge their mental health in terms of non-use of medications or hours of paid employment. Even within the research community, the conventional methods of outcome measurement have been questioned for some time. Harding (1994) who, with colleagues, conducted the seminal 'Vermont' study, cast doubt on whether the comprehensive protocol they had used comprised valid measures of recovery. Measures used in that study included: no signs or symptoms of psychiatric disorder; no psychotropic medications; working or age-retired after a work history; mutually satisfying relationships; no behavioural indicators of being a former psychiatric patient and full integration into the community (Harding *et al.*, 1987b). As we suggested in Chapter 1, these standards are higher than would be applied to many people who have not suffered any type of serious illness or disability. Harding (1994) pointed out that while there were people in the Vermont cohort who clearly fit these criteria, and others who clearly did not, there were also people who fell into a 'grey area'. First, over one-third of the cohort still had symptoms and mild impairment, but had learned to manage their symptoms; they were working, had satisfying relationships and a satisfying life. These individuals were described as 'significantly improved' in the study. Then there was a group who were sociable, had relationships and interests, and were happy, but did not work. Yet another group worked and were independent, but were self-described 'loners' (Harding, 1994). These latter two 'non-recovered' groups illustrate the value judgements that are often applied to outcome measurement in the field of mental health. Unquestionably, people with no history of mental illness, but who fit into these groups, would not be considered mentally ill based on their lifestyles.

In addition to measuring clinical outcomes, measurement tools are required for research into the process of recovery itself. While investigations have been conducted into the course of recovery, the intrapersonal and environmental factors that help recovery and to overcome barriers to recovery, there is, as yet, no widely accepted measure of recovery based on a theoretical model. We need to conceptualize recovery as consumers see it, to ensure that the working definition of recovery used by researchers incorporates the processes, views and aspired outcomes of consumers. To this end, we have explored what recovery means to those who have experienced mental illness and have struggled with their own recovery.

The Search for Common Ground

During the years 2000 through 2002, we gathered consumers' experiential accounts and theoretical articles about recovery (Andresen, Oades and Caputi, 2003). Because these narratives were published during the 1990s, they are not considered to be overly influenced by the emerging recovery research literature. The consumer stories were not always specific about their diagnosis, but were always referring to enduring illness; schizophrenia or bipolar disorder were the most often identified. (See Appendix 2.A at the end of this chapter for a list of the consumer literature reviewed.) We also included the findings of extant qualitative research in our review. (See Appendix 2.B at the end of this chapter for a list of this literature reviewed.) An overview revealed four important features in the literature:

- although there are different meanings of recovery, there is broad agreement amongst consumers;
- there are differences of opinion amongst consumers about a number of aspects of recovery;
- there are strong common themes among consumers' accounts of recovery;
- researchers have identified steps, phases or stages of recovery in qualitative work with consumers.

In the following sections, we first describe meanings of recovery already in use, and compare and contrast these with the definition we derived from the consumer-authored literature. We also discuss some aspects on which personal narratives differed, and which we took into consideration in developing this working definition of psychological recovery. Common themes are categorized into four component processes of recovery, which provided the foundation for the definition of psychological recovery and the conceptual model based on this definition. Finally, we examine the findings of previously existing qualitative research, which we synthesized to provide five stages of recovery. These stages provide added structure to the recovery model.

Meanings of Recovery in the Literature

Fitzpatrick (2002) summarized the recovery models in use by describing them as being on a continuum, with three identifiable points: (i) the medical model; (ii) the rehabilitative model; and (iii) the empowerment model. We elucidate these three models below in order to provide a background for our own findings.

The medical model

As we discussed in Chapter 1, this model assumes that mental illness is a physiological disease and, therefore, recovery refers to a return to a former state of health: the person is cured (Whitwell, 2000). Another use of this model is in describing recovery from a single episode of psychosis. Liberman *et al.* (2002) put forward that the abatement of symptoms – which was posited as an operational definition of remission (Andreasen *et al.*, 2005) – for a given period, coupled with improvements in psychosocial functioning, could be used as a definition of recovery. Longitudinal outcome studies have tended to use the medical model, focusing on symptom remission, freedom from medication, period without hospitalization and functioning (e.g. M. Bleuler, 1972/1978; Tsuang, Woolson and Fleming, 1979; Ciompi, 1980/2005; Huber *et al.*, 1980; Harding *et al.*, 1987a; DeSisto *et al.*, 1995a; Mason *et al.*, 1995; Sartorius *et al.*, 1996; Laurenen *et al.*, 2005). However, the medical definition is not the one used by the recovery movement: 'One of the biggest things I've had to accept is that recovery is not the same thing as being cured' (Deegan, 1997, p. 20). Nevertheless, the medical definition is the one that is understood in common discourse. In presenting the results of a qualitative study of 57 people who considered themselves recovered, Tooth, Kalyanansundaram and Glover (1997) found that professionals often questioned whether the participants could be considered as recovered, based on their level of functioning. Confusion can occur when either health professionals or consumers infer this meaning, so it is important for clinicians and researchers to be clear regarding their own meaning of recovery (Whitwell, 1999, 2000).

Paradoxically, because the medical definition of recovery requires a return to a former state, even people who would not be described by an outside observer as having a mental illness may not consider themselves recovered. Some reasons consumers have given for this are that:

• they continue to use medication or other illness management strategies;
• they do not believe that it is possible for people with a mental illness to get better;
• they do not feel like the same person that they were before.
                    (Ahern and Fisher, 2001; O'Hagan, 2004; Whitwell, 1999)

In addition, people who do not believe in the possibility of recovery can interpret normal emotional responses as illness symptoms (Tenney, 2000; Fox, 2002). The fact that apparently well people, who are participating fully in society by objective standards, do not think they have recovered highlights the pervasiveness of the medical model of recovery.

The rehabilitative model

The rehabilitative model holds that, although the illness is incurable, with rehabilitation efforts the person can return to a semblance of the life they had before the illness (Anthony and Liberman, 1992). This model, based on the disability model (e.g. Bachrach, 1992), implicitly assumes serious mental illness to be incurable, in much the same way as a permanent spinal injury.

The rehabilitation model focuses on functional disability, and presupposes that the person will always be disabled, but can learn to live well within the limitations of this disability (Ahern and Fisher, 2001). Psychiatric rehabilitation has traditionally focused on behaviour management through such interventions as symptom management, development of functional skills and case management, (e.g. Anthony, Cohen and Farkas, 1990; Schade, Corrigan and Liberman, 1990; Bachrach, 1992; Liberman, 1992). See Barton (1998) for a review. Hence, it has its foundations in the medical model; the focus on behaviour management reinforces the notion of chronicity, and the person may come to identify with the illness. However, 'Recovery is more than regaining external roles and functional skills, although these are certainly important; it is also about restoring the *self*. The consumer movement reaffirms the individual's **intentionality** . . .' (Barton, 1998, p. 172). According to the disability model of recovery, a person is never considered 'recovered', but having learned to live successfully with the illness is considered to be 'in recovery', requiring constant maintenance to avoid a relapse (Schiff, 2004).

The empowerment model

The empowerment model of recovery, as characterized by the National Empowerment Center in the United States, holds that mental illness does not have a physiological foundation. In a speech delivered to the World Mental Health Day Conference, Chamberlin (1996) stated, 'Despite all the research and all the theorizing, the schizophrenia gene or the schizophrenia germ has never been demonstrated. I believe that it never will; we can no more find the 'cause' of complex human behavior in brain chemistry than we can find the 'cause' of poetry'. Rather, mental illness is regarded as a sign of severe emotional distress in the face of overwhelming stressors (Ahern and Fisher, 2001; Fisher, 2003). This can interrupt normal development. How a person responds, and is responded to, plays a crucial role in their further development: 'With an attitude of optimism, understanding, trust and empowerment, people not only can restore their emotional balance, but also can heal past traumas. They are able to retain their expected role and avoid being labelled mentally ill' (Ahern and Fisher, 2001, p. 26). Advocates of the empowerment model are not satisfied with the notion of continued mental illness in recovery, and the strong version of this model denies the need for medical treatment (Fisher, 2003; McLean, 1995; Siebert, 2000). The Tidal Model of mental health nursing also eschews the medical model of mental illness, and encourages instead, the adoption of the construct 'problems of living' (Barker, 2001, 2003). According to this model, the most common form of disempowerment in mental illness is the failure to give a proper hearing to the person's story of his or her experience (Barker, 2003).

Which, if any, of these models best reflects the position of consumers who speak of their own recovery? To develop an understanding of what consumers mean by recovery, we examined first-person accounts of recovery, qualitative studies that addressed this issue and consumer-authored theoretical articles for definitions or descriptions of recovery. From this review, we developed a consumer-oriented conceptualization of recovery.

Consumer Descriptions – Psychological Recovery

Consumers' written accounts of their experiences rarely offered a definition of recovery *per se*. Indeed, attempts at eliciting a definition of recovery from consumers have been fraught with difficulty. In one qualitative study, volunteers from an ex-patients' support group, were interviewed to investigate the process and experience of recovery. Although the participants had identified themselves as recovered, they tended to see themselves as 'survivors', rather than recovered (Whitwell, 1999). Ongoing problems that they experienced included continuing symptoms, reduced tolerance of stress, stigma and a restricted lifestyle. Participants commented: 'Yes, but I will never be the same person again'; 'I have a made a good recovery, but I wouldn't say I have recovered. As to making a full recovery, I don't know if you ever do'; and 'I do consider that I have recovered, but I think it will take a little longer to forget' (Whitwell, 1999, p. 621). Two issues could be coming into play here. Perhaps these participants had *not* recovered in the consumer-movement's sense of the word. Alternatively, they are using different implicit definitions of recovery. When Tooth, Kalyanansundaram and Glover (1997) attempted to elicit a definition from participants – all of whom had identified themselves as recovered – they found that many had not even thought about the term prior to taking part in the study. Many participants were uncomfortable with the notion 'recovery' and preferred to think of themselves as 'getting on with life' (Tooth *et al.*, 2003). Still other consumers prefer alternative terms such as 'healing' or 'transformation', which they feel better communicates that they have grown through the experience, rather than having merely returned to some former state (Prior, 2000; Ralph, 2000a). Some consumers, however, have written articles that offer a definition of what recovery means for them. These quotes from consumer articles capture the essence of recovery:

> The need is to meet the challenge of the disability and to re-establish a new and valued sense of integrity and purpose within and beyond the limits of the disability; the aspiration to live, work and love in a community in which one makes a significant contribution. (Deegan, 1988, p. 54)

> It was being able to live in the community, to be able to work, to be accepted by myself and by others, it was taking responsibility for myself, it was learning how my mental illness was hurting people that loved me, it was a willingness to change myself to become all that I wanted to be. It was accepting the illness, but working towards health. (Schmook, 1994, p. 3)

These descriptions do not fit flawlessly into any of the three models described above. They clearly describe something that transcends a medical cure. They do not speak of accepting limitations imposed by a permanent disability. On the other hand, they do not make any claims regarding the aetiology of mental illness, as each of the other models imply. What they describe is recovery from the catastrophic effects of the illness (Anthony, 1993). They describe a change in attitude towards themselves, their lives and the illness itself.

What consumers are describing is *psychological* recovery. And this is the term we have adopted to mean the recovery movement's definition. Other terms have been used to differentiate between the consumer meaning and the traditional medical meaning of recovery. For example, in a review of the literature, Slade (2009) made the distinction between 'clinical' and 'personal' recovery. Davidson and colleagues (Davidson and Roe, 2007; Davidson *et al*, 2008), distinguished between 'recovery *in* mental illness', referring to reclaiming a full life whilst continuing to experience symptoms of mental illness, and 'recovery *from* mental illness' i.e. clinical recovery. Psychological recovery is similar to 'personal recovery' and the notion of 'recovery in mental illness', in that they are all different from 'clinical recovery'. Psychological recovery differs, however, in its specific emphasis on the psychological processes. The claim here is not that personal recovery or the notion of recovery in mental illness are necessarily problematic, rather that they have a slightly different focus.

Psychological recovery compared with other models

The pervasiveness of the medical model of recovery among professionals is illustrated by a claim by Remington and Shammi (2005), based on meta-analyses of the 'purported benefits of the newer antipsychotics', which stated that the case for recovery is overstated, since medications were unlikely to 'return patients to the vocational level predicted from their individual premorbid status'. Conversely, scientific evidence of the effectiveness of antipsychotic drugs in reducing symptoms may lead professionals to overestimate the value of medications (Lunt, 2002), and inhibit their exploration of other avenues to recovery (P. Brown and Tucker, 2005). Many consumers feel that medications did not help them, some even feel strongly that their medical treatment was part of the problem (e.g. Chamberlin, 1990; Deegan, 1990; Frese, 1997; Bassman, 2000; Mead and Copeland, 2000; Tenney, 2000; Fisher, 2003). In any case, recovery entails much more than bringing symptoms under control. As Lunt (2002) pointed out:

> A biochemical-based return to symptom-free 'reality' does not bring with it an understanding of that journey of return, does not explain the reality to which one is returned and fails to answer questions in search of personal meaning of future direction in one's life journey. (p. 33)

While the contrast between the medical model and the recovery model is reasonably clear, the difference between rehabilitation and recovery is somewhat more subtle. In the field of social work, Tower (1994) compared the philosophy of the rehabilitation model with that of a consumer-oriented model. The rehabilitation model was characterized as paternalistic, with solutions provided by professionals, the role of the client as that of a patient, and control of the process in the hands of the professional. Desired outcomes were safety, functioning and employment. In contrast, the consumer-oriented model of social work is based on self-determination, solutions are in the hands of the consumer, the role of the client is that of a consumer, and the desired outcomes are such things as independent living and quality of life (Tower, 1994). The flaw of the rehabilitation model of care is its grounding in the belief that psychotic disorders cause functional impairments and have no known cure. This disability model can paradoxically serve as a barrier to recovery, since it confers a permanent label of mental illness (Ahern and Fisher, 2001).

In contrast, recovery models are founded on the belief that people can redefine themselves through their life roles rather than by the disability (Noordsy *et al.*, 2000). While rehabilitation programmes often view the individual as a passive recipient, recovery implies that the person brings something active to the process (McGorry, 1992). Deegan explained that the fundamental difference is that recovery is what the person does, while rehabilitation provides the resources to help the person to recover (Deegan, 1994). 'We are not passive objects which professionals are responsible for "rehabilitating"' (Deegan, 1996a, p. 11). For rehabilitation services to be considered recovery-oriented, they need to shift away from a disability model and implement changes in policy and power distribution (Curtis, 2000). Recovery-oriented practice is a consumer-driven, clinician-facilitated change process with the goal of a meaningful life (Noordsy *et al.*, 2000).

The empowerment model, in comparison to the previous two models, makes a somewhat stronger statement than most consumers' meaning of recovery. The majority of consumers accepted the concept of mental illness, even if they did not see it as necessarily biologically based. Some consumers are comforted by the biological explanation, as it normalizes their experience by placing it within the framework of medicine, enabling them to separate the 'self' from the illness. For example, Fekete (2004) titled his story of recovery: 'How I quit being a "mental patient" and became a whole person with a neuro-chemical imbalance: Conceptual and functional recovery from psychosis.' The physiological explanation freed Fekete from his self-identity as less than a full human being, and enabled his recovery process to begin.

Although the empowerment model holds many of the same principles as the consumer descriptions of recovery, it makes strong statements regarding the aetiology of mental illness, questions the necessity for medication and, according to some (e.g. Ahern and Fisher, 2001), insists that the expectation should be the return to previously held career trajectories. These claims are at odds with the stories of many consumers. As illustrated by the consumer descriptions above, the recurrence of symptoms, the use of symptom-management strategies, medications or even inpatient services does not preclude a sense of recovery among those people who consider themselves recovered. Furthermore, many do not see the return to previously expected roles as a goal of recovery, but instead welcome what they have learned about their values and personal qualities through their journey to recovery.

The concept of *empowerment*, as opposed to the *empowerment model* espoused largely by opponents of the biomedical model of mental illness, is an important element of the consumer recovery discourse. Consumer empowerment encompasses personal empowerment – self-worth and self-efficacy in taking control of one's life, and social empowerment – the ability and opportunity to influence change in the community (Corrigan *et al.*, 1999a).

The importance of formulating a consumer definition of recovery from mental illness is highlighted in that not only are clinicians, researchers, carers and consumer advocates talking at cross-purposes, but consumers themselves are confused about what the term 'recovery' means. This was highlighted by Turner-Crowson and Wallcraft (2002), who explored reservations of consumers in Britain about the recovery concept. Some issues expressed were: Does speaking of recovery imply an acceptance of the medical model? Was the recovery movement like a 'born again' revival – can you fail at your recovery? Could the notion of recovery be appropriated by professionals, to force compliance in a 'recovery' programme? Others preferred to continue using terms already in use, such as 'strategies for living' (Turner-Crowson and Wallcraft, 2002).

Although the notion of recovery has gained acceptance in much of the English-speaking world, for example, in Australia, Israel, the United Kingdom, the United States and New Zealand, there is still no universal understanding of the recovery concept (Silverstein and Bellack, 2008; Slade, Amering and Oades, 2008). For most people who develop serious mental health problems, the first source of information is service providers. It is therefore important that mental health professionals have a clear understanding of the consumer-movement's concept of recovery. This will assist a dialogue around the various meanings of recovery with consumers.

Diverse Opinions on Some Aspects of Recovery

While the consumer definitions presented above give a good general account of what recovery means, and does not mean, to consumers, the review also revealed that not all consumers share the same implicit theory of mental illness. In addition, many consumers are adamant that recovery is a very personal, individual process and that no two people have had identical experiences of the recovery process. In formulating an inclusive consumer-oriented definition of recovery, we needed to take into account those issues on which conflicting views have been expressed. Some of these issues are outlined below.

Does recovery mean the return to a former state?

Although traditional meanings of recovery imply a return to a former state, and proponents of the empowerment model adopt this principle, many consumers do not feel the same as they did before developing the illness. This is not necessarily a negative thing. As Crowley explains: 'Much can be accomplished when we let go of who we were and get to know who we are now and who we can become' (Crowley, 2000, p. 11). Others are adamant that they do not want to be the same as they were before, as their earlier development had been hampered by the illness (D. Marsh, 2000; Ralph, 2000b). Harding (1994), in discussing issues surrounding the measurement of recovery, questioned whether a 35-year-old would want to be compared to their pre-morbid self, if that self was an 18-year-old. This notion is illustrated by McQuillin:

> The schizophrenia struck when I was nineteen, and a lot of normal maturation was suspended at that point. My experience at the Centre has enabled me to resume my growing up. I am still searching for a place in the world, but the task is coming clearer now. (McQuillin, 1994, p. 9)

Some consumers have even expressed that they had no 'before' (e.g. Ralph, 2000a). Even those who first became ill as adults do not regard being the 'same as before' as a criterion for recovery. Fekete (2004) was a doctoral student when psychosis first struck. He was awarded his PhD two years later. Although he says 'I like who I am now' (p. 194), he elaborates:

> I'm not sure that I have returned to the same person I was before my episode. This can be one of the most difficult aspects about recovery. We may not exactly 'recover.' We may become someone different from what we were. (Fekete, 2004, p. 193)

In fact, many consumers expressed no doubt that they are a better person for having experienced and recovered from the illness. For example:

> The struggle can enrich us or it can make us bitter. As I talk with others thus afflicted, it is my gut feeling that this struggle has not embittered most of us nor defeated us, but has made us more compassionate, sensitive and courageous. We have also learned some valuable lessons along the way. (Watson, 1994, p. 74)

> I'm not romanticizing the experience, as it is one of the most painful one can feel, but once you go through it, you can be as Dr. Karl Menninger said, 'Weller than well.' (Alexander, 1994, p. 39)

Clearly, returning to the way one was before the illness is not only often impossible, due to the growth that has taken place during the work of recovery, but to some people, undesirable.

Does recovery require the absence of symptoms?

Tooth, Kalyanansundaram and Glover (1997) reported that only 14% of respondents understood recovery as freedom from symptoms. Rather, it involves self-management of the illness: 'Many of us have learned to monitor symptoms to determine the status of our illness, using our coping mechanisms to prevent psychotic relapse or to seek treatment earlier, thereby reducing the number of acute episodes and hospitalizations' (Koehler, 1994, p. 199).

Further, although a number of consumers felt that their treatment was worse than the illness and had been detrimental to their recovery (Bassman, 2000; Frese, 2000; Mead and Copeland, 2000), and some saw their cessation of medication use as a mark of their progress (Anonymous, 1989; Schmook, 1994; Lynch, 2000), others see the controlled use of medications as fully compatible with recovery:

> Being in recovery means that I don't just take medications . . . Rather I use medications as part of my recovery process. In the same way, I don't just go to the hospital . . .. Rather I use the hospital when I need to. (Deegan, 1997, p. 21)

As Tenney (2000) says, it is a matter of choice:

> Now, sometimes I think that my life would be a lot easier if I just took the medication; it would make a lot of the noise stop. The side effects are really bad and that's what prevents me from taking the medication now. There's no black and white on this stuff. Recovery is a hard choice that does not end with just not taking medication. (p. 1443)

Although plainly the lack of symptoms is one form of recovery, from these quotes it is clear that some consumers do not see the lack of need for medication or the absence of symptoms as a necessary for recovery. Nor is the absence of symptoms necessarily sufficient for psychological recovery.

Does recovery entail the return to expected roles?

There is a history in rehabilitation of pressuring mental health consumers into demeaning work (Curtis, 2001), as was the case for (Bjorklund, 1998), and many others:

> Clearly these misguided goals were based on my label rather than on my past achievements or existing strengths. My every action and my future life goals were unnecessarily pathologized by myopic treatment plans . . .. (p. 654)

The empowerment model advocates a return to previous social and career roles without compromise (Ahern and Fisher, 2001), and this position should never be automatically dismissed. A number of articles were written by consumers who became, or continued to work as, professionals after the onset of serious illnesses such as schizophrenia (e.g. Deegan, 1994; Fisher, 1994; Frese, 1997 Ahern and Fisher, 2001). As Mead and Copeland assert:

> We have learned that we are in charge of our own lives and can go forward and do whatever it is we want to do. People who have experienced even the most severe psychiatric symptoms are doctors, lawyers, teachers, accountants, advocates and social workers . . .. (Mead and Copeland, 2000, p. 316)

However, most consumers did not appear to take the return to expected roles as a criterion of recovery. For example:

> Sometimes in the face of illness, our dreams blow up in our face. It is important to dream a new dream, and once you've done this to pick some aspect of it and begin working toward it in any increment. (Crowley, 2000, p. 16)

Although it is not necessary for everybody to aspire to highly socially-valued roles, it is important that the roles, goals or activities in which a person engages are valued highly by the individual. Evidently, the status of the social role in which a person is engaged is less important than the meaning, purpose and fulfilment that the role provides to the individual (Deegan, 1997). Deegan explains:

> They may tell you that your goal should be to become normal and to achieve valued roles. But a role is empty and valueless unless you fill it with *your* meaning and *your* purpose. Our task is not to become normal. You have the wonderfully terrifying task of becoming who you are called to be. (p. 24)

In light of the differences discussed in this section, the concept of psychological recovery is consistent with consumers' use of the term, allowing for recovery in the presence of ongoing management of illness. A definition of recovery needs to accommodate the diversity of opinions around these aspects of the recovery process. In order to formulate such a definition and conceptual model of psychological recovery compatible with the diverse perspectives of individuals, we conducted a thematic analysis, which stated simply, is analysis of narratives to find themes within the experiential and qualitative data to identify the key components of recovery.

Four Component Processes of Recovery

Although the authors of personal accounts did not necessarily claim to be 're-covered', and were generally not attempting to describe the process or definition of

Table 2.1   Concepts subsumed by each of the component processes.

Hope	Responsibility	Self and identity	Meaning and purpose
Optimism	Responsibility for	Restructured sense	Purpose in life
Hopefulness	recovery	of self	Meaningful work
Hope of others	Empowerment	Self-redefinition	Spirituality
Inspiration	Self-determination	Acceptance of	Change in values
Role models	Willingness	illness	Change in attitudes
Others' belief in	Determination	Self-acceptance	Change in goals
self	Attitude	Meaning of illness	Intrinsic values
Personal agency	Self-management	Overcoming	Self-worth
Hope for the	of illness	stigma	Meaning in the
future	Willingness to take	Integrated sense	illness
	risks	of self	
	Building	Taking stock of self	
	independence	Internal inventory	
	Discard patient	Self-knowledge	
	role	Relationship with	
		illness	

recovery, themes from their stories were mirrored in consumer theoretical articles and in the findings of qualitative research.

Four component processes of recovery were salient: (i) finding and maintaining hope; (ii) taking responsibility for life and wellbeing; (iii) redefining self and identity, and (iv) finding meaning and purpose in life. The concepts incorporated under each of these overarching themes are presented in Table 2.1. Each of these four psychological processes is described in the following paragraphs, illustrated with quotes from the first-person literature.

Finding and maintaining hope

The importance of hope pervades the literature on recovery. References to hope were found in 19 of the 29 consumer narratives, in nine of the 11 consumer articles and in all eight qualitative studies. Just as hopelessness is central to chronicity in schizophrenia (e.g. Davidson and Stayner, 1997; Deegan, 1997; Hoffmann, Kupper, and Kunz, 2000), so finding hope is the catalyst of the recovery process. We used definitions from theoretical literature on hope as a guide in categorizing quotes under this theme. Snyder's (1995) definition of hope comprises three distinct elements: a goal; envisaging pathways to the goal; and belief in one's ability to pursue the goal. Miller (1992) described hope as anticipation of a continued good state, an improved state or a release from perceived entrapment. In keeping with these definitions, themes such as sources of inspiration, personal agency, hope for the future, and the hopefulness of others represented the theme 'hope'. The first-person accounts described hope as commencing in a number of ways:

- stemming from within themselves,
- encouraged by a significant other, or
- triggered by a peer or a role model.

For Deegan (1996b) it was an awakening of self-determination in the face of having her life depicted as a 'closed book' (p. 92) at the age of 17:

> When my psychiatrist told me the best I could hope for was to take my medications, avoid stress and cope, I became enraged . . . just after that visit I made up my mind to become a doctor. (Deegan, 1996b, p. 96)

In contrast, a little hope in a professional can make all the difference. As Schmook (1994) recounts, 'I wanted to get better right from the beginning. However, I didn't find any support from professionals' (p. 1). And 'They told me I was denying my illness. I wasn't denying it. I accepted my illness' (p. 2). Then:

> I finally found a doctor who said 'I don't know' when I asked him if I could get better. For the first time, someone didn't tell me 'no' or that 'people with a mental illness did not get better.' He gave me hope. For the first time, I had a glimmer of hope! (Schmook, 1994, p. 2)

For some, it was the unflagging belief and support of loved ones that eventually encouraged the person to engage in the recovery process. 'It was [my mother's] perpetual optimism that kept me afloat, swimming with me until I was able to swim on my own' (Greenblat, 2000, p. 244). Or it could have been a caring professional:

> . . . it may have been because [my nurse] really seemed to pay attention to me . . . and I started waking up and I started knowing that there were possibilities for life outside that room and things really started opening up for me. (Betty, quoted in Davidson and Strauss, 1992, p. 135)

For others, inspiration came from a role model, as described by Unzicker (1994): 'Judi's book awakened in me a spirit of defiance, will and courage that I am still uncovering, like a perpetual birthday present' (p. 61).

Hope is not only the trigger for recovery, but is also necessary to maintain the recovery process: 'Growing hope involves having faith in what is possible; recognizing and building on the seeds of hope when they appear; and – most critically – not extinguishing it' (Crowley, 2000, p. 15). Hope is especially important to recovery, as it is depicted as the trigger for psychological recovery, and a necessary ingredient throughout the process. With hope, people were prepared to take on the struggle for recovery. Hopefulness for the future was also a characteristic of people who considered themselves recovered.

Taking responsibility for life and wellbeing

As important to finding hope is the realization of the need to take responsibility or control over one's treatment and one's life generally. Themes of responsibility appeared in 24 first-person accounts, 10 consumer articles and six qualitative studies. These themes included self-management of wellness and medication, personal empowerment, autonomy in one's life choices, accountability for one's actions, and willingness to take informed risks in order to grow. Realizing that one had to do the work of recovery for oneself was the first step:

> I now realize that I needed to take some responsibility for my recovery; I can't just wait for the pills to save me. . ..I've begun to make a start and I see some hope where I saw none before. (Anonymous, 1994a, p. 14)

This entails empowerment and self-determination, as highlighted by Mead and Copeland (2000):

> The person who experiences psychiatric symptoms should determine the course of his or her own life. No one else, even the most highly skilled health care professional, can do the work for us. We need to do it for ourselves, with your guidance, assistance, and support. (p. 328)

Taking responsibility requires taking risks, for example:

> It took me a long time to view failed attempts not as failures, but as learning experiences that should be used in future endeavours . . .. There is no learning that can take place without risk. (Tenney, 2000, p. 1443)

With hope and self-determination, the person can make changes to his or her life with which to build a positive sense of identity and provide meaning and purpose to life.

Renewal of the sense of self and building a positive identity

An horrific, and well documented, impact of mental illness is the loss of a sense of identity. This theme was represented by accounts of the loss of a sense of self, redefinition of self, loss of identity, and finding a positive identity. Themes of self and identity appeared in 26 of the experiential accounts, 10 consumer articles, and six qualitative studies. Bjorklund (1998) describes the immediate effects on identity conferred by a label:

> I entered the hospital as Robert Bjorklund, individual, but left the hospital 3 weeks later as a 'schizophrenic'. My individuality, which had taken years to form, now went through a rapid transformation. (1998, p. 654)

Whereas Deegan described the loss of her future self with the apparent unattainability of her goals: 'My teenage world in which I aspired to dreams of being a valued person in valued roles . . . I felt these parts of my identity being stripped from me' (Deegan, 1997, p. 16). The process of self-redefinition is therefore central to recovery. 'My illness eradicated my sense of self, and now I am engaged in the lifelong process of obtaining, maintaining and slowly modifying my sense of who I am' (Anonymous, 1994b, p. 25). Pettie and Triolo (1999) used case studies to illustrate the issues of identity and meaning in recovery. They described two approaches to reconciling one's self with the illness. First, the illness can be accepted as part of the self in a spirit of growth. An example of this approach can be seen in Alexander (1994), who accepted the experience as one to be treasured and not labelled as 'mental illness'. He explains: 'My identity was focused away from being a patient or ex-patient, but to my own life experience which was validated by literature and philosophy' (p. 38). Also:

> Now I don't see myself as being mentally ill but I do see myself now as a person who has a psychiatric condition, though I don't use it or treat it as a disability . . .. I consider myself a useful member of society . . .. (Roman, 1994, p. 43)

Alternatively, the illness can be seen as something that has to be lived with, but is separate from the 'true' self, (Pettie and Triolo, 1999). To quote one consumer (Anonymous, 1994b): '. . . the key . . . is to know yourself, know your illness and to know the difference between the two' (p. 25). Curtis (2000) described recovery as movement from being defined by the self and others *as* the illness to accepting the illness as but a small *part of the whole* self. Deegan (1997) explained how engulfment by the illness robs one of the sense of agency required to recover: 'Once you and the illness become one, then there is no one left inside of you to take on the work of recovering, of healing, of rebuilding the life you want to live' (p. 19). Closely connected to reconstructing a positive identity is finding meaning and purpose in life. As a person develops a positive sense of self, he or she begins to find means of self-expression. Alternatively, finding purpose in life can lead to a positive sense of identity.

Finding purpose and meaning in life

Having a purpose in life gives meaning to a person's recovery efforts. Twenty-six first-person accounts, eight consumer articles, and all eight qualitative studies described finding meaning or purpose in life as a task of the recovery process. Mary (1994, p. 45) found that her work giving in-service training to nurses gave her a reason to get out of bed in the morning: '. . . sometimes I don't feel confident. I just have to push myself. I don't allow myself to give in to that. If you're working you're expected to turn up' (p. 19). Often a person's previous life-goals are no longer available to them, and they face the task of reassessing their goals in life. As well, the non-availability of previous goals can lead one to reassess one's values and decide on different goals.

> It took several years to realize that I wasn't going to pick up the pieces and go back to graduate school. I did know what its like to have schizophrenia, though, and was willing to give presentations whenever asked. I wanted to prevent what happened to me from happening to others and started going into the high schools with a friend who has bipolar disorder. (Chovil, 2000, p. 746)

However, it must not be assumed by others that a person's prior goals are no longer attainable, as occurred for Bjorklund (1998):

> The treatment team and my family and friends adjusted their expectation accordingly . . . my medical records at age 15 revealed cautiously optimistic recommendations for vocational rehabilitation and assisted living. I was far too young to have the rest of my life predestined by one diagnostic label. (p. 654)

The danger in this is illustrated by Frese (2000), who tells how, for a year, he was unable to write a single sentence of his dissertation proposal. Nonetheless, three years later he was awarded his PhD, and became a registered psychologist. Similarly, Deegan (1997), who was diagnosed with schizophrenia as a teenager and spent years without hope, successfully attained a doctorate in clinical psychology. Both of these consumer advocates have been working in a professional capacity for decades, although still experiencing symptoms from time to time.

However, paid employment, often used as a measure of functioning, is not the sole provider of meaning. A person may find other ways of expressing their core values. Leete urged that personal growth be facilitated by 'discovering what makes life valuable and enriching to us as individuals' (Leete, 1994, cited in Schmook, 1996, p. 12). For example, Fox, while living 'a simple life, but a good life', embraces life to the full, and is grateful for 'my second chance to enjoy my family and pursue my dreams' (Fox, 2002, p. 365). For others, creative pursuits provide a sense of meaning or purpose (e.g. McQuillin, 1994). Moreover, the work of recovery can be meaningful in itself: 'I learned that I want to dedicate myself to this recovery process for myself and others . . .' (Armstrong, 1994, p. 53). Betty (cited in Davidson and Strauss, 1992), who had been about to commence a degree in art before her first psychotic episode, came to value the efforts she had made. Betty was 'too proud of the work she has had to do in improving to see herself simply as a failure in other, formerly important, areas of her life such as art' (Davidson and Strauss, 1992, p. 134). The work of recovery can also lead to other meaningful roles. Offering peer support or involvement in advocacy work is frequently mentioned, for example, Alexander (1994), Berman (1994), Chovil (2000), Unzicker (1994) and Weingarten (1994). As Lynch (2000) illustrates, 'I continued to start new self-help and advocacy organisations, investing my time and energy to help others regain their health. It all seemed so strange, my life's suffering led to my life's work' (p. 1431). Koehler (1994) explains, 'We ourselves are finding surprising depths of compassion and heights of inspiration in helping our peers. Demonstrating solidarity with others' suffering redeems our own suffering and turns it to good purpose (p. 23).

For some, spirituality gives meaning to the struggle. Watson (1994) believes God's love ensures that '. . . our courage will not be wasted or in vain. As we are strengthened by our courage, we shall ultimately emerge victorious to a life richer in joy, peace and love' (p. 75). Murphy (1998) captures the essence of finding meaning:

> An integral part of my recovery has been my search and discovery of meaning for my life. This is a philosophical and psychological issue that goes beyond mere chemical imbalances in the brain. In this search, I have developed a new world view. (p. 188)

These quotes illustrate that, while finding meaning in life is integral to recovery, the source of that meaning can vary greatly between individuals, and possibly over time.

The review of the consumer literature highlighted the commonalities in the experience of recovery in the form of four psychological processes. However, there were also a number of points of disagreement, and these needed to be considered in formulating a definition of recovery that would be universally acceptable.

A Definition of Psychological Recovery

Bearing in mind the differences of opinion between consumers on a number of aspects of recovery, and focusing on the commonalities within the experiential accounts exemplified in the four component processes, we formulated the following definition of psychological recovery:

> Psychological recovery refers to the establishment of a fulfilling, meaningful life and a positive sense of identity founded on hopefulness and self-determination. (Andresen, Oades and Caputi, 2003, p. 588)

This definition describes recovery from the psychological consequences of the illness. It is not grounded in any causal theory of mental illness, and is silent on whether symptoms of illness are still present in recovery. Although the empowerment model holds many of the same principles, it makes strong statements regarding the aetiology of mental illness, the lack of need for medication and the return to expected roles, which are at odds with the stories of many consumers. Nor does psychological recovery require changing goals or values, as the rehabilitation model of recovery implies (Anthony, 1993). It places no limitations on the possibilities for the person, and at the same time does not confine the definition of recovery to externally valued roles. The person is self-determined in their recovery and chooses the course that best leads to the fulfilment of his or her core values.

Psychological recovery is necessary whether mental illness is biologically based or the result of the exacerbation of emotional problems caused by stress. Even if symptoms can be controlled by medication, the journey of psychological recovery is still necessary. In a more recent article, a consumer explains this succinctly: '. . . the biochemical solution does not bring with it a dream, a goal, a journey, a direction, an inspiration, a faith or a hope. These are what are sought in recovery' Lunt (2000, p. 1).

The literature contains a number of explicit and implicit definitions of recovery. Although consumer authored literature rarely defines recovery, four component psychological processes were identified: finding and maintaining hope; taking responsibility for wellbeing and life as a whole; renewal of the sense of self and rebuilding a positive identity; and finding a purpose and meaning in life. These processes informed the development of a definition of psychological recovery that can accommodate diverse recovery visions, and are at the heart of recovery. In the next section, we review qualitative studies to determine the stages of recovery, which will provide a framework for a model of psychological recovery.

Steps Along the Journey of Recovery

As we mentioned earlier, a number of qualitative studies identified steps, phases or stages in the recovery process. We revisited these in order to gain a deeper understanding of the definition and description of steps or stages identified in each study. Parallels in the themes of each step or stage were sought which could be synthesized into a model of recovery that would lend itself to operationalization. The articles we reviewed (see Appendix 2.B) for descriptions of steps, phases or stages of recovery were: Davidson and Strauss (1992), Baxter and Diehl, (1998), Pettie and Triolo (1999), Young and Ensing (1999) and Spaniol *et al.* (2002).

Identifying and describing the stages of psychological recovery

The focus of these research projects varied: Davidson and Strauss (1992) focused on the role of the sense of self in recovery; Baxter and Diehl (1998) were interested in the emotional stages of recovery; Pettie and Triolo (1999) used case studies to describe the relationship between the meaning of the illness and identity; Young and Ensing (1999) conducted structured interviews and focus groups to identify components of the recovery process; and Spaniol *et al.* (2002) conducted a longitudinal study to investigate the processes of recovery. Although there was no consensus on the exact delineation of the stages, a pattern emerged that provided a model for further empirical investigation. A brief description of the research and the findings of each of these studies follows.

Davidson and Strauss (1992) conducted a series of interviews over a two to three year period. Participants were 66 people who had been hospitalized with serious mental disorders, 25 of whom had a diagnosis of schizophrenia. Participants were interviewed at bi-monthly intervals for one year and then at yearly intervals. Although the interview protocols were comprehensive, Davidson and Strauss focused their report on the theme of the sense of self in personal narratives. Nearly all of these individuals described themes of redefining or rediscovering an agentic sense of self over the course of their illness. Davidson and Strauss presented four aspects of this process, which they described as related and overlapping. These four aspects were:

- *Discovering the possibility of a more agentic sense of self.* This involves the awareness of latent aspects of the self, either through the rediscovery of parts of the self which remain unaffected by the illness, or the discovery of previously unrealized parts of the self. It may involve acceptance of the illness as separate from the self, allowing an identity separate from the illness, or a reawakening after a period of passivity and withdrawal.
- *Taking stock of one's strengths and limitations.* Once the person has gained renewed hope for a more active role in life, they need to determine whether they have the personal resources to pursue whatever goal they have in mind. This can be a cognitive appraisal of the individual's abilities and limitations, or a more intuitive sense of what is right for the person. Taking stock can involve step-by-step accumulation of the skills required to achieve a goal. It may also involve changing the goal to fit the person.
- *Putting aspects of the self into action.* Having acquired the skills considered necessary, the person attempts to achieve their desired goal. If successful, the person's strengths are affirmed, and his or her sense of self is enhanced. If unsuccessful, the person needs to reflect and integrate this into his or her sense of self. The important aspect of this process is that the goals must originate from the individual and the action must be taken by the individual, in order to establish a sense of agency, and the ability to take further steps.
- *Appealing to the self.* The enhanced sense of self separate from the illness can serve as a refuge from the effects of the illness such as stress and stigma. The agentic self can now be used as a resource in coping with the illness. There is a sense of a self that can be responsible for managing the illness and taking charge of one's life. The self can now monitor, manage and compensate for the illness in a social context.

(Davidson and Strauss, 1992)

Davidson and Strauss (1992) stress that a person may not progress through these phases in an orderly fashion; they describe the four aspects as related, overlapping and possibly interactive. However, they appear to have a logical sequence as presented.

Baxter and Diehl (1998) developed a semi-structured interview, based on constructs in the recovery literature. Content analysis was conducted on the responses from 40 mental health consumers, and the emotional stages of recovery were identified. Baxter and Diehl's model consists of three overarching psychological events, each of which are followed by a stage of recovery. These are:

- *Crisis – followed by a stage of recuperation.* The crisis may be psychosis, a suicide attempt, panic attack, manic episode or some other trauma accompanied by confusion. The Recuperation phase is a stage of dependence. Emotions include denial, negative feelings about the self and others, despair and/or anger. The person in this stage needs safety, food, rest, care and probably medication.
- *Decision – followed by a stage of rebuilding independence.* The decision to get going can occur from a few days to years after the crisis. This is followed by rebuilding the ability to take care of oneself and resume normal life roles. The person experiences successes and setbacks. Perseverance through this stage results in the development of a more integrated sense of self. During this stage, the person needs to be heard and accepted, needs to learn about mental illness, and develop recovery skills.
- *Awakening – followed by building healthy interdependence.* Awakening to a restructured personhood is followed by the stage of recovery and discovery involving rebuilding healthy interdependence. This stage is characterized by acceptance of self and others, confidence, helpfulness to others and anger at injustice. In this stage, the person needs a dream to strive for, good relationships, meaningful work, fun and may also advocate for self and others.

The three psychological events and emotional stages described by Baxter and Diehl (1998) are presented as ordinal in nature. Even so, the second stage involves times of success and setbacks, illustrating the sense in which consumers have described their recovery as non-linear.

Pettie and Triolo (1999) drew on the experiences of people with psychiatric disabilities to examine the effects of illness on identity. They used two case examples to illustrate the process of reconstructing identity, and the role of meaning in this process. They described two steps to the recovery process:

- *Why me?* This is a stage of identity confusion. The person struggles to reconcile his or her pre-illness identity with their new identity as a person with a mental illness. The person seeks the meaning of the illness. There are two main chosen meanings of the illness – illness as evolution, in which dealing with the illness results in personal growth; and illness personified, in which the illness is seen as a separate entity to the healthy self.
- *What now?* This is a stage of identity reconstruction. The person has found a meaning for the illness and moves on to the task of developing a new identity and positive sense of self. This may involve some changes to lifestyle and new values.

Pettie and Triolo (1999) concluded that the psychological response to illness is progressive; first the person must find an acceptable meaning for the illness, they can then use this meaning as a foundation on which to build a self which he or she can respect.

Young and Ensing (1999) used themes from a literature review and information from consumers and professionals to develop a protocol for individual interviews and focus groups to explore the meaning of recovery. Grounded Theory Analysis was used to analyse the data from 18 people, and three overarching phases of recovery, each involving a number of subcategories were described:

- *Initiating recovery – overcoming 'stuckness'*. This phase involves: (i) acknowledging and accepting the illness; (ii) having the desire and motivation to change; and (iii) finding a source of hope or inspiration, such as role models, other people or spirituality.
- *Middle phase – regaining what was lost and moving forward*. This includes: (i) discovering and fostering self-empowerment, including taking control and responsibility for one's life and developing empowering attitudes; (ii) learning and self re-redefinition, involving discovering new or lost parts of the self, insight of one's relationship with the illness and insight about living in the world; (iii) returning to basic functioning, involving taking care of self, being active and connecting with others.
- *Later phase – improving quality of life*. This includes: (i) striving for an overall sense of well-being, involving self-esteem, feeling at peace, feeling 'normal', caring about things; and (ii) striving to reach new potentials of higher functioning, involving finding meaning and purpose in life, improving standard of living, increased independence, maintaining a positive focus and symptom reduction.

Within each of the subcategories of these three phases are a number of tasks, themes or subprocesses. Young and Ensing (1999) point out that although each person follows a unique path to recovery, the results of their study highlighted the commonalities amongst consumers' experiences. Their labelling of the three main phases implies that they are conceptually sequential in nature.

Spaniol *et al.* (2002) conducted a longitudinal qualitative study. Participants were 12 people with schizophrenia who had previously been involved in a vocational skills programme. They were interviewed at four to eight-monthly intervals over four years. Themes and patterns were identified in the data and constructs were developed inductively. Three broad phases of recovery were identified from the interviews. A fourth phase, which was identified from the recovery literature, was not evident in the interviews:

- *Overwhelmed by the disability*. In this early phase, the person struggles with daily life. The person feels confused, out of control of his or her life, lacking in self-confidence and lacking connection with others. The person may fear becoming overwhelmed and is unable to articulate his or her goals.

- *Struggling with the disability.* In this stage the person formulates an explanation for his or her experiences, and accepts that they have a long-term problem. The person realizes the need to develop ways of coping with the illness, and managing symptoms. There is a fear of failure on new activities, and a focus on building strengths.
- *Living with the disability.* The person has accepted the disability and is confident in managing it. There is a stronger sense of self, and some control over life. The person has meaningful roles and realizes the possibility of a satisfying life within the limitations of the disability.
- *Living beyond the disability (conceptualized from the literature).* In this phase, the disability is a much smaller part of the person's life, and does not interfere with having a satisfying and contributing life. The person feels well connected to self and others and has a sense of meaning and purpose to life.

Spaniol *et al.* (2002) described recovery as a developmental process. They found that while some participants made steady fast or slow progress, others fluctuated. Sometimes periods of progress were followed by plateau periods of consolidation and integration.

Five Stages of Psychological Recovery

There are clear parallels between the findings of these qualitative studies. They identified from two to four superordinate steps, phases or stages, with the initial and/or final stages not being represented in all the studies. Although the phases and stages of the different studies overlap to some extent, there is a recognizable pattern to the findings, which can be conceptualized as a five-stage model of recovery. Table 2.2 shows the five stages of our model, and how they relate to the findings of each of the studies (Andresen, Oades and Caputi, 2003). The left-hand column shows the names we have given to the stages of the model. These stages are described in Box 2.1.

Conclusion

The model of psychological recovery consists of four overarching psychological processes of recovery and five stages of recovery. The final stage is ongoing and dynamic, and characterized by continued striving for personal growth. In the following five chapters, this model will be elaborated by integrating the four processes conceptually within each of the five stages of recovery. Aspects of each process will be illustrated with first-person quotes, including some from more-recent consumer literature, and will be discussed in view of the broader literature on recovery from trauma and loss.

Table 2.2 Comparison between recovery stages identified in five studies.

Stages of recovery according to:

Andresen, Oades and Caputi (2003)	Davidson and Strauss (1992)	Baxter and Diehl (1998)	Young and Ensing (1999)	Pettie and Triolo (1999)	Spaniol et al. (2000)
Stage 1 Moratorium		1. Crisis *Recuperation*		1. Why Me? *Meaning of illness*	1. Overwhelmed by the disability
Stage 2 Awareness	1. Awareness of a more active self		1. Initiating recovery		
Stage 3 Preparation	2. Taking stock of self 3. Putting self into action	2. Decision	2. Regaining and moving forward	2. What now? *Reconstructing identity*	2. Struggling with the Disability
Stage 4 Rebuilding	4. Appealing to the self	*Rebuilding independence*			3. Living with the disability
Stage 5 Growth		3. Awakening *Building healthy interdependence*	3. Improving quality of life		4. Living beyond the disability

Box 2.1 The Five Stages of Psychological Recovery

Moratorium

This stage is characterized by denial of the 'illness identity', confusion, hopelessness, powerlessness and self-protective withdrawal. It is called moratorium, because it seems 'life is on hold'.

Awareness

The person has a first glimmer of hope of a better life, and the realization that recovery is possible. This can be an internal event – an intrinsic drive, or it may be sparked by righteous anger, instigated by a clinician or significant other who displays hope, or by a peer role model. It involves an awareness of a possible self other than that of 'sick person': a self that is capable of recovery.

Preparation

The person resolves to start working on recovering. This stage involves taking stock of the intact self, and of one's values, strengths and weaknesses. It involves learning about mental illness and services available, learning recovery skills, becoming involved in groups, connecting with peers and building strengths and confidence.

Rebuilding

In this stage, the hard work of recovery takes place. The person works to forge a positive identity. This involves setting and working towards personally valued goals, and may require reassessing old goals and values. This stage involves taking responsibility for managing the illness and taking control of one's life. It involves taking risks, suffering setbacks and coming back to try again.

Growth

This final stage of recovery may be viewed as an outcome of the recovery process. The person is confident in managing the illness, resilient in the face of setbacks and maintains a positive outlook. He or she has a positive sense of self, lives a full and meaningful life, and looks forward to the future. Continued striving for personal growth, signifying psychological well-being, is a characteristic of this dynamic phase.

Summary

- A consumer-oriented definition of recovery describes the psychological recovery from the impacts of the illness and the diagnosis to a dynamic stage of growth
- Psychological recovery is an active, person-driven process of growth.
- Individuals have different ideas of what recovery means to them, and there are areas of non-consensus.
- Contrasting views are expressed on: the return to a former state; the presence of symptoms; the return to a former role.
- First-person accounts identify common themes which represent psychological processes of recovery:
     Finding and maintaining hope
     Taking responsibility for life and well-being
     Rebuilding a positive identity
     Finding meaning and purpose in life.
- A number of qualitative studies have identified phases or stages of recovery.
- Five stages of recovery were identified:
     Moratorium
     Awareness
     Preparation
     Rebuilding
     Growth.

Appendix 2.A: Summary of the Consumer Literature Reviewed

First-person accounts of recovery

Alexander, D. (1994). A death-rebirth experience, in *The Experience of Recovery* (eds L. Spaniol and M. Koehler), Center for Psychiatric Rehabilitation, Boston, pp. 36–39.

Anonymous. (1989). First person account: A delicate balance. *Schizophrenia Bulletin*, 15 (2), 345–346.

Anonymous. (1994). Coping and recovery, in *The Experience of Recovery* (eds L. Spaniol and M. Koehler), Center for Psychiatric Rehabilitation, Boston, p. 25.

Anonymous. (1994). The challenge of recovery, in *The Experience of Recovery* (eds L. Spaniol and M. Koehler), Center for Psychiatric Rehabilitation, Boston, pp. 13–17.

Armstrong, M. (1994). What happened and how 'What Happened' got better, in *The Experience of Recovery* (eds L. Spaniol and M. Koehler), Center for Psychiatric Rehabilitation, Boston, pp. 52–53.

Berman, R. (1994). Lithium's other face, in *The Experience of Recovery* (eds L. Spaniol and M. Koehler), Center for Psychiatric Rehabilitation, Boston, pp. 40–45.

Campbell, T. (2000). First person account: falling on the pavement. *Schizophrenia Bulletin*, 26 (2), 507–509.

Chovil, I. (2000). First person account: I and I, dancing fool, challenge you the world to a duel. *Schizophrenia Bulletin*, 26 (3), 745–747.

Cloutier, G. R. (1994). Overcoming the black garden, in *The Experience of Recovery* (eds L. Spaniol and M. Koehler), Center for Psychiatric Rehabilitation, Boston, pp. 29–34.

Deegan, p. (1988). Recovery: The lived experience of rehabilitation. *Psychosocial Rehabilitation Journal*, 11 (4), 11–19.

Deegan, p. (1996). Recovery as a journey of the heart. *Psychiatric Rehabilitation Journal*, 19 (3), 91–97.

Dickerson, G. (1994). Keeping time in chaos, in *The Experience of Recovery* (eds L. Spaniol and M. Koehler), Center for Psychiatric Rehabilitation, Boston, pp. 26–28.

Fox, V. (2002). First person account: a glimpse of schizophrenia. *Schizophrenia Bulletin*, 28 (2), 363–365.

Greenblat, L. (2000). First person account: Understanding health as a continuum. *Schizophrenia Bulletin*, 26 (1), 243–245.

John. (1994). In *Altered Lives: Personal Experiences of Schizophrenia*. Schizophrenia Fellowship of Victoria, North Fitzroy, Victoria, Australia, pp. 8–10.

Koehler, M. (1994). My road to recovery, in *The Experience of Recovery* (eds L. Spaniol and M. Koehler), Center for Psychiatric Rehabilitation, Boston, pp. 22–23.

Leete, E. (1989). How I perceive and manage my illness. *Schizophrenia Bulletin*, 15 (2), 197–200.

Leibrich, J. (1997). The doors of perception. *Australian and New Zealand Journal of Psychiatry*, 31, 36–45.

Lynch, K. (2000). The long road back. *Journal of Clinical Psychology*, In Session, 56, 1427–1432.

Lynn, D. (1994). My struggle for freedom, in *The Experience of Recovery* (eds L. Spaniol and M. Koehler), Center for Psychiatric Rehabilitation, Boston, pp. 50–51.

Mary. (1994). In *Altered Lives: Personal Experiences of Schizophrenia*. Schizophrenia Fellowship of Victoria, North Fitzroy, Victoria, Australia, pp. 15–19.

McDermott, B. F. (1994). Transforming depression into creative self-expression, in *The Experience of Recovery* (eds L. Spaniol and M. Koehler), Center for Psychiatric Rehabilitation, Boston, pp. 64–67.

McQuillin, B. (1994). My life with schizophrenia, in *The Experience of Recovery* (eds L. Spaniol and M. Koehler), Center for Psychiatric Rehabilitation, Boston, pp. 7–10.

Roman. (1994). In *Altered Lives: Personal Experiences of Schizophrenia*. Schizophrenia Fellowship of Victoria, North Fitzroy, Victoria, Australia, pp. 41–44.

Schmook, A. (1994). They said I would never get better, in *The Experience of Recovery* (eds L. Spaniol and M. Koehler), Center for Psychiatric Rehabilitation, Boston, pp. 1–3.

Unzicker, R. (1994). On my own: A personal journey through madness and re-emergence. *Psychosocial Rehabilitation Journal*, 13 (1), 71–77.

Watson, B. E. (1994). My self story, in *The Experience of Recovery* (eds L. Spaniol and M. Koehler), Center for Psychiatric Rehabilitation, Boston, pp. 68–75.

Weingarten, R. (1994). The risks and rewards of advocacy, in *The Experience of Recovery* (eds L. Spaniol and M. Koehler), Center for Psychiatric Rehabilitation, Boston, pp. 77–78.

Wentworth, V. R. (1994). From both sides: The experience of a psychiatric survivor and psychotherapist, in *The Experience of Recovery* (eds L. Spaniol and M. Koehler), Center for Psychiatric Rehabilitation, Boston, pp. 80–88.

Consumer-authored theoretical articles

Bassman, R. (2000). Agents, not objects: Our fights to be. *Journal of Clinical Psychiatry*, In session, 56 (11), 1395–1411.

Crowley, K. (1997). Implementing the concept of recovery, *Final report: Blue Ribbon Commission on Mental Health*, Wisonsin Department of Health Services, Madison.

Crowley, K. (2000). *The Power of Procovery in Healing Mental Illness*. Kennedy Carlisle, Los Angeles.

Deegan, p. (1997). Recovery and empowerment for people with psychiatric disabilities. *Social Work in Health Care*, 25 (3), 11–24.

Fisher, D. B. (1994). Health care reform based on an empowerment model of recovery by people with psychiatric disabilities. *Hospital and Community Psychiatry*, 45 (9), 913–915.

Frese, F. J., III. (2000). Psychology practitioners and schizophrenia: A view from both sides. *Journal of Clinical Psychology: In Session*, 56, 1413–1426.

Frese, F. J., Stanley, J., Kress, K., and Vogel-Scibilia, S. (2001). Integrating evidence-based practices and the recovery model. *Psychiatric Services*, 52 (11), 1462–1468.

Mead, S. and Copeland, M. E. (2000). What recovery means to us: consumers' perspectives. *Community Mental Health Journal*, 36 (3), 315–328.

Murphy, M. A. (1998). Rejection, stigma and hope. *Psychiatric Rehabilitation Journal*, 22 (2), 186–188.

Schmook, A. (1996). Recovery: A consumer/survivor vision of hope. *Psychiatric Rehabilitation Skills*, 1 (1), 12–15.

Tenney, L. J. (2000). It has to be about choice. *Journal of Clinical Psychology*, In Session, 56, 1433–1445.

Appendix 2.B: Summary of Qualitative Studies Reviewed

Baxter, E. A. and Diehl, S. (1998). Emotional stages: Consumers and family members recovering from the trauma of mental illness. *Psychiatric Rehabilitation Journal*, 21 (4), 349–355.

Davidson, L. and Strauss, J. S. (1992). Sense of self in recovery from severe mental illness. *British Journal of Medical Psychology*, 65, 131–145.

Jacobson, N. and Greenley, D. (2001). What is recovery? A conceptual model and explication. *Psychiatric Services*, 52 (4), 482–689.

Ralph, R. O. (2000). Recovery. *Psychiatric Rehabilitation Skills*, 4 (3), 480–517.

Ridgway, P. (2001). ReStorying psychiatric disability: Learning from first person narratives. *Psychiatric Rehabilitation Journal*, 24 (4), 335–343.

Spaniol, L., Wewiorski, N., Gagne, C. and Anthony, W. A. (2002). The process of recovery from schizophrenia. *International Review of Psychiatry*, 14 (4), 327–336.

Tooth, B. A., Kalyanansundaram, V. and Glover, H. (1997). *Recovery from Schizophrenia: A Consumer Perspective*. Final Report to Health and Human Services Research and Development Grants Program. Department of Health and Aged Care, Canberra:

Young, S. L. and Ensing, D. S. (1999). Exploring recovery from the perspective of people with psychiatric disabilities. *Psychiatric Rehabilitation Journal*, 22 (3), 219–231.

Part II

Elaboration of the Model: From Hopelessness to Flourishing

3

Moratorium: The First Stage of Psychological Recovery

Overview

This chapter examines the psychological and social mechanisms that lead to the loss of hope, relinquishment of responsibility for one's life, loss of a sense of identity and the loss of meaning in life in the first stage of the recovery model, Moratorium. These processes are discussed in the context of the wider literature, and illustrated with quotes from consumers. An understanding of the moratorium stage lays the foundation for understanding the processes of recovery proper.

Negative Symptoms or Psychological Sequelae?

Contributing to the pessimistic attitude towards schizophrenia is the apparent lack of motivation in some people with the illness. This is often seen as a symptom of the illness. Lack of motivation, or 'avolition', is one of the negative symptoms of schizophrenia. However, a number of factors that are not essential to the illness can contribute towards this loss of motivation. Harding (1987) summarized possible causes of chronicity in schizophrenia other than the symptoms of the illness. These were:

- the effects of institutionalization;
- adoption of the patient role;
- lack of rehabilitation;
- social and economic status;

Psychological Recovery: Beyond Mental Illness, First Edition.
Retta Andresen, Lindsay G. Oades and Peter Caputi.
© 2011 John Wiley & Sons, Ltd. Published 2011 by John Wiley & Sons, Ltd.

- medication effects;
- staff expectations; and
- self-fulfilling prophecies.

Today, medications have improved, long-term hospitalization is no longer the norm (Warner, 2004) and policies promote rehabilitation and recovery. However, consumers continue to report the iatrogenic effects of medication, poor community care, the pessimistic attitude of mental health workers, stigma, adoption of the patient role and loss of hope as contributing to their apparent lack of motivation (e.g. Bassman, 2000; Bjorklund, 1998; Fekete, 2004; Frese, 2000; Henderson, 2004; Lally, 1989; Mead and Copeland, 2000). Strauss *et al.* (1989) described several psychological and environmental sources of negative symptoms, including:

- fear that involvement in enjoyable activities could lead to a relapse into positive symptoms;
- problems with losing the structure provided by the sick role to develop a 'non-patient' identity;
- self-protective withdrawal in the face of overwhelming conditions;
- institutionalization; and
- stigma leading to the acceptance of the role of mental patient.

These socially-induced negative symptoms can then affect the course of the disorder (Strauss *et al.*, 1989). It is clear that these factors may be present for people with serious mental illnesses other than schizophrenia. In this chapter, we examine how each of the component processes of recovery is absent in the Moratorium stage, and how this contributes to withdrawal, helplessness and the apparent lack of motivation.

Hope in the Moratorium Stage: Hopelessness

In the first stage of recovery, hopelessness abounds. Consumer accounts are rife with descriptions of the hopelessness that follows diagnosis and/or treatment. Those who are trying to help the person can paradoxically have the opposite effect. As noted in Chapter 1, the hope of consumers can be undermined by the lack of hope of their treating clinicians and programmes that are geared towards stabilization and maintenance (Harding, 1987). Many clinicians have been taught that people with schizophrenia never improve, and this is reflected in some psychoeducational programmes (Bassman, 2001; Chadwick, 1997; Strauss, 2005). As Strauss (2005) says, people are often told, 'You have a disease like diabetes. You will have it all your life. You will have to take medications all your life and there are certain things you will never be able to do' (p. 51). Chadwick (1997) explains that this analogy to chronic illness can underpin beliefs that there is no chance of recovery. Thus, consumers and their carers learn hopelessness from the attitudes of those trying to help them (Warner, 2004; Strauss, 2005). Bassman (2000), who held a Master's Degree in Psychology, relates:

> He was emphatic in alerting all of us to the chronic life-long course of my disease and explained how I would have to learn to live with my limitations. If I did become able to work, future employment would have to be in a low-pressure, low-stress job. (p. 1401)

Bassman later earned a Doctorate and at the time of his account had been working in a professional capacity for over 20 years (Bassman, 2001). Hope has been found to be unrelated to the severity of psychotic symptoms (Resnick, Rosenheck and Lehman, 2004). And hopelessness predicts poor rehabilitation outcomes for people with schizophrenia, even when the influence of negative symptoms is taken into account (Hoffmann, Kupper and Kunz, 2000). Hoffman and colleagues found that having already 'given up' – as evidenced by depressive-resigned coping strategies – was as strong a predictor of a person's poor outcome as were negative symptoms.

Hope theory describes hope as '. . . a positive motivational state that is based on a . . . sense of successful (a) agency (goal-directed energy), and (b) pathways (planning to meet goals)' (Snyder, Irving and Anderson, 1991, p. 287). 'Pathways thoughts' are the person's perceived ability to generate routes to goals. That is, the person believes he or she can find a way of attaining his or her goals. 'Agency thoughts' represent the person's belief that he or she will be able to make progress towards a goal. Thus, agency is the motivational component of hope theory (Snyder, 2000a). So in order to hope, the person has to have a goal, perceive a route to the goal, and have the motivation to pursue the goal. Goals are vital to hope; they provide the endpoints of mental action sequences (Snyder, 2000b). There can be no hope if there is no goal, and many people diagnosed with schizophrenia feel that their valued goals in life have been taken from them:

> Our pasts deserted us and we could not return to who we had been. Our futures appeared to us barren, lifeless places in which no dream could be planted and grow to reality. (Deegan, 1988, p. 55)

All purposeful human behaviour is goal-directed (e.g. Snyder, 2000b). Avolition, or the inability to initiate and persist in goal-directed behaviour, is one of the negative symptoms of schizophrena. However, rather than representing a symptom, avolition may represent goal-directed 'self-protective withdrawal' by someone whose dreams and aspirations have been shattered (Davidson and Stayner, 1997; Deegan, 1996b). Rodriguez-Hanley and Snyder (2000) described the loss of hope when a person's goals are blocked, tracing a route through rage, despair and finally apathy. Although these hypothesized stages of loss of hope do not map perfectly onto the consumer accounts of loss of hope in serious mental illness – for some, rage marks the returning of hope (e.g. Unzicker, 1994; Deegan 1996b) – the final stage, apathy, resonates with consumer descriptions. Apathy is a state of loss of interest in things that would normally be appealing or important, a lack of emotions or feelings, and passivity.

> Anguish is a death from which there appears to be no resurrection. It is inertia
> which paralyzes the will to do and to accomplish because there is no hope. (Deegan,
> 1988, p. 56)

Descent into apathy depends both on the importance of the goal and the perceived magnitude of the barriers to the goal (Rodriguez-Hanley and Snyder, 2000). Clearly, these factors are immense in the case of serious mental illness. The impediments to a person's goals are often portrayed as insurmountable – as illustrated by the earlier quotes of Bassman (2000), Bjorklund (1998), Deegan (1988) and others, who had been advised to abandon the aspirations they had and replace them with more 'realistic' goals.

In a review of the concept of personal hopefulness in the context of psychiatry, Nunn (1996) described hope as having three components: *temporality*, or future orientation; *desirability*, or the wished-for future; and *expectancy*, or the belief that the desired future is possible. Expectancy has to be strong enough to result in behaviour directed towards the desired future. Therefore, in line with Snyder's definition, hope is the general tendency to *construct* and *respond* to the perceived future *positively* (Nunn, 1996). When expectancy is weak, however, the person will not take action towards the goal. Nunn describes four components of personal hopefulness. These are: (i) mastery – consisting of personal responsibility, personal efficacy, and environmental responsiveness; (ii) purpose in life – the capacity to make sense of one's experience; (iii) future support – hope borne in the trust of others; and (iv) perceived future self. These components of personal hopefulness suggest links between the four components of recovery described by consumers. Hopelessness ensues when negative events are attributed to internal and global personal inadequacies that are projected onto the future self (Abramson, Metalsky and Alloy, 1989; Nunn, 1996). Nunn's and Snyder's formulations of hope and the descent into hopelessness are instructive on the loss of hope in the Moratorium stage.

Hopelessness develops when the person perceives the disorder and its consequences to be beyond his or her control, becomes demoralized, and gives up believing in a successful outcome (Hoffman, Kupper and Kunz, 2000). The person feels helpless, eventually abandoning responsibility and active coping strategies:

> It is a time of real darkness and despair. Just like the sea rose in January and February, it
> is a time when nothing seems to be growing except the darkness itself. It is a time of
> giving up. Giving up is a solution. Giving up numbs the pain because we stop asking
> 'why and how will I go on?' Even the simplest of tasks is overwhelming at this time. One
> learns to be helpless because that is safer than being completely hopeless. (Deegan,
> 1996a, p. 5)

Responsibility in the Moratorium Stage: Powerlessness

As suggested in Nunn's (1996) explication of hope, the agency component is linked to responsibility. People in the Moratorium stage feel powerless in almost all aspects of life. Chronic illness, whether physical or mental, in which a person feels a loss of control over the illness, can bring about a sense of powerlessness that can result in a cycle of poor self-esteem, depression and hopelessness (Miller, 1992). Furthermore, psychiatric symptoms themselves rob the person of a sense of control over themselves (e.g. Williams and Collins, 1999; Chovil, 2005). Dependency and the adoption of the sick role reflect the loss of a sense of agency and abandonment of responsibility for one's life. The following quotes suggest a path to loss of motivation, starting with the symptoms of the illness, through the negative effects of treatment on motivation and on to acceptance of the patient role: 'My illness attacked my self-esteem and motivation. I felt powerless, unable to improve my life' (Anonymous, 1994b); 'People have gotten used to their identities and roles as ill, victims, fragile, dependent and even as unhappy. Long ago we learned to "accept" our illnesses, give over control to others and tolerate the way of life' (Mead and Copeland, 2000, p. 321), and 'It's appealing to be taken care of and give up responsibility and indulge in hospitalisations, confusion and rejection of accountability for me and my life' (Dickerson, 1994, p. 28).

The sick role, which was conceptualized in the context of acute illnesses, allows a person temporary exemption from social roles, with the understanding that the person's responsibility is to get well by seeking, and complying with, the professional treatment. As Kelly and Millward (2004) point out, the sick role is not always appropriate in chronic illnesses, as it is based on the assumption that the condition can be cured by the doctor, and is only a temporary departure from one's usual roles and responsibilities.

The notion that people with a mental illness need to take responsibility for their own lives and wellness is not to be misunderstood. It is important to emphasize that this does not imply that the person is in some way responsible for their illness, or for the consequences of the illness. Although lack of autonomy has been shown to lead to depression, Waller (2005) warns against confusing increased autonomy with moral responsibility. Waller makes the distinction between moral responsibility, or being to *blame* for the condition, and 'take charge' responsibility, that is, responsibility for management of illness. Consumers have described the struggle with the loss of control over their lives, brought on by the illness ...

> My whole life had collapsed around me and it seemed like there wasn't anything I could have done to prevent it. But living with mental illness the rest of my life was not something I wanted to do. I wanted to sleep all the time, making it difficult to function on a daily basis. The simplest tasks were no longer easy to perform. My frustrations gave way to tears, self-pity, and resentment. I wanted answers and the mental health system didn't have any. (Schmook, 1994, p. 2)

... and by their treatment and care:

> Whereas most healthier people have had choices, I've had none. My choices were made
> for me by other people – parents, housing directors, hospital and staff psychiatrists.
> (Lynn, 1994, p. 51)

> ... the real tragedy of that time [in hospital] was the day-to-day tedium and boredom
> and wearing down of the human spirit – not being able to decide when to get up or go
> to bed, when to eat, with whom to talk, not being able to send or receive uncensored
> mail, to make a phone call, to eke out an instant of privacy – these were the more subtle
> results. (Unzicker, 1994, p. 61)

The role of this loss of choice in recovery from illness has been elaborated in Self
Determination Theory (e.g. Deci and Ryan, 2002; Sheldon, Williams and Joiner,
2003). Lack of autonomy in one's goals can undermine intrinsic motivation: the
inherent drive to learn, master and grow (Ryan and Deci, 2000b). Behaviour that is
controlled by others does not generate the same levels of energy and persistence as do
self-determined goals. Nor is the pursuit of controlled goals associated with the same
levels of well-being as autonomous personal goals (Sheldon and Kasser, 1998; Ryan
and Deci, 2000b). Treatment for physical and mental illnesses can often involve
treatment regimes, rehabilitation efforts and life goals that are not those of the
person trying to recover. Pettie and Triolo (1999) challenge us to imagine being a
participant in a game show:

> Come on down! ... way down ... to your new life as a mental health client. You lost
> your job, car, apartment and boyfriend, but just wait until you hear about one of the
> dazzling new goals we have in store for you in your new life! Your new goal is to drag
> yourself out of bed to get showered, dressed, and fed in time so you're no more than an
> hour late to the first group of your new day program! (p. 258)

Efforts to motivate people to non-autonomous goals by using controlling methods,
such as fear or coercion, paradoxically undermine motivation (Sheldon, Williams
and Joiner, 2003). Leibrich (1997) writes that the purportedly top-quality hospital,
which had been her last hope for asylum, maintained a hierarchy in which the
patients were treated as second-class citizens: patients' feelings and self-expressed
needs were understood in terms of mental illness. Leibrich says, 'I became mute,
almost catatonic' (p. 38).

The sense of powerlessness experienced by patients was one of the instigations
behind the consumer movement, which adopted 'consumer empowerment' as a
primary goal (McLean, 1995). The ex-patients' movement arose from gross abuses
of patients' human rights within the mental health system. Leibrich (1997) describes
how a group of patient representatives on a hospital staff–patient committee posted
a patients' 'bill of rights' on notice boards. It criticized lack of choice of treatment,
drug regimes and abuse of patients. The administrator's response the next morning
was to divide the patient representatives up so that they could no longer

communicate with each other. Leibrich (1997) was put in seclusion and drugged. The ex-patients' movement has two equally important objectives according to Chamberlin (1990). One is the development of self-help programmes as an alternative to professional treatment, although many people who attend these programmes simultaneously utilize traditional mental health services (Chamberlin, 1990). The other objective is advocacy for political change, such as the removal of all laws and practices which limit the rights and responsibilities of people who have been labelled with a mental illness (Chamberlin, 1990). Self-help groups have made great strides in combating stigma and increasing involvement of consumers in decision-making processes at all levels of the mental health system (Chamberlin, 1990), and one would hope that abuses of basic human rights are now rare in the mental health system. Nonetheless, consumers continue to suffer the effects of authoritarian organizations and power differentials between clinician and client (e.g. Barker, 2001; Fekete, 2004; Fisher, 1994; Lynn, 1994; McLean, 1995; Torgalsboen, 2001; Unzicker, 1994).

For consumers receiving care within the mental health system, the primary concern is for autonomy in personal treatment and rehabilitation decisions, and antecedent to this is the need for *personal* empowerment. Corrigan *et al.* (1999a) identified two superordinate factors to empowerment in a consumer population: community orientation and self-orientation. Community orientation to empowerment included the factors of community action, powerlessness and effecting change – variables which are clearly related to the aims of the survivors'/ex-patients' movement. Self-orientation to empowerment involved self-efficacy, optimism/ control over the future and self-esteem. These latter, intrapersonal, variables are demonstrably the more relevant to consumers struggling to regain responsibility for themselves and control over their lives. People describing their experience of the Moratorium stage have expressed feelings of complete powerlessness: 'When one lives without hope (when one has given up) the willingness to "do" is paralysed as well' (Deegan, 1994, p. 56).

The rediscovery of the *possibility* of a more active self is therefore necessary before a person can begin to take an active role in his or her own recovery (Davidson and Strauss, 1992). We will now explore the mechanisms and consequences of the loss of a sense of self.

Identity in the Moratorium Stage: Loss of Sense of Self

The loss of sense of self and one's identity is one of the most devastating consequences of serious mental illness. In the Moratorium stage, the person feels as though they no longer know who they are as a person. For example:

My illness eradicated my sense of self, and now I am engaged in the lifelong process of obtaining, maintaining and slowly modifying my sense of who I am. (Anonymous, 1994b, p. 25)

Two schools of thought exist as to the role of loss of self in schizophrenia (Estroff, 1989). The first, a clinical view, is that the illness *constitutes* the loss or absence of a sense of self. This concept has been examined from the perspectives of psychoanalytic self-psychology (e.g. Kohut and Wolf, 1978; Pollack, 1989), personal construct psychology (e.g. Gara, Rosenberg and Mueller, 1989; Rosenberg, 1993) and neuro-psychology (e.g. Hemsley, 1998; Vogeley *et al.*, 1999). In a case study investigating the loss of volition, Lysaker and Bell (1995) proposed that a fundamental disturbance of identity was the basis of the person's inability to pursue a direction in life: activity derives its meaning from the individual's sense of identity. Deprived of a sense of one's self, there is no basis for purposeful choice of activity. The second, social psychological view of loss of identity, is that the illness *results* in a loss of, or change in, the sense of self (e.g. Goffman, 1968; Erikson, 1975; Charmaz, 1983). This explanation was elaborated in relation to physical illness (Charmaz, 1983), and was applied by Pettie and Triolo (1999) to explain loss of identity in serious mental illness. Another theory of the loss of self in schizophrenia is the phenomenological view (Davidson, 1994). Davidson described a fundamental loss of a sense of self as stemming from symptoms such as hallucinations and thought insertion, which cause the person to feel that he or she can no longer trust his or her own perceptions, and can lead to a feeling of external control (Davidson, 1994). While not denying the possibility of the aetiological explanation of the relationship between the self and schizophrenia, or ignoring the phenomenology of a loss of sense of self, the consumer literature clearly focuses on the *psychosocial* effects of mental illness on the sense of self and identity.

Erikson (1968) described a person's identity as a 'progressive continuity between that which he has come to be during the long years of childhood, and that which he promises to become in the anticipated future' (p. 87). When a person loses the sense of continuity of the self, they suffer a crisis of identity (Erikson, 1968). Erikson described how some Second World War veterans seemed to lose their sense of identity: 'They knew who they were; they had a personal identity. But it was as if, subjectively, their lives no longer hung together—and never would again' (Erikson, 1963, p. 42). Kelly and Millward (2004) differentiate between two forms of identity: *the self* – referring to private identity; and *identity* which refers to social identity – or identity as it relates to others. With the onset of a severe and enduring mental illness, a number of processes come into play to undermine the sense of continuity of the self and of the social identity. First, the symptoms of the illness can include memory impairments that disrupt the person's sense of self through the loss of a sense of continuity between past, present and future identity (Davidson, 2002). Then, as described by Charmaz (1983), chronic illness – whether physical or mental – may rob the person of his or her close relationships, educational and/or occupational aspirations, social life and autonomy, thus undermining his or her social identity. Leibrich (1997) explains:

> I tried to pick up what was left of my life. But in the course of my illness and treatment I had lost my studies, my marriage, my home, and most of my friends. I returned to a community where I didn't belong any more . . .. (p. 39)

When a person's goals for the future are lost through uncontrollable events, their hoped-for possible self is also lost (King, 1998). Therefore, a person with a mental illness may find it impossible to imagine a positive 'future self' (Pettie and Triolo, 1999). Deegan (1997), at 17 years of age, had yet to start on her adult life course when her dreams were negated: 'My teenage world in which I aspired to dreams of being a valued person in valued roles ... I felt these parts of my identity being stripped from me' (p. 16).

And for an established professional, the effects are no less devastating, as made clear by Wentworth (1994), who had practiced many years as a psychotherapist before developing bipolar disorder. She writes:

> At the age of forty-three ... I was hurled into a new arena ... far into the side of life I had tried to help my clients avoid, the brutal, the ugly, the shadow side. I found myself in the space of the marginal, the deviant, the disabled .... I had landed myself in Hell. There I felt stark terror, the pain of rejection by people I trusted the most, isolation, deprivation, and unworthiness. The loss of power and respect was like being in a black hole where I had to fight my way out using all the skills and strengths I could summon. (p. 80)

Diagnosis and treatment, with the concomitant conferring of the 'mentally ill' label, robs the person of his or her sense of identity as a valuable and functioning member of society (e.g. Murphy, 1998; Henderson, 2004). According to Estroff (1989), schizophrenia can cause a more profound sense of loss of self than other chronic illnesses, as it may entail 'becoming a schizophrenic'. Bjorklund (1998) told in Chapter 1 how he left hospital, after only three weeks, as 'a schizophrenic'. Thus, the illness becomes part of the known self and of the social identity. The pre-illness self is usually perceived as 'successful, reliable, healthy, well and better .... The present self ... is perceived as unreliable, unsuccessful, sick, weird and worse' (Pettie and Triolo, 1999, p. 256). For example:

> The locked doors of the psych ward separating us from 'normal' people became my dominant metaphor. I was a resident of the psych ward wherever I went geographically. Me as 'crazy' now replaced every other image I had formed about myself – scholar, musician, poet. (Fekete, 2004, p. 190)

Labelling a person's problems as schizophrenia has a negative affect on the response of others towards that person, and engenders social distancing (Angermeyer and Matschinger, 2003). This stigma contributes to the poor outcomes of people with mental illness (Arboleda-Florez, 2003; Couture and Penn, 2003). Here Murphy (1998) describes stigma as the source of helplessness:

> No, the psychotic symptoms were not the cause of my despair. It was realizing that, because there is no cure for schizophrenia, I must wear this label for the rest of my life, and as a result of it, be considered different and treated as an inferior being. (p. 186)

Loss of a positive identity can also be engendered by *self*-stigma: previously internalized negative conceptualizations of people with a mental illness applied to the self (Lally, 1989; Corrigan and Watson, 2002). For example: 'But accepting the diagnosis was, for me, most difficult because I had to overcome my *own* stigma about being one of *them*' (Henderson, 2004, p. 85), and 'In my own mind I thought I was less than a part of the human race. I was on the other side of the wall between "normal" people and "crazy" people. I had left society and become a "mental patient."' (Fekete, 2004, p. 190)

These negative attitudes are then projected onto others. The person expects rejection in social situations, and so avoids them – even if the expectation of rejection is not justified by any actual experience of stigma (Lally, 1989). For instance: 'In fact, I carried the stigma myself! And had I not isolated myself by my own self-image, I felt assured that other people would isolate me if they found out I was a mental patient.' (Fekete, 2004, p.190)

This self-protective avoidance illustrates another contribution to the withdrawal seen in the Moratorium stage. An anonymous author provides this interesting insight on passivity in the face of an unacceptable identity:

> As someone who had not only produced and functioned professionally, but felt I was worthless if I didn't do so, it was quite a comedown when the medication stopped working. Thus my tendency in the past was to sit out life until I could be my ideal self, unwilling to acknowledge my imperfections and limitations or discuss them with my therapist. (Anonymous, 1994a, p. 15)

Stigma can be exacerbated by the attitude of clinicians and staff in treatment facilities (Frese, 2000; Sartorius, 2002). Deegan (1990) described the abuse of people in institutions as an underlying cause of despair. But overt physical or psychological abuse is not necessary for the transmission of stigmatizing attitudes. Chaplin (2000) found that psychiatrists often hold the same prejudices about people with mental illness as the wider population. Leibrich (1997) described earlier how the communication barrier between staff and patients led her to become 'almost catatonic' (p. 38). She continues: 'So people tried to pull me out of my darkness. Some tried to coax me out, others shame me out, drug me out, and get me into their light. Get me out of . . . my . . . self' (p. 38; ellipses in original). Fekete (2004) describes a more subtle effect of the power imbalance between the practitioner and the client: 'Her clinical posture deprived me of a feeling of full personhood and reinforced the doctrine that I was her "mental patient"' (p. 191).

The perceived inability to reaffirm an identity or sense of belonging can lead to defensive internalization of the illness identity (Rooke and Birchwood, 1998). Acceptance of the 'mentally ill' label can lead to engulfment in the patient role (Estroff, 1989; Lally, 1989; Gray, 2002). This entrapment in the patient role stems from the perception that relationships, core roles and autonomy are no longer available (Rooke and Birchwood, 1998). With this loss of a sense of self, and the emergence of the patient role, the person's expectations of him or herself are lowered

(Hayward and Bright, 1997), contributing to the loss of motivation seen in this stage.

Given the consequences of the stigma engendered by the label, a person, while accepting that his or her experiences are not normal, may reject the diagnostic label (e.g. Lally, 1989; Schmook, 1994; Pettie and Triolo, 1999; Bassman, 2000). Often construed as denial, this can be a self-protective reaction to the new identity that is inherent in the diagnosis: 'Our denial was an important stage in our recovery. It was a normal reaction to an overwhelming situation. It was our way of surviving those first awful months' (Deegan, 1988, p. 55).

When the self is under threat, strategies of reality negotiation are employed to protect the self-image (Snyder, 1989). The person distances him- or herself from information that has negative implications for the self, while maintaining beliefs that enhance the self (Snyder, 1989). The above quotes from consumers bring into question the wisdom that acceptance of the illness is an important precursor to coping with illness. Instead, acceptance can be a barrier to the active recovery process by encouraging resignation and passivity (Lally, 1989).

Deegan (1997) asserted that acceptance of the patient role resulted in there being 'no-one left inside' to do the work of recovery. A person's sense of self and identity provides a basis for the meaning in one's goals in life (Lysaker and Bell, 1995), and in the following section we will explore the loss of meaning and purpose in life in serious mental illness.

Meaning in the Moratorium Stage: Loss of Purpose in Life

The occurrence of serious mental illness is a traumatic event. A traumatic event challenges a person's basic beliefs about him or herself and about the world, creating a crisis of meaning (Emmons, Colby and Kaiser, 1998; Janoff-Bulman, 1992). There are two broad categories of the use of the word 'meaning' in the recovery literature. First, there is the meaning of the illness: What does the illness mean about me as a person? (e.g. Bjorklund, 1998; Murphy, 1998; Deegan, 1997; Pettie and Triolo, 1999; Chovil, 2000; Fekete, 2004; Henderson, 2004). This question clearly ties in with the sense of identity, but is also related to how the person reacts to the illness, and can influence his or her recovery (Davidson and Strauss, 1995). The second sense of the term relates to meaning in life or purpose in life. The loss of meaning in life has been investigated in other forms of loss or trauma (e.g. Jaffe, 1985; Elliott, Kurylo, and Rivera, 2002). It refers to the loss of purpose resulting from the loss of the constellation of goals and roles around which the person had structured his or her life (Emmons, Colby and Kaiser, 1998; King, 1998).

The effect of the construed meaning of the illness was explicated by Davidson and Strauss (1995). In explaining the necessity for understanding a person's relationship with the illness, Davidson and Strauss demonstrated how the meaning attributed to the illness can affect how a person reacts. In a case study, 'Mr J', whose illness first manifested after his divorce, viewed the illness as punishment for being a poor husband. Therefore, when each subsequent failed relationship initiated another episode of the illness, his theory that he was 'condemned to failure as a man' (p. 8) was further confirmed. When the person sees the symptoms of the illness as coming from a higher power, he or she can feel unable or even unwilling to avoid the symptoms. An early question a person asks when struck by mental illness is, Why did this happen to *me*? (Pettie and Triolo, 1999). If the person believes the answer is that he or she somehow deserved the illness as punishment, this can be detrimental to recovery, as the person is not sure that he or she is worthy of any gains in success or happiness (Pettie and Triolo, 1999). Janoff-Bulman (1992), in her theory of adjustment to trauma, distinguished between *characterological* self-blame and *behavioural* self-blame, claiming that the former explanation undermines self-worth, while the latter implies some control (Janoff-Bulman, 1992). Watson (1994) expressed such self-doubt: 'I have asked myself, as unfortunately do many mental patients, was this period of anguish punishment from God for my sin and rebellion' (p. 71).

Chovil (2005) describes another way in which the meaning of the symptoms can lead to helplessness. He tells of his delusions that powerful aliens had chosen him as the future of humankind. After a time, these 'aliens' had complete control over him. Chovil explains that to doubt the authority behind such hallucinations can be a test of faith, as the person has invested heavily in their reality. He writes that 'frightened individuals become helpless face to face with these powerful forces' (p. 70). When the person eventually chooses to defy these forces, and seek help, they may transfer their dependency to mental health services. Chovil (2005) suggests that this path to dependence and helplessness is possibly more relevant in the current climate than institutionalization caused by long-term hospitalization. Mental health services, he suggests, rather than *engendering* helplessness, are *responding* to helplessness.

When a person does come to a medical or psychosocial understanding of the illness, they then face the prospect that it may be a long-term problem (Spaniol, Gagne and Wewiorski, 2002). The acknowledgement that one needs professional help is a difficult step to take towards recovery, because the person is confronted by the loss of independence and sense of control (Young and Ensing, 1999). Then, when the person has achieved some stability, he or she may find it difficult to take steps towards engagement in new activities, due to fear of failure or of a return of symptoms (Strauss *et al.*, 1989; Spaniol, Gagne and Wewiorski, 2002).

This brings us to the second sense of meaning used in recovery – purpose in life. This use of meaning is the more prevalent one in the consumer accounts of recovery. Harvey (2000) defines a 'major loss' as one in which one's sense of self is fundamentally changed, and which disrupts a person's beliefs about his or her reasons for being (Harvey, 2000). Serious mental illness represents such a loss. The loss of one's important goals in life is one of the greatest and well-documented hurdles in coping with any chronic illness or acquired disability (e.g. Emmons, Colby and Kaiser, 1998; Lukas, 1998; Elliott *et al.*, 2000). Our long-term goals imbue our lives and our daily tasks with meaning. Clinging to unattainable goals can cause depressive symptoms, and ruminating on lost goals can lead to reductions in daily functioning and increased psychological distress (Klinger, 1975). This is particularly poignant when the goal that has become unattainable is central to a person's life and sense of identity (Brandtstadter, 2009).

Early in the illness, not only are previous meaningful life roles and goals lost, but the person can also have difficulty formulating and pursuing new goals. Spaniol *et al.* (2002) quote 'Mr F' as describing his life as 'like a revolving door. One minute it's one way, next minute it's another way' (p.330). Although prior to the illness he had worked professionally in a scientific laboratory, Mr F now had an irregular work history in menial jobs (Spaniol *et al.*, 2002). The loss of meaning when no longer able to pursue previous goals is illustrated by Fekete (2004), who experienced a psychosis whilst writing his dissertation. The psychosis caused written language to appear as a secret code that he could not understand, rendering him unable to continue with his scholarly work:

> Everything had lost its significance for me. Everything seemed meaningless. There was no enjoyment in things that used to amuse me . . .. There seemed no point in doing anything . . . . I saw myself as old, physically deteriorated and, basically, done with life. I seemed to myself to have succeeded at nothing. (p. 191)

And the impact of the loss of future goals is captured in this passage, in which Deegan (1997) looks back on herself as a 17 year-old:

> No, this is not mental illness I am seeing. I am witnessing the flame of the human spirit faltering. She is losing the will to live. She is not suicidal, but wants to die because nothing seems worth living for. Her hopes, her dreams, her aspirations have been shattered. She sees no way to achieve the valued roles she once dreamed of. (p. 17)

This loss of future goals then impacts on motivation in the present:

> As for the present, it was a numbing succession of meaningless days and nights in a world in which we had no place, no use and no reason to be. (Deegan, 1988, p. 55)

The person's interpretation of his or her symptoms, the chosen meaning of the illness to the person, and the loss of meaningful roles therefore conspire separately, or in combination, to rob the person of any motivation to work towards recovery.

Conclusion

By examining the Moratorium stage of psychological recovery in the light of the broader literature, we can see how psychological and sociological mechanisms can contribute to behaviour that may be misconstrued as negative symptoms of mental illness. A cycle of hopelessness ensues and becomes a self-fulfillng prophecy. In Chapter 4, we will explore how the components of recovery manifest themselves in the Awareness stage, in which the person realizes that recovery is possible.

Summary

- Understandable psychological ramifications of diagnosis can lead to self-protective withdrawal that is misinterpreted as a symptom of the illness.
- This apparent lack of motivation contributes to the pessimistic attitude towards serious mental illnesses such as schizophrenia.
- The lack of hope amongst professionals can be transferred implicitly to the consumer and others.
- Loss of motivation is reflected in each of the four processes of recovery.
- Hope can be undermined by the loss of goals and a lack of self-efficacy.
- Consequent adoption of the patient role can lead to abrogation of responsibility for recovery and for one's well-being.
- The loss of important roles in life and the stigma attached to the diagnosis contribute to the loss of identity
- The loss of important goals and valued roles also leads to a lack of meaning in life
- A cycle of hopelessness leads to a self-fulfilling prophecy of failure to recover psychologically.

4

Awareness: The Second Stage of Psychological Recovery

Overview

In this chapter we look at the turning point in recovery. In the Awareness stage, there is a dawning realization that life is not 'over'. Hope for a more fulfilling life may come from within the self, or be triggered by something, or someone, external. The person recognizes a sense of identity separate from the illness, and feels the need to take responsibility for his or her own recovery. There is renewed awareness of an intact 'self' and desire for a purpose in life.

Hope in the Awareness Stage: The Dawn of Hope

If hopelessness is a cause of chronicity, then hope has been identified as both the catalyst and the linchpin of recovery. Hope is an expectation that something good will happen in the future. Hope springs from a sense of 'the possible' (Adams and Partee, 1998, p. 31). A number of sources of hope for recovery were described in the consumer accounts. The hope of significant others often had a gradual healing effect on the person, bringing him or her to realize that life did not have to continue as a meaningless cycle of illness and treatment. Sometimes this 'sense of the possible' came from a professional, as Betty relates in Davidson and Strauss (1992):

> [My nurse] knew I had potential and talent and all this and that I could get better, and I knew it too. And I just woke up. I wasn't hallucinating as much, and I was active and eager, and I was also more social. (p. 135)

Psychological Recovery: Beyond Mental Illness, First Edition.
Retta Andresen, Lindsay G. Oades and Peter Caputi.
© 2011 John Wiley & Sons, Ltd. Published 2011 by John Wiley & Sons, Ltd.

Sometimes a family member's unwavering belief instils hope, as told by Greenblat (2000): 'It was [my mother's] perpetual optimism that kept me afloat, swimming with me until I was able to swim on my own' (p. 244).

Hope can also be inspired by peers who have recovered. Often this inspiration comes from the published stories of people with mental illnesses. Unzicker (1994) describes how another's recovery story provided the spark of hope for her: 'But there on the pages was another person's story, Judi Chamberlin's story of suffering and survival; it was her story that jump-started my rage' (p. 60). Others mentioned the stories of people with acquired physical disabilities who went on to achieve great things in life, such as the renowned physicist Stephen Hawking (Anonymous, 1994a), or those who demonstrated great courage and determination, for example Christopher Reeve, the actor who suffered quadri-plegia as the result of an accident (Pettie and Triolo, 1999). Support and self-help groups also provide peer role models who are further ahead in the recovery process (Pettie and Triolo, 1999; Young and Ensing, 1999; L. Brown, Wituk and Lucksted, 2010). When Tenney (2000) decided to change the patterns in her life, she found self-help and peer support more helpful than therapy. In fact, she says, 'It was basically what I would have liked therapy to be about – sharing as equals …' (p. 1442).

The will to recover can be the result of inner determination, as it was for Deegan (1996b), who described how her 'angry indignation' (p. 96) at the suggestion that she was destined for a life of 'maintenance' set her on the path to becoming a health professional.

Leibrich was inspired by the approaching new year to start a new life: 'The end of the year was close … I was possessed by the idea that I had to leave the hospital by New Year's Eve, a new decade' (Leibrich, 1997, p. 39). Leibrich tells how she discharged herself and spent the night alone, writing, and watched the sun rise in the distance, heralding a new decade.

For many, spirituality provides a source of hope and inspiration (Young and Ensing, 1999; Torgalsboen, 2001; Spaniol *et al.*, 2002; Wilding, May and Muir-Cochrane, 2005). Young and Ensing found that spirituality was the source of hope for the majority of participants in their study, faith in God providing a source of inner strength, peace and healing.

> Having faith in God has also given me hope. By participating in religious practice, including the disciplines of prayer and meditation, I have gained new strength and a new outlook on life. Granted I still have my problems, but my attitude has become one of optimism. (Murphy, 1998, p. 188)

Chadwick (1997) has highlighted the importance of taking spiritual issues into account and working from within the client's belief system. Spirituality does not necessarily imply religiousness. Lapsley, Nikora and Black (2002), in conducting qualitative research in New Zealand, found Christian and Maori traditional practices, as well as more 'New Age' and philosophical approaches were mentioned as bringing about the 'turning point' in recovery.

Snyder's hope theory (Snyder, Irving and Anderson, 1991; Snyder *et al.*, 1991) fittingly explains the leap of hope that occurs when the individual realizes that recovery is possible. In terms of hope theory, hopefulness can be restored with the emergence of a new goal, the emergence of a new pathway or skill, or an increased sense of agency (Snyder, 1998). Goals have been defined as '. . . internal representations of desired states . . .' (Austin and Vancouver, 1996). The Awareness stage of recovery in effect presents the person with a goal. This goal may be clear and concrete, as it was for Deegan (1996b). One participant in Kirkpatrick *et al.* (2001) explained: 'The seed of hope is when you want something, whether it's a job or a family or if you want some type of help in some area . . . you need something to hope for' (p. 49). For others, it is no more than a somewhat vague, distant goal of a 'better life' (Davidson and Strauss, 1992). For example, Koehler (1994) says: 'It was more like an inkling, a hunch, an intuition, one of those feelings that defies description . . . that told me this decade would be better than the last' (p. 22).

The person may experience any of the three components of hope first in the Awareness stage of recovery. The person may not yet have formulated pathways to the goal of recovery, but rather he or she realizes that pathways exist, because others with mental illnesses have managed to navigate them. For some, agency seems to come first, a sudden determination to get on with life: 'My inner spirit finally burst through and I convinced my medical team . . . that any possible period of "real life," indeed I had forgotten what this was, was worth any cycling I might sustain' (Berman, 1994, p. 42). Still for others, the care and belief of others seems to open up pathways to recovery before a future goal has been formulated, as described above by Greenblat (2000) and Betty (Davidson and Strauss, 1992). Byrne *et al.* (1994) found that a good relationship with a therapist who believed in the person's abilities could be a catalyst for change and a powerful motivator. Such a relationship was experienced by Watson (1994): '[My therapist] offered me, and continues to offer me . . . warmth, nurturance, brilliant insights and a dedication to, and intense belief in, my capacity to heal and grow' (p. 70).

Agency and pathways thoughts are both additive and iterative, so when one component occurs, the other component follows in an upward spiral (Snyder, 2002). According to hope theory, emotions follow cognitions about goals. When goals can be pursued without barriers, positive emotions result, while obstacles to goals produce negative emotional responses. As noted in Chapter 3, the association of successful pursuit of personal goals and subjective well-being has been explored by a number of researchers and theorists, including Brunstein *et al.* (1999), Deci and Ryan (2002), Diener *et al.* (1999), Emmons (1999b), King (1998), Omodei and Wearing (1990) and Sheldon and Kasser (2001). Since psychological well-being is an important feature of recovery, it comes as no surprise that the expectation of goal attainment would be a first rung on the recovery ladder – the kernel of hope. The advent of hope brings with it the sense of personal agency that is necessary for taking responsibility for recovery.

Responsibility in the Awareness Stage: The Need to Take Control

In the Moratorium stage, the person has the sense of having no control over his or her life. He or she has forfeited responsibility: their treatment, and their lives generally, are in the hands of carers and professionals. However, the person is experiencing an existential crisis; life lacks meaning and purpose and he or she has lost the sense of personal coherence. The second stage of recovery is heralded by an awareness of the need to take control of one's life, and this suggests that, even though the person may not have formulated clear goals, the individual is acutely aware that his or her life is 'going nowhere'.

For some, it was the feeling of not making progress in their mental health. Being a receiver of treatment was not enough – they realized that they would need to do more for themselves:

> What I can say about my recovery is that I had to accept that I played a role in my wellness . . .. I knew I had to have a working relationship with a therapist and accept my part of the job. I carry with me today the question I was asked several years ago: 'Are you ready to be well?' I wasn't then, I am now. (Greenblat, 2000, p. 245)

> I now realize that I needed to take some responsibility for my recovery; I can't just wait for the pills to save me . . .. It hasn't been easy to change, but I've begun to make a start and I see some hope where I saw none before. (Anonymous, 1994a, p. 14)

> I was very frustrated waiting for this psychiatrist to perform the necessary miracles . . . I faced the fact that if my situation was going to improve, I would have to do it myself. (Chovil, 2005, p. 70)

Nor does control of symptoms constitute recovery. Recovered consumers realized that more was required, and it had to come from themselves. Fox (2002), describes how, after the medication started to work, she still questioned whether to 'embrace the world of thought or to continue to believe in [her] inner voices' (p. 365). She eventually made a conscious choice to let go of the world of voices and 'embrace the world where [her] children and mother were' (p. 365).

Even in the midst of illness, some people experienced an awareness that they had to decide to be well. After a failed suicide attempt, Watson (1994) tells, 'I vowed "never again" I would endure to the end' (p. 70). While Simon, quoted in Thornhill, Clare and May (2004), related how something just 'dawned on him' and he decided to let go of being mad. Simon described the feeling as like a moment of 'grace'.

As we discussed in the previous chapter, personal empowerment is needed in order to take responsibility. The power differential that exists in some therapeutic relationships can hinder the personal empowerment of the consumer. However, the actions or attitude of the mental health practitioner can enable a person to take charge of their recovery. Leibrich (1997) illustrates the subtle nature of the power imbalance, and how simply this can be overcome with a person-centred approach:

> But one day something changed. I was assigned to a therapist who said the most astonishing thing. In all the time I had been unravelling inside, no-one had ever said this: 'Let me come in there with you. Show me what its like.' (p. 38)

Leibrich goes on to explain that for the first time she felt safe to talk about what was going on inside, and she 'began to emerge' (p. 38).

A compelling example of the effects of an empowering attitude among staff is provided by one of the case studies reported by Davidson and Strauss (1995). After 15 years of schizophrenia involving eight hospitalizations, divorce and unemployment, 'Mr. J' turned his life around when an aide on the inpatient unit pointed out to him that he could still make something of his life if he so wanted. Mr J reported that this restored some hope for a better life, and placed responsibility for change on his own shoulders. Five years later he was studying, parenting his young child, working two part-time jobs, socializing with a number of friends and his cognitive functioning had improved considerably. This is a powerful illustration of a turning point.

Frankl (1984) pointed out that only the individual has the power to imbue his or her life with meaning by setting meaningful goals. He maintained it was the *responsibility* of everyman to make life meaningful in this way, and moreover, that this is the *primary motivating source* in human beings. The stories of consumers illustrate how powerful this drive is, when, in the midst of serious mental illness, individuals will look deep within themselves to find the resources to take on that responsibility. The significance of even tiny acts of personal responsibility is illustrated by Betty (Davidson and Strauss, 1992), as she talks about her new-found ability to 'nurture' herself, by listening to jazz music on the radio: '*I* turn it on, *I'm* responsible, *I* enjoy the music, *I* make notes and draw while I'm hearing it . . . then I turn it off . . .' (p. 138). Betty explains the importance of doing this herself, and for herself, thus providing evidence that she is capable of having control over some aspect of her life (Davidson and Strauss, 1992).

Betty's experience reveals the importance of a sense of control and autonomy in recovery from serious mental illness. A sense of control has also been found to be an important factor in recovery from serious physical conditions, such as chronic illness (Jaffe, 1985; Sidell, 1997) and acquired disability (Dunn, 1996), as well as traumatic events (Taylor, 1983) and bereavement (Stroebe and Stroebe, 1993). The ability to 'choose life' in the most debilitating circumstances is illustrated by Simpson (1982, cited in Jaffe, 1985). Simpson was recovering from a coma, which left her with almost total amnesia as well as physical disabilities. She was in a deep depression after returning home and felt victimized: 'I felt that for arbitrary reasons I was being picked on and abused.' Seeing no escape, she wondered if she could just lie down and die. However, she wrote, 'One must squeeze the victim out of oneself . . .

Choose for vigor. Opt for life.' This same attitude of choosing between life and death can be seen in those who have recovered from serious mental illness:

> At age 40, I reached a point in my life where I knew there were only two choices: to live or to die. Dying would be an easy way out of the relentless chattering that continued in my head. Living would take courage. (McDermott, 1994, p. 65)

Responsibility, personal empowerment and agency reflect the growing sense of an agentic self (Davidson and Strauss, 1992) that occurs in the Awareness stage, along with the realization of the possibility of a positive identity.

Identity in the Awareness Stage: I Am Not the Illness

In this stage of recovery, the person realizes that there still exists an 'intact self' capable of taking action on one's own behalf (Davidson, 1994). Davidson and Strauss (1992) found that for some people, there is a realization that there remain healthy parts of the self that are not affected by the illness. Others become aware of personal resources of which they were previously unaware. Deegan (cited in Spaniol and Gagne, 1997) explained the need to be become aware of one's inner strengths before being able to accept the illness:

> How can we accept the illness when we have no hope . . .. Why should one pile despair on top of hopelessness.. . . So perhaps people are wise in not accepting the illness until they have the resources to deal with it. (p. 76)

As Estroff (1989) proposed, denial of illness, even while acknowledging symptoms, can be a plea for recognition of the persisting healthy self trying to survive. There is an enduring 'core' self that has developed over time, that the person is trying to distinguish from the negative social identity bestowed by the illness (Estroff, 1989; Charmaz, 1999). 'Mr A' described the 'part of me that is well no matter what situation I get myself into, the aspect of me that loves myself without any conditions attached ...' (Duckworth *et al.*, 1997, p. 229). In the Awareness stage, there is a breaking away from the feeling that the illness must dictate who one is, as the person comes to realize the possibility of a self independent of the patient role. As noted in Chapter 3, the sick role is legitimate in acute conditions, allowing the person to become dependent on necessary care and to receive exemption from his or her usual roles (Kelly and Millward, 2004). However, in the case of chronic illness, the hierarchical relationship between patients and professionals is more appropriately replaced by a collaborative relationship; and the person may wish to retain social roles which may be abandoned in the sick role (Charmaz, 1999).

Pettie and Triolo (1999) have identified two positive explanations of mental illness a person may adopt. The first they describe as 'illness as evolution' (p. 260). In this explanation, illness is seen as a way of learning about the self and developing previously unrecognized strengths. This meaning of the illness helps to instil hope for a positive future, and provides a reason to work towards recovery. Curtis (2000) described recovery as a process of moving from being defined by the illness, to integrating the illness as a small part of the whole self. People reconstruct a sense of self, in which the illness is seen as only one aspect of a complex self (Young and Ensing, 1999). Illness as evolution is one way of accepting the illness as part of the self. A second way of accepting the illness is to regard it as a separate entity, or 'illness personified' (Pettie and Triolo, 1999, p. 260). This implies a relationship between the self and the illness, and allows the person to develop an identity separate from the illness (Strauss, 1989; Davidson and Strauss, 1992; Pettie and Triolo, 1999). Pettie and Triolo explain that 'illness personified' gives the person some control over their part of the relationship: that is, in how they respond to the illness. Strauss (1989) found that a key turning point evident in interviews of people with schizophrenia was a change of attitude in which the person accepted the illness and decided to have a life in spite of the illness. Acceptance did not take the form of resignation, which would denote helplessness, but rather, the determination to work towards a better life (Strauss, 1989). People who are in positions where they have little control over events, choices or outcomes, can adopt a stance of applying their remaining resources to do what they can (Jaffe, 1985, p. 113).

For some people, this separation of self from the illness was facilitated by adopting a biomedical explanation of illness (e.g. Anonymous, 1994b; Armstrong, 1994; Berman, 1994; Fekete, 2004; Henderson, 2004). Fekete (2004) says 'I distinguish between bipolar disorder and what I mean by me, or my identity. My illness is a separate, alien thing from my identity' (p. 192). However, many individuals vehemently deny the medical model of mental illness, claiming that this explanation is fraught with determinism and hopelessness (Thornhill *et al.*, 2004). The medical model leaves them without hope of recovery, and tied to a future of medication, treatment and merely coping (e.g. Bjorklund, 1998; Schmook, 1994; Unzicker, 1994). Some people described hardships or childhood trauma which they felt were causal factors in the illness (Anonymous, 1989; G. Dickerson, 1994; Lynch, 2000; Lynn, 1994), whereas others adopt the biopsychosocial model (Anonymous, 1994a; Leete, 1989; McDermott, 1994; Wentworth, 1994). For example, an anonymous consumer says, 'I have gotten a lot of insight into how my background shaped my personality, and I can see where I got some 'raw material' for developing my particular brand of delusions, paranoia, and other symptoms' (Anonymous, 1989, p. 346).

Miriam (cited in Thornhill, Clare and May, 2004) rejected the medical model being imposed on her, and says 'I had a very passionate feeling that I needed help with a great many human problems' (p. 188). This enabled her to escape from the illness identity and was more important to her than getting over the psychosis itself. While for Alexander (1994) the psychosis represented a spiritual journey:

> Important to my healing, was the realization that I had an experience that was to be treasured and not labeled as a 'mental illness'. My identity was focused away from

being a patient or ex-patient, but to my own life experience which was validated by literature and philosophy. (p. 38)

Whether adopting a medical, psychosocial, biopsychosocial or spiritual model, the person takes comfort in an explanation of the illness that relieves him or her of the stigma of mental illness: 'I have often told friends that the key to overcoming schizoaffective disorder is to know yourself, to know your illness, and to know the difference between the two' (Anonymous, 1994b, p. 25).

Freedom from the patient identity enables the person to imagine a more positive possible future self. As described by Jaffe (1985), this response is in contrast to the 'victimization' response, characterized by helplessness, and is at the core of self-renewal after traumatic experiences.

Meaning in the Awareness Stage: Need for a Purpose in Life

In the Awareness stage, the person strives to assimilate the illness into their 'world view', developing an understanding of why it occurred and what the implications are for his or her future (e.g. Emmons, Colby and Kaiser, 1998). In the section on Identity, above, we saw how the adoption of an explanation of mental illness enabled a person to separate the self from the illness. Seeking a meaning of the illness in the Awareness stage can be explained by theories of cognitive control, in which one tries to understand unexplainable negative events by finding a reason for them (e.g. Taylor, 1983; Jaffe, 1985; Janoff-Bulman, 1992). For example, people with serious physical illnesses try to determine the cause of the illness, thus enabling them to take action in curing, managing or preventing a recurrence of the illness (Taylor, 1983). In the case of mental illness, the 'chosen meaning' provides a foundation for the person to start working towards recovery (Pettie and Triolo, 1999, p. 260).

Agentic, rather than resigned, acceptance of the illness goes hand-in-hand with the need to find meaning in life. Awareness of an agentic self, and the possibility of a positive identity, accompanies the perception that life as a 'mental patient' is empty and meaningless. The person is acutely aware of the loss of, or failure to acquire, meaningful goals and roles. Chovil (2005) describes how, once he stopped believing in his delusions, he realized the damage that had been done to his life:

> What if Saint Francis d'Assisi had one day realised that there was no God, that he had been talking to the birds instead of acquiring career training, courting his future wife, building equity to buy a home, and ultimately raising a family. What if he realized that he had nothing concrete to show for the last ten years of his life . . . and now he was face to face with the one person who specialized in his loss, a psychiatrist? (p. 70)

Chovil went on to explain that he eventually realized that neither the psychiatrist, nor anyone else, could undo the damage that had been done, and that it was up to him to improve his situation. While continuing psychiatric care and medication, he took responsibility for solving the problems of his life.

For Berman, it was a sense that meaningful life had been passing him by whilst he had struggled for 20 years to maintain professional employment in 'marshmallow-clouded concentration' on lithium:

> Finally, too much, much too much of life had passed me by while I dwelled in a semi-alive state. Barely functioning .... Never really being able to enjoy the rather rare pleasant things that came my way .... Life, as I experienced it, was through my marshmallow .... (Berman, 1994, p. 42)

Berman explains that he decided to go off medication, as any chance of experiencing a satisfying life was worth the risk of continued symptoms. The need for a more meaningful life can require a change of attitude that can involve some very difficult and threatening decisions. For Berman it involved giving up hope of further professional employment and considering himself retired. At the other end of the scale, another author, who had worked professionally before the onset of illness, writes of a change of attitude which saw him accept participation in a rehabilitation programme, involving work in a sheltered workshop, as a first step towards returning to meaningful employment (Anonymous, 1994a). Acceptance of his illness and his limitations enabled him to consider the rehabilitation process as 'just a phase' (p. 16).

Leibrich (1997) explained how, her life in ruins after having received all available help without recovering, suicide had seemed like a rational decision. A failed attempt and subsequent hospitalization provided the catalyst for her recovery:

> But I failed and there was another hospital admission. This time I went less willingly. Once again I was forced to take drugs I didn't want. Now I felt imprisoned within a prison within a prison. For the first time, I realised that the treatment was becoming a disease. (Leibrich, 1997, p. 39)

While some people never had the opportunity to secure meaningful adult roles prior to the illness, others lost high-status positions and families because of the illness. Against professional advice, Schmook (1994) desperately clung to her roles as mother and provider, and sought a doctor who would support her efforts to get well:

> My therapist tried to convince me to go on welfare; to get food stamps; to get housing assistance; to get aid for families with dependent children. I told her that, in good conscience I couldn't do that. I wanted to get better. (p. 2)

As we noted in Chapter 3, our personal goals imbue our lives with meaning (Emmons, Colby and Kaiser, 1998; King, 1998; Little, 1998). In the Awareness stage, the desire for a better life, the separation of self from the illness, and an emerging sense of agency are manifestations of goal-directed thinking. Frankl (1984) asserted that the 'primary motivational force' (p. 121) in human beings is the 'will to meaning' and this is manifested by finding a purpose. Purpose in life is a key component of psychological well-being, which has been conceptualized as striving to reach one's full potential (Ryff and Keyes, 1995). The consumer stories illustrate how, even in the depths of despair, this need for meaning and purpose in life can break through, providing the motivation to work towards a fulfilling life, by establishing goals that transcend coping with, and management of, the illness.

Conclusion

The Awareness stage, then, represents the person's dawning realization of the possibility of a more fulfilling life, that it is they who have to make this become a reality, and that they may indeed possess the internal resources to recover. For some people, a clear concrete goal emerges, while for others, it is a more vague goal of a 'real' life. Still others simply have a feeling that he or she could 'do better' (Davidson and Strauss, 1992). This is the turning point in recovery. 'Hope is the turning point that must quickly be followed by the willingness to act' (Deegan, 1988, p. 56). This brings us to the Preparation stage, which we discuss in Chapter 5.

Summary

- The Awareness stage marks the turning point in the recovery process.
- The catalyst can be a significant other, a role model or an inner drive.
- The person finds hope in the form of a goal, a sense of agency or a realization that there are pathways towards recovery.
- Goals may be clear and concrete, or a vague 'general' goal of recovery.
- There is a re-awakening of the need to take control of one's life.
- There is a realization that, even with effective medication, real recovery comes from within the person.
- The person becomes aware of his or her intact core self.
- Illness may be seen as either separate from, or incorporated into, the whole self.
- A desire for meaning and purpose in life becomes manifest.

5

Preparation: The Third Stage of Psychological Recovery

Overview

In the third stage of recovery, the Preparation stage, the person lays the groundwork for recovery. This groundwork may take the form of introspective preparation, identifying one's strengths and values, as well as practical steps towards utilizing whatever resources are available.

Hope in the Preparation Stage: Mobilizing Resources

> From that point on, I reinvested in life, in my own recovery process. I was no longer just a 'mental patient' who would recycle in and out of hospitals the rest of my life. I dared to begin to think of the present and make future plans instead of dwelling on the past. (Lynch, 2000, p. 1430)

This quote is a fitting introduction to the Preparation stage of psychological recovery. We can continue to utilize Snyder's theory to describe hope in the Preparation stage. Hope can be seen in the mobilization of both personal and external resources to foster agency and find pathways to goals. Agency involves building on inner strengths, while finding pathways can take the form of gathering knowledge and information, utilizing resources such as rehabilitation services and/ or seeking peer support.

Psychological Recovery: Beyond Mental Illness, First Edition.
Retta Andresen, Lindsay G. Oades and Peter Caputi.
© 2011 John Wiley & Sons, Ltd. Published 2011 by John Wiley & Sons, Ltd.

The notion of 'taking stock' of personal resources and building on strengths is a recurring theme of the Preparation stage of recovery (e.g. Davidson and Strauss, 1992; Young and Ensing, 1999; Mead and Copeland, 2000; Lapsley, Nikora and Black, 2002; Lunt, 2002; Spaniol *et al.*, 2002). This idea was colourfully illustrated by Betty (in Davidson and Strauss, 1992), who used the analogy of baking a cake:

> I have a good will . . . [but] the kitchen has to be right, so to speak, before I . . . do the endeavours. The feeling . . . has to be right . . . everything has to be right before you can make a cake . . . . If you don't feel like buying the flour for six months . . . then you don't feel like it. Then you get your flour, and then you notice you don't have enough cinnamon, so you wait a while. (p. 137; ellipses in original)

Betty's story relates to building inner resources, rather than finding external sources of support. Her words describe building on the agency component of hope. The development of a wide range of personal skills was identified by the participants in Young and Ensing's (1999) research, including: learning to live in the moment – not being preoccupied with the future or the past; learning to be honest with self and others; learning to be assertive; learning to accept what you need from various resources; and learning that there are many productive ways to use time and energy. Changing self-destructive behaviours has also been identified as important in nurturing hope during recovery (Kirkpatrick *et al.*, 2001).

During this period, the use of information resources can be important in helping people to understand both their illness and the resources available to help them to grow beyond the illness (Armstrong, 1994; Frese, 2000; D. Marsh, 2000; Mead and Copeland, 2000). Berman (1994) spent many years during his illness as a leader of a peer support group, while battling with the blunting effects of medication. In this role, he organized a strong educational programme, and relates the value of seeking knowledge about the illness:

> For me this played a crucial role in building a background of knowledge and understanding upon which I grew, even significantly enough to question my continued use of lithium. In my opinion, knowledge and understanding are the foundation for all successful coping. (p. 43)

The theme of seeking out resources and building the necessary skills for recovery was echoed in a number of stories and studies. For example, Thornhill, Clare and May (2004), in their analysis of recovery narratives, relate the experience of Simon, who, after deciding to 'let go of being mad' (p. 189) started on his journey of recovery by taking on unskilled work, and exploring mental health resources and alternative avenues to wellbeing. In terms of hope theory, Simon's story represents an example of finding new pathways. Schmook (1996) tells us 'As one begins to take action and experiences small triumphs, which may or may not be noticed by anyone else, hope of recovery begins to be internalized' (p. 14).

While the person is building on his or her strengths, developing skills and learning about resources, they may not yet have a clearly defined goal. Although in the Awareness stage the person may have developed a goal of recovery, this may as yet be a somewhat nebulous idea. Hopeful thinking has been associated with concrete goals rather than vague goals, and there is less likelihood of achieving a poorly defined goal (Snyder *et al.*, 2006). Identifying a goal may sometimes require abandoning long-held aspirations, and taking small steps towards a new goal, as we saw plainly expressed by Crowley (2000) in Chapter 2.

Therefore, in the Preparation stage, the person may have a highly motivating long-term goal, or alternatively, may set him or herself short-term, incremental goals. King (1998) notes that when a person's life goals become unattainable, day-to-day goals can provide a buffer and a sense of agency while the long-term goal changes. Whatever the level of goal chosen, the tone of the consumer stories is that it is *approach* rather than *avoidance* goals that are in the spirit of recovery. That is, goals directed towards attaining desirable outcomes rather than avoiding negative outcomes (e.g. Higgins *et al.*, 1994; Elliot, Sheldon and Church, 1997). The nature of the recovery stories is that there is a determination to break free of a life ruled by the illness (e.g. Crowley, 1997; Young and Ensing, 1999; Mead and Copeland, 2000; Tenney, 2000; Lunt, 2002). Therefore, a goal of avoiding stress, for example, does not reflect the recovery ethos as does the goal of learning to self-manage one's illness. Approach goals have been associated with higher levels of hope (Snyder *et al.*, 2000), wellbeing (Emmons, 1999b), goal attainment (Elliot and Church, 1997) and perceived confidence in illness management (Elliot and Sheldon, 1998). The development of approach-oriented goals or tasks implies hope for the future and entails a budding sense of agency – a necessity for taking responsibility.

Responsibility in the Preparation Stage: Taking Autonomous Steps

Movement from the Awareness stage to the Preparation stage requires determination to realize the goal of recovery. The process of moving from the question 'Why did this happen to me?' to the question 'How do I proceed from here?' requires taking responsible action (Lunt, 2002). To be empowered in one's recovery necessitates making informed decisions and, to enable this, the person needs to acquire an understanding of the illness and its management. Learning about the effects of the illness is one of the steps towards taking responsibility:

> As a result of hard work in therapy and other support, during my fourth hospitalization, I began to acknowledge that I have a chronic and serious mental illness and discuss specific limitations and how I might deal with them. (Anonymous, 1994a, p. 16)

> I ... have found education invaluable in understanding my illness, coming to terms with it and dealing with it. We must conscientiously study our illnesses and learn for

ourselves what we can do to cope with the individual disabilities we experience. (Leete, 1989, p. 199)

Learning about the illness can improve the ability to recognize, monitor and manage symptoms, and to monitor medications and make treatment decisions. Aside from these illness-related activities, the nature of recovery is in taking charge of one's life as a whole. Agency is cultivated by rebuilding independence in basic areas of life, such as self-care and care of the living environment, which provide proof to the person of his or her ability to live in the world (Davidson and Strauss, 1992; Baxter and Diehl, 1998; Young and Ensing, 1999). The person becomes aware of the importance of self-nurturing, taking time for the self and looking after one's own needs: 'I now try to do things for myself. I go for walks and just do things for me. I know that sounds selfish, but that is what you have to do' (in Young and Ensing, 1999, p. 223). Learning about one's illness and its management, making lifestyle changes, and utilizing psychological methods such as meditation have also been found to instil a sense of control associated with better adjustment in cancer patients (Taylor, 1983). In preparation for rebuilding independence, the person may also utilize available resources to work on social and vocational skills (Baxter and Diehl, 1998; Young and Ensing, 1999). For example, Henderson explains how she prepared for employment:

> There were things I had to do to make certain my success in these activities. I established routines for ensuring good nutrition (three squares a day), adequate sleep, regular exercise, continued compliance with taking my medication and keeping therapy appointments. My increased socialising helped me feel more comfortable around people . . . I collected information relevant to my work history. I considered the appropriateness of my wardrobe for interviewing, and the kinds of work I like to do. (Henderson, 2004, p. 86)

Tenney (2000) found that involvement with a peer support group provided her with the psychological resources needed to advance with her recovery:

> Something incredible happened – I began to take responsibility for my actions. I found myself getting excited about my life and creative about my choices. For me the change had happened. (p. 1442)

All of these efforts towards self-empowerment, control of life and management of illness require the courage to take risks. Davidson and Strauss (1992) reported that participants emphasized the need for a sense of *possibility* of change before taking new risks. Therefore, consumers stress the importance of the support of others in their efforts to access the internal resources required to challenge entrenched assumptions about their limitations (Mead and Copeland, 2000). Empowerment in recovery can be fostered by empowering attitudes of professionals and caregivers:

> Yet too many times our efforts to cope go unnoticed or are seen as symptoms themselves . . .. Unfortunately, our progress continues to be measured by professionals

with concepts like 'consent' and 'cooperate' and 'comply' instead of 'choose' insinuating that we are incapable of taking an active role as partners in our own recovery. (Leete, 1989, p. 200)

Identity in the Preparation Stage: Taking an Internal Inventory

'Taking stock' of the self during preparation for recovery is mentioned frequently by consumers and by researchers (e.g. Davidson and Strauss, 1992; Williams and Collins, 1999; Mead and Copeland, 2000; Sells, Stayner and Davidson, 2004). In the Awareness stage the person recognizes that there exists a part of him or her that is not affected by the illness (Davidson and Strauss, 1992). During the Preparation stage, the person takes stock of his or her skills and strengths in order to build on them to rediscover a positive sense of identity.

> Ultimately we must conquer stigma from within. As a first step – and a crucial one – it is imperative for us as clients to look within ourselves for our strengths. These strengths are the tools for rebuilding our self-image and thus our self-esteem. (Leete, 1989, p. 199)

The idea of taking stock of the personal resources necessary for a task was illustrated by Betty (Davidson and Strauss, 1992) in the passage on Hope, above. Mead and Copeland (2000) described the need to rebuild a positive sense of self by testing out one's internal resources. This involves taking risks in trying out new activities to re-establish a sense of self that is not limited by beliefs about the illness. The person not only rediscovers lost aspects of the self, but may also discover new aspects, which are then incorporated into a new sense of self (Davidson and Strauss, 1992; Young and Ensing, 1999).

However, it is not only strengths and limitations that are assessed during the Preparation stage – the person also needs to develop a durable sense of self – that is, a sense of being the same person one was before the illness (Sells, Stayner and Davidson, 2004). As one of Young and Ensing's (1999) participants expressed:

> It feels like I haven't lost touch with me altogether. That I am still wandering around in there and that I just have a little more work to do to find me, but you know maybe if I get up and go and search I'm there somewhere. And little by little I will find me again. (p. 226)

The person needs to separate thoughts and emotions that were caused by the psychosis from their core beliefs (Williams and Collins, 1999). This appears to be the process described here by Wentworth (1994):

> The internal definitions of reality (my assumptions, beliefs, attitudes, thinking) that I held when I first got manic had to be changed for me to heal though

> I didn't realize it consciously at the time. I had to grow in understanding. That took a lot of work and a lot of time. I took a long time turning understanding into behavioral change. (p. 83)

The rediscovery of his or her positive qualities and deeply held values forms the basis for setting goals which uphold these values. For example, Schmook (1994) vividly describes her process of taking an internal inventory:

> I began to believe in myself. I accepted myself just as I was. I wrote things down on paper about myself; things that I needed to change and things I couldn't change. I started to think about the things I wanted to do with my life when I got better. (p. 2)

This inner search may involve reassessing one's values and finding them wanting. New values may then be adopted and new goals identified. A reordering of values is well recognized as a form of coping and adjustment to life circumstances (e.g. Taylor, 1983; King, 1998; Emmons, 1999c; Coursey *et al.*, 2000; Elliott and Kurylo, 2000; Calhoun and Tedeschi, 2001), and this phenomenon is well documented in the popular press. John (1994) found that he had to re-examine the values he grew up with: 'Where I grew up, the ideal was to be tough, sporty and sexually successful ... . I am regarded as the disabled one. But I have gone beyond these standards and found other qualities in life' (p. 8).

Learning from others' experience is another source of inspiration, and the need to connect with others is a frequent theme in the recovery literature. Peer support groups can provide a safe arena for challenging oneself in a non-stigmatizing environment (e.g. Schmook, 1996; Spaniol and Gagne, 1997; Young and Ensing, 1999; D. Marsh, 2000; Mead and Copeland, 2000; Tenney, 2000). As in the Awareness stage, the possibility of a positive identity can be inspired by prominent successful people:

> The walls of the psych ward crumbled further in my mind as I came to see that others with my illness had contributed to society. I found out that my two favourite writers, Hemmingway and T. S. Eliot, each had a neuro-chemical disorder .... the significance of this fact can hardly be overestimated ... these great writers not only lived in society but they had a hand in shaping the society in which they lived. (Fekete, 2004, p. 192)

The dual tasks of taking an internal inventory of one's core values, and taking stock of one's strengths and weaknesses, mirrors Waterman's (1984) two metaphors for identity formation: discovery and creation. The former applies to the process of discovering the 'true self'; the second implies there is no pre-existing self, so the person needs to create an identity. Both of these processes can be seen as occurring in the Preparation stage. The person needs to examine his or her values, changing them if deemed necessary, and then seek ways in which to live up to these values by setting appropriate goals. When the individual rediscovers what makes him or herself truly valuable, he or she gains a sense of the possibilities of a positive identity (Pettie and Triolo, 1999). Fekete (2004) explains:

After the soul-shattering experience of a psychotic episode and the personality distortions that come with it, no issue is more compelling than the question of identity, and this question can be divided into two parts. The first question is 'Who am I?', or self-concept. The second question is 'What am I?' or 'What have I become?' This is the issue of symptoms. (p. 190)

In Lysaker and Bell's (1995) case study of work and volition, a participant illustrated how a sense of self is a prerequisite to building a meaningful life. 'R' explained that he was unable to make plans or set goals for himself as he had no self-understanding. He had no coherent sense of self to provide a 'foundation for meaning and eventually give his energies a shape' (p. 397).

Meaning in the Preparation Stage: Reassessing Goals

While the inner search for one's positive qualities and resources can be the foundation for establishing a positive sense of self, living in keeping with one's values is the basis for a meaningful life. The process of introspection in the Preparation stage includes the identification of one's core values. These values represent higher-order goals (Emmons, Colby and Kaiser, 1998), and can be thought of as one's 'valued directions' in life (Hayes and Strosahl, 2004). 'Taking stock' during this stage leads some people to decide that they no longer have the personal resources to continue the pursuit of their valued goals, or at least, not at the same level as they had before the illness:

> I had to realize a change in my career goals. I hold a BS degree in biology and completed an additional two and a half years toward an MD degree. The stress of medical education overwhelming me, I withdrew from medical school. (Henderson, 2004, p. 85)

When circumstances rob a person of their anticipated future, they need to 'dream a new dream' (King, 1998). Abandoning goals that are no longer attainable, rather than signalling resignation and failure, can represent a healthy adjustment to a changed situation, enabling resources to be applied to attainable goals (Brandtstädter, 2009). This can serve to preserve psychological well-being. Many abandon their careers or education early in the illness, and so, during recovery, need to reassess their capacity to re-establish their former goals, or find alternative ways to pursue their valued directions. This process is described here by McDermott (1994):

> [I] realized that I was on the planet for a purpose, and through meditation and introspection, probed for my life purpose and developed short-term and long-term goals to serve the purpose. (p. 65)

Living according to one's valued directions gives meaning to the work of recovery, and for this reason, some people hold on tenaciously to their goals. For example, Schmook (1994), a divorced mother, was told by her therapist that if she did not go on welfare she would fail and lose her children. However, she had a strong work ethic and believed strongly in providing for her family herself. She tells:

> I told her I could not see her any longer because she was trying to force me to go against my conscience. I knew what I had to do to get better. What I wanted was to find a doctor and therapist who would support my desire to be healthy again. (p. 2)

The courage behind this decision cannot be overstated, as at this time, Schmook, who had been diagnosed with paranoid schizophrenia, had never heard of recovery and had been told that 'people with mental illness did not get better' (p. 1). In a later article, Schmook (1996) cites Leete (1994) as stating: 'We must each facilitate personal growth by discovering what makes life valuable and enriching to us as individuals' (p. 12).

The reordering of values and priorities has often been construed as a benefit of loss, illness or disability (e.g. Schaefer and Moos, 1992; Tedeschi and Calhoun, 1995; Davis, Nolen-Hoeksema and Larson, 1998; Emmons, 1999a). Davis, Nolen-Hoeksema and Larson (1998) identified two construals of the concept of 'finding meaning' in loss. These are *sense-making* – making sense of the event; and *benefit-finding* – finding some good in the experience. Davis *et al.* asserted that sense-making was important in the early days of adjustment, while benefit-finding was more important later. The chosen meaning of the illness discussed in the Awareness stage can be associated with sense-making, while the reordering of priorities in the Preparation stage is akin to the process of benefit-finding. In Elliott, Kurylo and Rivera's (2002) model of positive growth following acquired disability, adaptive people often 'look inward to exercise control over internal states when external events are beyond their control' (p. 692). Those who try to accept their situation and find positive meanings tend to show better adjustment, while those who ruminate and take a 'victimization' stance may fail to find meaning and direction in their circumstances. Sometimes the benefit found in mental illness is the ability to help others who are struggling with similar problems. This often provides a meaningful goal for the person. For example, Armstrong relates:

> I learned that I want to dedicate myself to this recovery process for myself and others . . .. I am able to keep going forward learning real job skills, which I never had from those years on the streets, in the psychiatric rehabilitation field. (Armstrong, 1994, p. 53)

Although the reordering of priorities and setting of new goals is well-documented in adjustment to various forms of loss and trauma, Emmons, Colby and Kaiser (1998) found that goal conservation is also a common response. Lack of goal change was found to be associated with recovery from loss. There are at least two possible explanations for these results. First, the nature of the loss or trauma experienced may not have necessitated goal change (e.g. the loss of a parent).

The second explanation is that those goals that were of a 'higher order' may not have required changing. For example, Emmons *et al.* found that spiritual goals were associated with recovery from loss or trauma.

A person's strongly held values provide guiding principles for the identification of value-congruent lower-order goals. Such goal congruence is associated with well-being, satisfaction with life and meaning in life (e.g. Emmons, Colby and Kaiser, 1998; Little, 1998; McGregor and Little, 1998; Sheldon and Kasser, 2001). McDermott (1994) explains how she scaled down her goals, while continuing to reflect her core values:

> [I] gave up the grandiose idea that I could 'save society' and concentrated on seeking inner peace and harmony by being a constructive influence with my family, peers and professionals. (p. 66)

As Henderson (2004) says, 'One must give serious thought to what he/she wants out of life and define what recovery means for him/herself – and pursue it' (p. 87). Once the person has an increased sense of agency and a sense of direction for their life, they are ready to take more concrete steps towards getting their life back on track.

Conclusion

During the Preparation stage, the person conducts an introspective exploration of his or her internal resources and values, and a search for environmental resources. These internal and external resources are then employed in laying the groundwork for rebuilding a fulfilling and meaningful life. In Chapter 6, we will examine this Rebuilding stage.

Summary

- The Preparation stage provides the foundation for building a meaningful life.
- The person takes stock of his or her internal resources.
- External sources of support are sought.
- The person seeks knowledge about the illness.
- Information about treatment enables empowered decision-making.
- Change involves taking risks.
- The core self is examined and core values identified and reassessed.
- Goals are re-examined, and new goals may be set.
- Valued directions, which give life meaning, can be retained in new goals.

6

Rebuilding: The Fourth Stage of Psychological Recovery

Overview

The Rebuilding stage can be thought of as the 'action' stage of recovery, in which the person takes the necessary steps to work towards his or her goals in rebuilding a meaningful life. This may include such things as becoming involved in occupational or educational pursuits, practising illness management and promoting wellbeing. The person builds on rediscovered strengths and values to develop a positive identity. Taking responsibility is characterized by small steps, trial and error, perseverance and hard work. During this stage the person builds resilience against set-backs.

Hard Work and Hopefulness

The Rebuilding stage of recovery is characterized by hard work, small victories and set-backs. Perseverance is a core feature of recovery . . .

> I find that just staying with the struggle is halfway to winning the battle. Important also is patience: refusing to be hurried, awaiting my own timing. (Koehler, 1994, p. 23)

> My life didn't turn out the way that I thought it would when I was eighteen. Neither did anyone else's life that I know. We are left to pick up the pieces and go forward every day, week, month and year. (Armstrong, 1994, p. 53)

coupled with hope and hard work . . .

Psychological Recovery: Beyond Mental Illness, First Edition.
Retta Andresen, Lindsay G. Oades and Peter Caputi.
© 2011 John Wiley & Sons, Ltd. Published 2011 by John Wiley & Sons, Ltd.

> I have met people who have healed from this disorder and what has distinguished them from others was their belief that they could heal. They were also determined to do the necessary work. (Wentworth, 1994, p. 83)

Rebuilding requires agency and personal responsibility, in order to take the risks necessary to pursue those goals that give life meaning and purpose.

Hope in the Rebuilding Stage: Active Pursuit of Personal Goals

After laying the groundwork in the Preparation stage, the person starts taking concrete steps towards his or her goals in the Rebuilding stage. These steps may involve tasks in pursuit of concrete high-level or distal goals. Alternatively, the person may decide to pursue the goal of recovery 'one step at a time', as he or she feels ready. An anonymous consumer who had been employed successfully in a technical position for a number of years, while attending regular therapy and a support group explains:

> I can't say that my life now is as I had expected it to be before my break, but as things have improved for me since then, I have some hope that maybe I can have a more satisfying life in the future (Anonymous, 1989, p. 346).

Although he clearly does not consider himself 'recovered', this person is looking forward to a future more fulfilling life, despite not having a clear goal. Sometimes it is necessary to reformulate poorly defined or difficult goals into smaller, attainable steps. Setting specific, proximal goals can increase feelings of self-efficacy when striving for a distant goal (Latham and Locke, 1991). Koehler (1994) also describes this stage of rebuilding hope:

> Eventually, I got a job as a cashier at a convenience store, and moved out on my own. This was a very stressful time, but I found within myself the strength and stamina to keep it all going. ... As a result of these challenges, I felt much more confident in the face of the public ... and I felt rather matter-of-fact about keeping my living situation running smoothly. (p. 22)

With achieving incremental successes, one's sense of personal agency increases. Davidson and Strauss (1992) noted that the 'dawning of hope' (p. 136), which occurs in the early stages of recovery, recurs during the course of recovery. The perception of success in the pursuit of meaningful goals provides this spiral of hope.

As we saw in Chapter 4, Emmons, Colby and Kaiser (1998) found that for some, perceived recovery from loss was associated with the ability to retain, rather than change, important goals. Similarly, some consumer authors are adamant that recovery from mental illness involves the ability to retain personal goals, or – given that many people succumb to mental illness in young adulthood – to aspire to and achieve similar goals and roles as others of the same demographic (e.g. Curtis, 2000;

Mead and Copeland, 2000). Indeed, Mead and Copeland pointed out that many people who have been diagnosed with schizophrenia or other serious mental illnesses are pursuing professional careers. This is amply demonstrated by the number of authors we have cited, for example, Bassman (2001), Chadwick (1997), Deegan (1988), Frese (2000), Schiff (2004) and Wentworth (1994), who were working in a professional capacity at the time of their respective publications.

It would be a mistake, therefore, to assume that a person with a serious mental illness should necessarily set lower-level goals. On the other hand, while distal or higher-level goals provide a source of meaning in life, proximal or interim goals are a source of agency (King, 1998; Little, 1998). Shortening one's pathways thinking preserves agentic thought (Snyder, 2000a). With the attainment of incremental goals, pathways to goals are affirmed and agency increases. Thus, the attainment of small goals builds hope (Snyder, 2002). F. Dickerson (2000) describes how she is pursuing her goals hopefully, and at a pace with which she feels comfortable, by making use of resources at a rehabilitation centre:

> Here, I have been able to explore my dreams and abilities. I have always wanted to be a professional in the human services field. With help from the Center staff I was able to get accepted to the Counseling Psychology Program [at college]. (p. 28)

Dickerson relates that she suffered a set-back when the course touched on issues that she was still working through in therapy, necessitating a leave of absence. However, she continues: 'I hope to return to the graduate course in the near future. I will also be investigating how to handle confusing and painful feelings with [my therapist]' (p. 28).

Until now, this discussion has centred on working towards career goals. However, many consumers find fulfilment in non-career roles, volunteer work or personal development: 'There is a vast spectrum of ways to live and love life with a neuro-chemical imbalance' (Fekete, 2004, p. 194). Goals including creative pursuits, physical fitness and connection with others were also mentioned in the consumer stories. For example, Henderson (2004) describes how involvement in recreational activities opened up a new world of creative self-expression for her, and how these activities contribute towards her recovery:

> I had never thought about doing arts and crafts projects, but now I enjoy them very much. I enjoy language and am an avid reader, as well as interested in writing. Listening to music, as well as playing the keyboard, is uplifting and/or soothing, depending on how I feel at the time. These activities help me unwind and relax as well as build up my self esteem. (p. 82)

An anonymous writer (Anonymous, 1994a) describes how regular exercise in the form of jogging contributed to his wellbeing, in addition to the physical health benefits:

> This not only provided me with a certain amount of structure, but the activity itself reduced stress and thus helped even out my moods. In addition, my self-worth

improved as my times gradually improved, and I soon recognized that I was functioning in a way I had previous to my hospitalizations. (p. 15)

While Berman (1994) describes rebuilding his social life:

> Most important [of the rehabilitation programs] perhaps was the several hours per day that I would spend in the coffee shops, hours of growing friendship and conversation with people who could understand. Here were people, not patients, sharing our concerns . . .. As I climbed the path towards recovery I became interested, almost obsessed with the desire for a social life. (p. 43)

Berman then joined a singles club where he met a large variety of men and women, some of whom became good friends. He continues: 'And on this dual social program I progressed towards wellness' (p. 43).

King (1998) has described the reinstatement of agency after the loss of one's life goals as 'a process of reconstructing and reinvesting in a future toward which to strive' (p. 122). The recovery stories demonstrate how the attainment of, or progress towards, goals in all domains of life contribute to building hope, thereby promoting wellbeing and recovery.

Responsibility in the Rebuilding Stage: Taking Control

Through setting and working towards goals, the person begins to actively take control of his or her life; not only management of symptoms, but also enlisting social support, improvement of self-image, handling social pressures and building social competence. This involves empowerment in treatment decisions, learning to recognize and manage symptoms, making autonomous choices about career or other goals, and gaining control over all aspects of one's life: 'We rebuilt our lives on three cornerstones of recovery – hope, willingness and responsible action' (Deegan, 1988, p. 56). Even those who found that medications worked well for them expressed the necessity of taking an active role in psychological recovery:

> Medication can help alleviate some of the symptomology, but the illness still remains and we have to deal with it. Medications make it possible to work toward a more productive life, but medication doesn't do the work, we do! (Anonymous, 1994b, p. 25)

An integral part of the recovery process is taking control of one's treatment decisions and illness management. Learning to manage symptoms and to take control of the illness by identifying warning signs is the foundation of recovery. As Leete (1989), says:

> Many of us have learned to monitor symptoms to determine the status of our illness, using our coping mechanisms to prevent psychotic relapse or to seek treatment earlier, thereby reducing the number of acute episodes and hospitalizations. (p. 199)

The attitude and support of the mental health professional can provide the impetus for this process. Weingarten (2005) tells of the effect of being 'put in the driver's seat':

> The first pillar in my recovery foundation came when my therapist ... put me in the driver's seat in my efforts to recognize the problems I was experiencing ... What emerged from this effort was a three-step coping method: identifying, evaluation and doing something to offset the problems. (p. 77)

A number of consumers recounted the symptom management measures they learned and practiced. For example, reframing voices ...

> I am, however, coming to understand that what sounds to me like an outside commentary is from my own thinking ... I can rephrase it to myself. I shift from third person to first person. (Greenblat, 2000, p. 244)

stress management techniques ...

> Coping mechanisms may include withdrawing and being alone for a while; obtaining support from a friend; socializing or otherwise distracting myself from stressors; organizing my thoughts through lists; problem-solving around specific issues; or temporarily increasing my medication. (Leete, 1989, p. 200)

and changing self-defeating behaviours ...

> So I switched to being a social smoker, only taking marijuana once every few weeks. Then on the 28th March, 1986 I decided it was getting me nowhere and I gave it up forever. I gave up nicotine on 29th April 1987 and then a year later I gave up alcohol. (Roman, 1994, p. 43)

Later, Roman explains: 'It was because I had been so ill and don't want to be that ill again, that's given me the strength to give up [substance use]' (p. 43).

Taking responsibility for one's life involves taking risks. Deegan (1996b) points out that risk-taking is an important aspect of personal growth, and to protect a person from taking risks is to deny a human right:

> Each person must find what works for them. This means that we must have the opportunity to try and to fail and to try again .... Professionals must embrace the concept of the dignity of risk, and the right to failure if they are to be supportive of us. (p. 97)

The process of personal development by taking responsibility for one's choices is amply illustrated by Henderson (2004), who says, 'I'm taking responsibility for myself, setting goals and challenging myself to do more, taking risks. I feel like a 'real person', taking on the responsibilities of adulthood' (p. 68). Furthermore, taking risks and persevering through set-backs are important processes in rebuilding personal empowerment, as Koehler (1994) explained:

> Prevailing as I did through these challenges brought to my awareness that with determination and commitment such as mine there's a lot of power and ability in the disabled that's waiting for an opportunity to prove itself. (p. 22)

However, taking responsibility does not preclude accepting the help and advice of others. Rather, involving others when necessary is an act of responsibility in itself. Choosing to use mental health resources after recognizing signs of developing symptoms is a reflection of responsible action by the consumer, for example, 'I know my healthy personality and I know when my illness is interfering with it. I take precautions and alert my treatment team when I am slipping out of balance' (Anonymous, 1994b, p. 25). And also:

> However, now I do not just take medication or go to the hospital. I have learned to use medications and to use the hospital. This is the active stance that is the hallmark of the recovery process. (Deegan, 1996b, p. 96)

The support of others during recovery can be important in enabling the person to build their agency and empowerment. Some consumers recognized the need to trust others' observations of their wellness, rather than to rely totally on their own perceptions. For example, Henderson (2004) relates:

> I'm now very aware that I cannot rely on purely subjective thoughts and feelings to determine the state of my mental health. I hope I will remain trusting of others to clue me in when I seem headed for problems. (p. 85)

Fox (2002) values the opportunity that she now has of a new life, and uses professional monitoring of her symptoms to ensure she stays in control:

> I am aware that I must be careful with my illness. I must take care of myself and must be monitored . . .. I recognize I have been given a second chance at life and try never to take it for granted. (p. 363)

Taking on responsibility for one's life necessarily involves suffering set-backs and having the courage to learn from one's mistakes:

> Fortunately, through many years of trial and error, I have learned what medication works for me and when to take it to minimize side effects based on my daily schedule. (Leete, 1989, p. 199)

Perseverance in the face of challenges and set-backs gradually builds resilience. One consumer described how he dealt with uncertainty about himself with others, and about discussing his medical or employment history:

But as you continue to face these issues, often in more challenging situations, you get better at it and it becomes less of a burden. At the same time, I realize that I must proceed here in an orderly fashion, while being constantly aware of any mood shift. (Anonymous, 1994a, p. 17)

Weingarten (2005) describes persevering with work through difficult times, while battling for 19 years with untreated dysthymia:

I managed to hold down many part-time and full-time jobs. I knew I wasn't functioning at my best but I pushed through the depression and anxiety and proved to myself that I could be effective even when I was less than 100%. This was an important step and it was risky. (p. 78)

Taking control of one's life involves more than controlling symptoms and identifying goals. Another important aspect of taking responsibility is taking care of the self in order to maintain psychological strength for the battle for recovery. Many approaches to wellbeing may be utilized in this process:

It took me eight years to learn all the things I needed to learn in order to regain my mental health. It wasn't just changing my eating habits, or taking vitamins that did it. It was a combination of many things that I had to learn to change me so I could be healthy. (Schmook, 1998, p. 3)

This includes keeping active and involved in enjoyable activities. Participants in Young and Ensing's (1999) research warned against 'living the illness', allowing it to sap all of one's energy. One participant noted the need to find a focus outside of the illness: 'I've been a person that just stayed in suspended animation for so long I find it's helpful just to go somewhere. Just do something, anything' (p. 227).

In the Rebuilding stage then, the person puts into action the nascent sense of agency that was rediscovered during the Awareness stage and nurtured during the Preparation stage. The person begins to exercise choice and to demonstrate control over his or her life and management of the illness. Taking responsibility for one's wellbeing, health, and life as a whole demonstrates an inherent drive towards growth, as described by Deci and Ryan (2002). In articulating Self Determination Theory, Deci and Ryan claim that autonomy, or the opportunity to make self-determined choices, is a basic need for personal growth (Deci and Ryan, 2000, 2002). This is reflected in the work of Davidson and Strauss (1992), who described the utilization of the rediscovered agentic self to become an active and responsible agent in one's recovery.

Identity in the Rebuilding Stage: Self-redefinition

Rebuilding a positive identity requires first developing a positive sense of self that is not defined by the illness. Introspection in the Preparation stage results in the person reaffirming his or her personal strengths and core values that are still present despite the illness (Davidson and Strauss, 1992). Having tested his or her new-found agency on simple tasks, the person acquires the confidence to pursue more complex and important goals (Davidson and Strauss, 1992). In this manner the person elaborates and enhances his or her sense of identity.

> The third and final pillar of my recovery was discovering how to summon my own personal strengths and resources to go back and reclaim my personal voice and keep my place at the table . . . like professional meetings and social gatherings. (Weingarten, 2005, p. 79)

As we discussed in the Awareness stage in Chapter 5, finding an explanation for the illness that is acceptable to one's sense of self is an important step. Fekete (2004) found that the medical model of illness enabled him to reclaim his identity:

> As I grew to understand the medical model of bipolar disorder, I was able to overcome the stigma associated with my illness and to redefine my person as it relates to my illness. . . . I am an ordinary person with a physical disorder. (Fekete, 2004, p. 192)

However, as we have noted, others find the medical model limiting and stigmatizing, as they feel it gives them no option of wellness (e.g. Davidson and Strauss, 1995; Thornhill, Clare and May, 2004). Wentworth (1994) elaborates:

> The medical model is especially harmful in how little vision and hope it offers to the mentally ill. The 'mentally ill' are as varied as any population and even if most don't at this time use their 'illness' as a vehicle for working to understand and learn to grow, we should be given the opportunity to do so. (p. 88)

Either way, Curtis' (2000) description holds true:

> [The spirit of the recovery process is]: I am no longer defined by myself or by others as my mental illness or disability, nor am I limited in opportunity, responsibility or direction. It is not who I am – though it may be a small part of me at times. (p. 4)

Having found a recovery-congruent explanation for the illness, the person can move forward in developing a positive identity. Fekete (2004) talked of a pilgrimage: 'The pilgrimage I refer to is the overwhelming crisis of identity that psychosis brings as one begins to recover' (p. 189).

Rebuilding a positive identity often requires changing a previously held identity. This can mean either letting go of the 'illness identity' and building a more positive sense of self, or it may require incorporating the illness into a previously held very positive identity and constructing a new 'future self'. Crowley (2000) echoes a number of consumer-authors with this sentiment:

> Much can be accomplished when we let go of who we were and get to know who we are now and who we can become. Instead of trying to figure out, 'Why did this happen to

me?' 'What could I have done to prevent it?', 'What did I do to deserve it?' it is often more productive to ask, 'What can I do about it?' and to move forward. (p. 11)

'This is the paradox of recovery: in accepting what we cannot do or be, we begin to discover who we can be and what we can do' (Deegan, 1988, p. 56).

A number of consumers we have quoted have described how the illness itself, and the journey of recovery, provided them with a new vocation in life, for example, Armstrong (1994), Anonymous (1994a), Berman (1994), Koehler (1994), Lynch (2000), Weingarten (1994) and Wentworth (1994). Berman (1994), mentioned earlier, who was by age 60 also coping with physical illness, decided to discontinue lithium and abandoned his career goal to replace it with a retirement goal. He describes his decision as a change of attitude. The decision to retire did not take the form of helpless resignation. Rather, the tenor of his quote is hopeful for the future:

It was obvious that I could not return to work in a meaningful manner because of my age and multiple infirmities, thus I concluded that having had two careers, the first in chemistry and the second as a lithium-blunted manic-depressive, the time had come for me to regard myself as retired rather than disabled and to rebuild a new life on this basis. (p. 43)

Berman was determined to once again experience 'real life' without the dulling effects of medication. An anonymous consumer, a qualified attorney, writes that it took much introspection to realize that he was projecting his insecurities about himself onto others (Anonymous, 1994a). Challenging these assumptions then freed him to move forward: 'I've begun to loosen up and become more accepting of myself as I am' (p. 17). As he gained confidence, he moved out of his parents' home, began volunteer work, began continuing education with other lawyers and renewed contact with extended family and friends. He continues: 'And significantly, I've developed some relationships with people whereby my sense of humanity and worth have been reaffirmed' (Anonymous, 1994a 'p. 17').

McDermott (1994) also highlights the importance of others' affirmation of the self in recovery, writing that, amongst other things, she 'chose to be with nurturing, non-shaming people in healthy environments' (p. 66). McDermott also writes that, in order to develop positive relationships with others, she attended many courses to 'develop my self esteem, reduce my shame, increase my assertiveness and learned how to deal with anger appropriately' (p. 66).

Success in battling with illness while at the same time holding down a responsible position can be in itself a source of self-affirmation. One consumer prides himself on his ability to draw on the healthy part of the self. In the absence of role models of heroes with a mental illness, he says, 'I look at myself as my own hero, working on my illness while educating my students with well-thought-out lectures. I give myself a lot of credit for letting my healthy side predominate and for reaching out to help others' (Anonymous, 1994b, p. 25).

For many people, the illness strikes before they have commenced adult life or formed a mature sense of identity. One such person is McQuillin (1994), who developed schizophrenia at age 19, and writes that this 'suspended normal maturation' (p. 9). He says:

> I am still searching for a place in the world, but the task is becoming clearer now. I recently completed an evening course in the Principles of Marketing at the local community college. I received an A in the course, which gave me self-confidence and pride. I plan to take further courses next term, maybe day courses. (p. 9)

The importance of being patient with oneself, knowing when to slow down, and rebuilding one step at a time was a recurring theme. Koehler (1994) describes his approach:

> One of the coping skills I use is pacing. For instance, I reassure myself ... that if I reduce my expectations, my performance will improve.... I take frequent breaks at work ... I have a long-range vision of myself several months into the future, so that minor problems can get put in perspective and don't become catastrophes. (p. 23)

In the Rebuilding stage, then, 'the individual's personal path of redefinition through action' (Lunt, 2002, p. 39) takes place. Lunt stresses that the person is empowered in this process by the help of others. Mead and Copeland (2000) emphasize the importance of the attitude of mental health staff in nurturing the personal agency required for the task of reconstructing a positive identity:

> Our only hope for accessing internal resources that have been buried by layers of imposed limitations is to be supported in making leaps of faith, redefining who we'd like to become, and taking risks that aren't calculated by someone else. (p. 321)

The importance of supporting personal goals is a core tenet of Self Determination Theory (Ryan and Deci, 2002). The 'innate tendency to develop an increasingly elaborated and unified sense of self' (p. 5) entails the pursuit of goals that are reflective of one's values (Ryan and Deci, 2002). Autonomous goals are more than merely self-chosen goals; autonomous goals are those that are self-integrated, that is, they are an expression of the person's core values (Ryan *et al.*, 1996). Autonomous goals, rather than goals chosen for extrinsic reasons – for example, to please others – induce greater motivation, leading to enhanced goal attainment (Sheldon and Elliot, 1998). When a person has examined his or her core values and developed a sense of self, then support in choosing and working towards value-congruent goals is likely to lead to greater commitment, greater success and a positive sense of identity.

Meaning in the Rebuilding Stage: Valued Goals

The developing sense of identity, and having self-congruent goals, endows life with a sense of purpose. In the day-to-day sense, Mary (1994) found that working gave her a reason to get up in the morning and to stay with the struggle:

For example, I find it hard to get out of bed and sometimes I don't feel confident. I just have to push myself. I don't allow myself to give in to that. If you're working you're expected to turn up. (p. 19)

In the context of recovery the need for a reason to start each day is not trivial. However, in the Rebuilding stage, people also begin to find purpose in the more philosophical sense of finding a meaning in life. Their occupations provide them with more than a reason to get out of bed; they provide a reason to live. A vocation is often born of the experience of illness or recovery itself. After many years of trauma counselling, and with support from professionals, family and peers, Lynch (2000) was able to gradually give up all medications. In time she was able to begin working with children who, like herself, had been abused:

Most importantly, I began to invest in myself, I felt hopeful again. Eventually I resumed working with children who were abused. I began doing part-time consulting work [in mental health]. I continued to start new self-help and advocacy organizations, investing my time and energy to help others regain their health. It all seemed so strange. My life's suffering had led to my life's work! (p. 1431)

Finding a meaningful role can be a catalyst to, rather than an outcome of, the recovery process, and such roles can be instigated by people in the helping professions:

A dramatic turn in my coping occurred about seven years ago when Dr. Cole asked me to form some sort of patient group at McLean Hospital .... After some research I discovered the National Depressive and Manic-Depressive Association and was given their approval to form a chapter... I devoted every ounce of my energy to this project .... (Berman, 1994, p. 43)

Imperative to providing impetus to recovery is that the role must be autonomous: it should be integrated with the person's sense of self, and therefore intrinsically motivating. As such, the person finds joy in performing the role. Simply doing a mundane job because it is part of the rehabilitation programme is not sufficient. Unzicker (1994) forcibly makes the point that professionals must not redefine what success means for their clients:

If a client is working six hours a week in a janitorial service, run by a mental health center ... the case manager writes a report to the stage/funder which claims a wonderful programmic success. Nobody ever asks the poor guy sweeping the floors if he wanted to do that in the first place. (p. 63)

Similarly, John (1994) makes clear:

People who are disabled deserve to grow and learn to the best of their abilities. I think they can be an asset – an inspiration – to people in the community .... My life now is great. I've done the first year of a two-year part-time course and I'm enjoying it immensely. I enjoy learning, especially in the caring field. (p. 10)

An example of an intrinsically motivated goal is provided by Alexander (1994), who found writing therapeutic, providing a purpose intensely meaningful to him:

> I had experienced another world that I believed needed to be communicated. I rewrote it over the years, compiling manuscripts. This ritual put me in touch with my underlying dynamics, the message of my experience. It culminated recently in its publication .... (p. 39)

The search for meaning in the wake of mental illness can also be a deeply introspective process. Some have related how it entailed the reconstruction of their understanding of the world. For example:

> An integral part of my recovery has been my search and discovery of meaning for my life. This is a philosophical and psychological issue that goes beyond mere chemical imbalances in the brain. In this search, I have developed a new world view. (Murphy, 1998, p. 188)

Murphy explains that discussing her views about the world was part of her therapy, and describes the respect shown to her by her psychiatrist as 'a prerequisite for hope' (p. 188). As well as purely philosophical understanding, many described a spiritual element that was important to their recovery. One such person is Watson (1994), who found strength for the struggle through her faith:

> [God's] love insures that our courage will not be wasted or in vain. As we are strengthened by our courage, we shall ultimately emerge victorious to a life richer in joy, peace and love. Rejoice in yourselves. Rejoice in your courage. (p. 75)

King (1998) has stated that, following loss, the new 'possible self' must be as 'elaborate and emotionally engaging' (p. 123) as the one it replaces, in order to give life meaning. Reflect back for a moment to the issue of identity. Two metaphors for identity formation were discussed in the Preparation stage: *discovery* and *creation* (Waterman, 1984). Waterman's conceptualizations can be utilized again in the Rebuilding stage. According to Waterman, discovery involves the individual discovering, developing and living in accordance with his or her highest potentials, or intrinsic character. This endeavour brings meaning and purpose to one's life. In contrast, creation implies there is no 'true self', but that the person chooses from endless possibilities with which to build something of value. Waterman likens creation to finding 'something to do', and discovery to finding 'someone to be' (Waterman, 1993). Rebuilding identity can be seen as having an element of creation, in that the person finds a worthwhile occupation. However, this occupation may not necessarily be in keeping with his or her true character. In order to build a meaningful life, the person must find ways of expressing their innate qualities and the chosen values that they have rediscovered – or perhaps redefined – in the Preparation phase. Waterman describes this as 'personal expressiveness' – engaging in activities that give a feeling of personal fulfilment. This concept of personal expressiveness resonates with Deci and Ryan's (2002) description of intrinsic motivation – the pursuit of goals that are self-concordant, or stem from one's core values.

Finding meaning, then, is more than finding a valued occupation, but rather is more akin to finding a way to live. This may include, but is not limited to, vocational goals. It includes examining one's spirituality or philosophy of life. The journey is, in itself, a source of meaning for many. Watson (1994) expresses this in spiritual terms:

> Most of us do not see ourselves as courageous, but I do see us all making these heroic choices that speak of a closeness to God and an affirmation of His love for each and every one of us. This love insures that our courage will not be wasted or in vain. As we are strengthened by our courage, we shall ultimately emerge victorious to a life richer in joy, peace and love. (p. 75)

Risk-taking, Perseverance and Resilience

The rebuilding stage entails actively managing the illness and taking steps towards one's goals. It is a step-by-step effort to construct a positive identity, define personally meaningful goals and to pursue them incrementally, building hope, personal empowerment, and life meaning through the journey. This process is characterized by risk-taking, as Lynch (2000) says, 'I could begin to risk again; risk going off Social Security disablement entitlements, risk going to work again, risk returning to school. Risk giving up my identity as a "career mental patient"' (p. 1431).

Taking small, calculated risks and persevering in the face of set-backs helps to build resilience. A question that has arisen in the literature is whether resilient qualities are enduring traits of the person that enable them to overcome adversity, or whether resilience is a process during which the person learns from life experiences (Rutter, 2000). In a qualitative study of women who had successfully adapted to a major life event, Wagnild and Young (1993) identified five personality character-istics associated with resilience: *Equanimity* (composure and equilibrium under tension); *Perseverance*; *Self-reliance*; *Meaningfulness*; and *Existential Aloneness* (the need for each of us to find our unique path in life). However, Rutter (2006) asserts that, rather than being considered a stable personality trait, resilience is built through a dynamic process. Rutter holds that resilience develops from controlled exposure to risks and successful coping with challenges. The consumer literature on recovery certainly reflects this view. The key, however, is not simply successful coping, but perseverance through failures and set-backs. For example, 'Building my social life and career slowly, step by step, sometimes losing ground, sometimes gaining, has been an essential process to recovering from my illness' (Anonymous, 1994b, p. 25). And also:

> I continued to be mentally ill; I continued to break down; but there were long stretches in between the breaks and they didn't last as long as the ones before. I was beginning to get healthier as my thinking became healthier. ... I began to believe in myself. I accepted myself just the way I was. (Schmook, 1994, p. 2)

More than recovering from acute stressors, the process of building resilience in mental illness involves *sustainability* (Zautra, 2009). Sustainability refers to the ability to maintain psychological wellbeing in the face of ongoing challenges, and requires appraisal, planning and action (Zautra, 2009). This entails intentional risk-taking to promote learning and personal growth:

> Learning, like laughter, makes life fun and exciting. There is no learning that can take place without risk. We need to start rewarding calculated risks. I think if anything can teach us something about ourselves and others it is worth learning, even if it is painful. (Tenney, 2000, p. 1443)

> I may have taken only small steps but I feel I have made significant strides that both time and therapy have enabled me to do. And of course, most of all, just learning from the past, growing up, living life, trusting life, have all helped give me the experience I often need. (Lynn, 1994, p. 51)

Willingness to take risks and learn from failures requires a great deal of courage and determination. Consumers wrote of their strength of will in their efforts to recover. As Wentworth (1994) says, 'While my intention to heal never wavered, everything else did, my feelings, my behavior, and my situation. My intention was the thread I held on to' (p. 83). And Watson (1994) explains:

> First, most of us choose not to give up. We choose to continue to try to overcome that which challenges us, to hang on to hopes, to work and learn, to reach out to others and let others reach out to us. (p. 74)

> If we didn't accept our journey as a difficult one, we'd spend all our time and energy damning the journey, having nothing left to take on and overcome and heal the illness that makes that same journey so momentarily painful and challenging. (Watson, 1994, p. 75)

The quotes in this section reflect two strands of resilience: returning from set-backs, and deliberate, considered risk-taking in the service of moving forward. As one consumer was quoted as saying, 'psychotic people can learn from mistakes, too' (Davidson and Strauss, 1992, p. 143). Resilience is a vital element in, and outcome of, successful recovery.

Conclusion

The Rebuilding stage, then, is a time of hard work and step-by-step progress towards one's goals, including trial and, frequently, error. Weingarten (2005) described three strategies he used in his recovery. These were: successful coping with stressors through a process of recognizing and working through his emotional responses, calculated risk-taking, and discovering and developing his personal strengths and resources. This all took courage and required support. The process of learning and building resilience culminates in personal growth. In Chapter 7, we will look at the processes of the Growth stage, and consider the role of resilience in thriving and the gaining of wisdom.

Summary

- The Rebuilding stage involves step-by-step rebuilding of one's life.
- Perseverance and hard work are key characteristics of this stage.
- The person builds agency by pursuing achievable goals.
- Taking responsibility in this stage involves taking risks in order to take charge of one's life.
- A positive identity is developed by pursuing goals that are in keeping with one's values in life.
- Activities that express one's core self provide meaning in life.
- Spirituality can be another important source of meaning.
- Calculated risk-taking, resulting in successes and failures, provides learning experiences and personal growth.
- Overcoming failure and set-backs builds resilience in the face of future obstacles.

7

Growth: The Fifth Stage of Psychological Recovery

Overview

Although the entire process of recovery is clearly a growth process, those who are in this final stage feel confident and demonstrate an established and positive sense of self, and enthusiasm about the future. This stage is characterized by resilience, wisdom and flourishing. To call Growth the 'final' stage of recovery, is somewhat misleading, as this is a dynamic stage in which the person continues to seek personal growth and self-actualization.

It has been clear throughout the elaboration of the model that the elements of hope, responsibility, positive identity and meaning in life, are inextricably intertwined. In this discussion of the Growth stage, therefore, quotes under each subheading frequently span more than one of these processes. These quotes often contain a message of recovery for others with a mental illness or for professionals.

We conclude this chapter with a discussion of the relationships between resilience, personal growth and wisdom, and revisit the concept of wellbeing.

Hope in the Growth Stage: Optimism About the Future

In the final stage of recovery there is a sense of optimism and the promise of a rewarding future. For some people, keeping a positive focus involves commitment to a particular goal, however, for others it is a matter of maintaining a positive attitude regarding moving forward in their recovery (Young and Ensing, 1999).

Psychological Recovery: Beyond Mental Illness, First Edition.
Retta Andresen, Lindsay G. Oades and Peter Caputi.
© 2011 John Wiley & Sons, Ltd. Published 2011 by John Wiley & Sons, Ltd.

Mead and Copeland (2000) sum up the overall change in attitude from hopelessness to hopefulness that is characteristic of successful recovery:

> There is hope. A vision of hope that includes no limits. . . . It is only when we believe that we are fragile and out of control that we find it hard to move ahead. (Mead and Copeland, 2000, p. 317)

While the Rebuilding stage represents getting life 'back on track', the Growth stage is characterized by looking ahead from this platform towards the future. The skills that have been nurtured during the Rebuilding stage can now be applied with confidence:

> Therapists will say that a move to another city to go to graduate school is about a 10 on the stressor scale. I know this all too well. I also know that I have the tools to manage this life event. (Greenblat, 2000, p. 245)

Young and Ensing (1999) reported that, in the final recovery phase, the person strives 'to reach new potentials of higher functioning' (p. 227). This is expressed by Weingarten (2005; see Chapter 6) when he describes how his three recovery strategies contributed to his personal growth. He writes: 'Using these strategies and working hard every day I've found is rewarded with new skills, including discipline, greater self-confidence and self esteem, better social interactions, job satisfaction and the joy of self fulfilment' (p. 79). Chovil (2005), also describes the fruits of his recovery efforts:

> I would never have believed fourteen years ago that I would be enjoying the quality of life I have now. I have a home, a job, a car, and fairly good health. I've won national, provincial and municipal awards . . . . I was surprised given the stigma of mental illness, that any community would recognize someone with schizophrenia for their contribution to the community. (p. 71)

Snyder *et al.* (2006) highlighted the role of an orientation towards future goals in successful rehabilitation. They found that focusing on negotiating pathways to the desired future leads to enhanced physical and mental wellbeing in recovery from losses caused by injury and physiological conditions. The perceived attainability of goals, and making progress towards goals, has been associated with subjective wellbeing (Emmons, 1986; Brunstein, 1993). The successes achieved in the Rebuilding stage engender further agency and positive attitudes, which continue to drive the recovery process. Mary, a participant in a large New Zealand study of recovery (Lapsley, Nikora and Black, 2002), stated, 'I know now what my work is and . . . I'm not sure how I'll do it for the rest of my life, but I know I will do it' (p. 91). This statement reflects the spirit of optimism and vision of the future that characterizes the Growth stage.

While a general goal of 'getting better' does not provide a great deal of inspiration for recovery, envisaging a valuable benefit of getting better can be a powerful motivator (Snyder *et al.*, 2006). Self-transcendent, or higher-order, goals such as reaching out to others, and spiritual goals, have been associated with greater subjective wellbeing and recovery from loss and trauma (Emmons, Colby and Kaiser, 1998). Schmook (1994) vividly illustrates a future-oriented, self-transcendent goal:

> As I stated when I was in the mental hospital, I made up my mind that I would get better and that I would help others know that they could too . . .. I am developing a speaking business to promote mental health and to educate and train professionals, patients, families, communities, corporations, and religious organizations . . .. I look forward to the opportunity to provide my service on a national level and, one day, internationally as well. (p. 3)

The most rewarding goals are not always extrinsic goals representing occupation or other accomplishments. After listing many educational, vocational and recreational achievements, Cloutier (1994) was especially delighted with his restored relationships with his family and his many new friends: 'I feel vibrant, happy and alive!' (p. 34).

Hopeful thinking, that is, finding pathways around obstacles to goals, and the agency to negotiate such pathways, promotes 'optimal levels of functioning and satisfaction' (Snyder *et al.*, 2000, p. 262). Snyder and colleagues suggest that in moving from a prevention approach to an enhancement approach, hopeful thinking moves towards building on strengths to reach 'peak levels of functioning and wellbeing' (p. 262). They discuss the role of hope in the *secondary enhancement* of psychological wellbeing. While *primary enhancement* refers to the role of hope in achieving optimal functioning and satisfaction, secondary enhancement furthers this to optimal levels of wellbeing. This is achieved by finding meaning in life through the pursuit of self-actualizing or self-transcendent goals (Snyder *et al.*, 2000). Quotes from the Growth stage reflect this concept of secondary enhancement.

Responsibility in the Growth Stage: In Control of Life and Wellbeing

Consumers who considered themselves recovered described being in control of the illness and of their lives generally. This control is the result of a long struggle to understand and cope with the illness, and to develop personal resources: 'Taking responsibility for my life and developing coping mechanisms has been crucial to my recovery' (Leete, 1989, p. 197). An anonymous consumer, while acknowledging that medications helped to relieve the symptoms, expressed strongly the level of hard personal work involved in taking responsibility for his recovery:

> Statements like 'your illness is getting better,' 'your therapist has done wonders,' or 'your medication has cured your illness' infuriate me. Statements like this take the

credit away from the mental health consumer and instead bestow the thanks on outside sources. Illnesses don't get better in most cases; instead clients sweat blood and tears and fight heroically to cope with the symptoms and re-enter mainstream society to the greatest extent humanly possible. (Anonymous, 1994b, p. 25)

Achieving control requires sustained commitment in the face of set-backs, as noted by Mary (1994): 'I feel correct medication is important for people with schizophrenia. Unfortunately this involves trial-and-error. What's kept me going is that I am determined to live a normal life' (p. 18). Although they may continue to use medications or mental health services, people in the Growth stage feel empowered regarding which treatments or services they use, and in choosing when to use them, as described by Deegan (1997) in Chapter 2, and here expressed by Lynn (1994):

> Now, I am finally living where I want, on my own, and I am my own caretaker. I decide when I need hospitalization. No one pushes me in involuntarily. I still have this voice problem which sometimes interferes with my life, but, fortunately, over the years, I've developed a network of good friends who all constitute a great part of my support system. (p. 51)

As Lynn demonstrates, in taking responsibility for their own lives and living autonomously, people are not seeking to live independently of others in the sense that they refuse help and advice. Williams (2000) explained the difference between the meanings of autonomy and independence as the terms are used in Self Determination Theory: autonomy refers to feeling volitional in choosing and pursuing goals (Ryan and Deci, 2000a), and this may require the support of others, whereas independence implies acting without reference to, or support from others (Williams, 2000). Mead and Copeland (2000) highlight that, while consumers can take responsibility for their lives, they need the cooperation and support of those who would help them to succeed in this endeavour:

> The person who experiences psychiatric symptoms should determine the course of his or her own life. No one else, even the most highly skilled health care professional, can do the work for us. We need to do it for ourselves, with your guidance, assistance, and support. (p. 328)

And the importance of the positive and empowering attitude of the clinician in this process is illustrated by Greenblat (2000):

> Later in my treatment, Dr. Alaoglu gave me more rein in my recovery, listening to my input about the level of medication I was on and taking me seriously when I asked for a decrease or even an increase in my medications. I felt empowered in my recovery. (p. 244)

These lessons in the need for control have been noted by researchers and authors in the other areas of loss. For example, Dunn (1996) investigated well-being following amputation, and found that optimism and a sense of control over the disability was associated with lower depression scores and higher self-esteem. Similarly, Taylor (1983) found, in work with chronic illness patients and victims of other life-threatening events, that regaining mastery over the event and over one's life generally was an important element in the readjustment process. This could take the form of either cognitive or behavioural control (Taylor, 1983). Jaffe (1985) also observed that survivors of trauma, including natural disasters and internment in concentration camps, took direct action to overcome the traumatic experience. The rejection of the role of victim reflected the 'will to live', and represented the retention of personal power over the current situation and future events (Jaffe, 1985). Jaffe asserted that the rediscovery of psychological control over one's life was central to self-renewal, and to physical and psychological well-being.

In a qualitative study, Williams and Collins (1999) found that the struggle for control was an important aspect of coping with schizophrenia. They reported that active coping with the illness and life generally was necessary for a person to consider him or herself recovered in the face of possible relapse. They noted that people who had had more experience of relapse learned from each episode and built on their competence in one or more of the areas of symptom management, self-image, social competence, and others' expectations (Williams and Collins, 1999). Development of these skills then dampened the destabilizing effects of relapse. Taking responsibility for wellness and taking control of one's life, then, develops the resilience and sense of competence characteristic of the Growth stage. Recovered consumers invariably say that the outcome was worth the struggle:

> If we do acknowledge and seriously study our illnesses; if we build on our assets; if we work to minimize our vulnerabilities by developing coping skills; if we confront our illnesses with courage and struggle with our symptoms persistently – we will successfully manage our lives and bestow our talents on society, the society that has traditionally abandoned us. (Leete, 1989, p. 200)

> I do not believe in magical cures for illnesses like mine. It takes very hard work to recover from a series of acute episodes. The problem is compounded by the fact that my will-power was damaged by the illness and my reaction to it. Now that my life is better it is so clear that it was worth it. I hope a lot of people get the help that they need and that their lives become more satisfying and enjoyable. (Anonymous, 1994b, p. 25)

Identity in the Growth Stage: An Authentic Self

In the Growth stage, the person has a strong, positive sense of self and of identity. Introspection in the Preparation stage and putting one's values into practice during the Rebuilding stage have led to a firm sense of self-worth. Often the loss of goals with the onset of illness results in a self-exploration that many people who do not experience such loss will never undergo (see Watson, 1994, above), resulting in a stronger sense of self, for example:

> [I] know where I stand on issues and know what I am about. It used to be that every time I encountered someone with strong opinions I would feel confused . . .. Unless I know what I stand for, everyday events will confuse me and my behaviour will be erratic at best. (Anonymous, 1994b, p. 25)

> Now, when I speak or write, I do so as a total self, a whole person, and I do not worry about my illness or sick self 'showing'. In fact, I feel very good about myself and what I am doing. (Weingarten, 2005, p. 77)

People who have an enduring sense of self, represented by stable, value-congruent goals, are better at setting adaptive goals after the onset of disability (Elliott *et al.*, 2000). Deegan exemplifies this idea of goal flexibility within a stable framework of values when she says, 'But now, rather than being an occasion for despair, we find that our personal limitations are the ground from which spring our own unique possibilities' (1994, p. 56). Leibrich (1997), for example, describes how freedom from medications enabled her to develop that important part of her self that is a poet:

> I have a home again, friends, love, work, a family. I also have my poetry and have come to see that the very part of me that was once drugged away is what makes me write. And after all being a poet is an easier role than a psychiatric patient! (p. 44)

On the other hand, Fekete (2004) tells how medications and a medical understanding of the illness have enabled him to rebuild a positive identity. He says that, although he is not sure that he is the same person as he was before the illness, he likes who he is now. After listing his many successful endeavours since he developed the illness, Fekete offers this hopeful message to others:

> I have a good life. Having a neuro-chemical imbalance is not the end of life as we knew it. There is a vast spectrum of ways to live and love life with a neuro-chemical imbalance . . .. Never give up. Never, never give up. (p. 194)

And recovery is not necessarily a matter of fulfilling the roles traditionally valued in our society. More important than aspiring to fulfil the expectations of others, then, is striving to live an authentic life:

> They may tell you that your goal should be to become normal and to achieve valued roles. But a role is empty and valueless unless you fill it with *your* meaning and *your* purpose. Our task is not to become normal. You have the wonderfully terrifying task of becoming who you are called to be. (Deegan, 1997, p. 24)

As noted in Chapter 2, many consumers have reported feeling that they are a better person as a result of their struggle with the illness. Participants in Lapsley *et al.*'s

(2002) research reported developing personal qualities, including: strength and courage; more confidence in the self; resourcefulness and responsibility; a new philosophy of life; compassion and empathy; a sense of self-worth and being happier and more carefree. Very few people noted negative changes, and those who did generally said that they were now more cautious (Lapsley *et al.*, 2002). The process of recovery, and the re-examination of values and assumptions, therefore fosters personal growth. For example, John (1994), who earlier described the culture of sport and sexual prowess in which he was raised, tells how his change of values improved his sense of self: 'I look on my schizophrenia as a source of growth rather than as something I have to manage. There can always be growth out of trauma' (p. 8). An interviewee in Young and Ensing's study went so far as to say recovery should be referred to as 'a better me through the recovery process' (1999, p. 226), and this is echoed by another consumer, who is quoted as saying 'I'm more of a person now than I ever was before the illness' (Pettie and Triolo, 1999, p. 260).

The stories of recovered consumers can be understood in terms of 'narrative identity' (McAdams, 2001). A person constructs a story that links their past, present and future in a way that brings them to an understanding of how they fit in with the world, thus imbuing their lives with a sense of unity and purpose (McAdams, 2001). People can learn and grow from their negative experiences, and this ability to learn from one's experiences promotes personal adjustment, stress-related growth and maturity (J. Singer, 2004). In Waterman's (1993) terms, the person has truly found 'someone to be'. Young and Ensing (1999) found that people in the final stage of recovery reported being well enough to 'strive for ideals that are often associated with stable psychological health and self-actualization' (p. 227). We discussed in the Rebuilding stage how, when life goals have been lost, a person needs to rebuild a future that is as meaningful as the previously imagined future (King, 1998). This process requires an internal search for one's core values, and a redefinition of goals that are in keeping with these values (e.g. King, 1998). Therefore, although the specific goal may change, it nonetheless serves the same higher value that represents the core self.

Meaning in the Growth Stage: Living a Meaningful Life

While finding a purpose in life is an important aspect of recovery, those in the Growth stage exhibit a deeper sense of meaning. People often describe achieving a sense of serenity and peacefulness (Young and Ensing, 1999). Some find meaning in the experience of illness itself, and for some it takes the form of a spiritual awakening:

> I do not think [God] could have given me a more gracious gift, especially gracious since I am in no way worthy of it. I might have opted for the gift of 'no pain' but somehow I now feel a difficult journey shared is better than a solitary one that is painless. (Watson, 1994, p. 70)

> I have a great respect for life and for the deadliness of my illness, yet I embrace life fully and am thankful for each day of health of mind. I live a simple life, but a good life; and I am very grateful for my second chance to enjoy my family and pursue my dreams. (Fox, 2002, p. 365)

> I live on the edge of the sea and walk on the beach. That's how I find my strength. Some say it's when the universe is talking. Others, it's about being close to God. (Leibrich, 1997, p. 44)

Watson (1994) describes how the almost obligatory reassessment of values can lead to finding a deeper meaning in life:

> In a very real way we are blessed we don't have to spend a lifetime finding out what's really important. Most of us know. In this way our pain has been a good teacher. Somehow we just know that a kind heart is worth more than a Mercedes, that learning, loving and growing touches our deepest longing much more than status, power or TV-style 'success' ever could. (p. 74)

In the Growth stage, as suggested in the passages on Identity above, occupational activities do more than provide a purpose in life; they can reflect a meaning in life (Young and Ensing, 1999). According to Singer (1996) we create meaning in our lives by identifying those things that we see as valuable and work towards some ideal. Some consumers have used the experience of illness and recovery to find new, more deeply meaningful occupations, often in a peer-support, advocacy or educational role:

> Experience with mental illness 'from the inside' is not necessarily a liability; it can also be an asset. More and more, the professional world is coming to realize the potential that recovering people have to bring their skills and understanding, healing, empowering and advocacy to the lives of recovering peers. (Koehler, 1994, p. 23)

Consumers who perform a professional role find themselves in a uniquely powerful position to educate consumers and other professionals about the experience of mental illness and recovery:

> I now see my experience as valuable, if very painful, and will try to use it, along with my professional and educational experience, to help other such disabled individuals. (Anonymous, 1994a, p. 17)

> The question becomes: Why be employed in a toxic system taking toxic drugs to maintain myself in that system? It doesn't make a lot of sense except that it is an opportunity to have some effect in promoting empowerment of mental health consumers . . . . What kind of opportunity is this? A risky one. (Wentworth, 1994, p. 88)

There is mutual benefit in these roles as mental health workers, educators and advocates, as they provide opportunities for growth and a meaning in the illness:

Finding my role as an advocate was like being in the dark, wintry North and finding my way to the Interstate where I hitched a ride with a big semi-trailer headed for the sunny South. That truck carried me where I wanted to go, and with my health much improved, I am still hitching rides. (Weingarten, 1994, p. 78)

We ourselves are finding surprising depths of compassion and heights of inspiration in helping our peers. Demonstrating solidarity with others' suffering redeems our own suffering and turns it to good purpose. (Koehler, 1994, p. 23)

It is worthy of note that so many recovered consumers mentioned goals that were either helping others, or transcending the self in a spiritual or philosophical way, and these types of goals have been found to be related to self-reported recovery from loss (Emmons, Colby and Kaiser, 1998) and adjustment in ageing (Lapierre, Bouffard and Bastin, 1997). Self-transcendent goals provide one with a meaning for the illness and, in so doing, represent a form of benefit-finding (Davis, Nolen-Hoeksema and Larson, 1998). Benefit-finding has been associated with adjustment to loss of a loved one (Calhoun and Tedeschi, 2001) and other forms of trauma such as amputation (Dunn, 1996) and breast cancer (Taylor, 1983), in which people reported that some good had come of the experience, and that they considered themselves better adjusted than before.

Resilience, Personal Growth and Wisdom

The process of finding benefit in a negative event, and learning from it, thus giving meaning to the experience, results in the acquisition of wisdom (Bluck and Glueck, 2004). Wisdom is the ability to use the lessons learned from past experiences in negotiating new challenges (Bluck and Glueck, 2004; J. Singer, 2004). The ability to appreciate what one has learned by successfully responding to a negative event can enhance a person's sense of competence and self-efficacy (Bluck and Glueck, 2004). The stories of recovered consumers reflect this notion of gaining wisdom by dealing with adversity. By tapping previously unrealized strengths in order to reclaim a meaningful life, the person gains an enhanced sense of self, which provides resilience in facing future challenges (Davidson *et al.*, 2005). For example, 'Hula', a participant in Lapsley *et al.*'s (2002) study, demonstrated her optimistic outlook towards setbacks during recovery: 'If I get a bit down, I don't actually get right down anymore because I know there is hope, I know I've got power' (Lapsley *et al.*, 2002, p. 94). Her statement illustrates a sense of competence and personal empowerment. Deegan (1997) noted that her bid to grow involved risking relapse due to increased stress. However, her attitude towards relapse has changed:

I have found that although my symptoms may look the same or even worse, relapsing while in recovery is not the same thing as 'having a breakdown'. When I relapse in recovery I'm not breaking down, but rather I am breaking out or breaking through . . . . It means that I am growing, breaking out of old fears and *breaking through* into new worlds . . . . (p. 21)

Deegan's statement is a powerful illustration of resilience borne of wisdom. Resilience does not always entail the tenacious pursuit of long-held goals. Brandtstädter and colleagues (e.g. Brandtstädter and Rothermund, 2002; Brandtstädter, 2009) have developed a dual-process model of adjustment in which the abandonment of unattainable goals can protect against loss of well-being. Acceptance of one's limitations is a core component of wisdom, and this can include finding benefit in the current state of affairs (Linley, 2003; Brandtstädter, 2009). In later life, when personal resources are diminished, wisdom is reflected in a shift from extrinsically motivated goals to more intrinsically valuable goals, such as altruism, spirituality and intimacy (Brandtstädter, 2009). We have seen many consumer quotes in which recovery features these types of self-transcendent goals. The key to resilience is in striking a balance between commitment to previous goals and adjusting goals while maintaining one's valued directions in life.

After experiencing disruption to his or her life, a person may reintegrate dysfunctionally, reintegrate with loss, return to homeostasis, or achieve *resilient reintegration*, in which new insights or growth occurs (Richardson, 2002). Richardson claims that the energy for resilient reintegration is an innate force within all human beings that drives a person to seek self-actualization, altruism, wisdom and spiritual harmony. Personal growth rather than return to homeostasis has been referred to as 'thriving' within the fields of stress-related growth and post-traumatic growth (e.g. Carver, 1998; O'Leary, 1998). Losses that render important goals unattainable, causing confusion about the meaning of life, initially cause great emotional distress and rumination, a decline in the ability to cope and changes to the sense of identity (Calhoun and Tedeschi, 2001). However, some people manage to use the experience of trauma as a 'springboard to further individual development or growth' replacing lost goals and beliefs, and creating a new and better life than the one they had before (Tedeschi, Park and Calhoun, 1998, p. 1). Domains of growth outlined by Calhoun and Tedeschi (2001) include an enhanced sense of self, improved relationships and existential or spiritual growth. Schmook (1996) demonstrates the progression from loss to thriving in recovery from schizophrenia:

> Recovery happens in small ways, starting moment by moment, hour by hour, leading to one day at a time. Lives are rebuilt that way until one fully realizes that survival is possible. . . . The process of recovery then moves from survival to realizing individual potential with its transforming power of personal growth. (p. 12)

The preceding models of wisdom, resilience and post-traumatic growth echo the views of Frankl (1984). Inspired by his personal experiences and observations of survival in Nazi concentration camps, Frankl criticized theories of mental health that were based on the need for homeostasis, or absence of tension. He stated 'What man actually needs is rather the striving and struggling for a worthwhile goal, a freely chosen task. What he needs is ... the call of a potential meaning waiting to be fulfilled by him' (Frankl, 1984, p. 127). Furthermore, Frankl asserted that one can *only* find true fulfilment by self-transcendence, that is, in the service of some thing or somebody outside oneself. This view has been supported by empirical research: people with spiritual or self-development goals have been found to be more likely to consider themselves recovered from loss, and to have found meaning in it, than those with extrinsic goals (Emmons, Colby and Kaiser, 1998).

Conclusion

Our discussion of the Growth stage has illustrated that recovery from serious mental illness is more than staying out of hospital or a return to some arbitrary level of functioning. It is more than merely coping with the illness. In this last stage, the notion of well-being replaces that of wellness. While wellness implies the absence of illness, well-being refers to a more holistic psychological experience of a fulfilling life. In Chapter 6 we talked about building a meaningful life through personal expressiveness, that is, living in a way that reflects one's true values (Waterman, 1984). Waterman described this as the path to 'eudaimonia', that is, living a deeply satisfying life associated with feelings of rightness, sense of purpose and competence. This is in contrast to hedonia, which essentially means feeling happy. Happiness does not necessarily equate to psychological health. In seeking to define psychological health, Ryff (1989) reviewed philosophical and psychological literature on the topic to develop a theory of psychological well-being. The resulting concept consists of six components: autonomy, environmental mastery, personal growth, positive relations with others, purpose in life and self-acceptance (Ryff, 1989). It is immediately clear how these constructs are reflected in the literature on recovery. A state of superior mental health, involving high levels of emotional, psychological and social well-being has been dubbed *flourishing* by Keyes (2003). People who are flourishing 'have an enthusiasm for life and are actively and productively engaged with others and in society' (Keyes, 2003). Although we may not expect everyone (including those who do not have a mental illness) to reach the highest levels of self-actualization, we can expect that all people have the opportunity to develop a positive sense of self and identity and to live a meaningful life filled with purpose and hope for the future. Schiff (2004) painted this picture of recovery:

> To me, being recovered means feeling at peace, being happy, feeling comfortable in the world and with others, and feeling hope for the future. It involves drawing on all my negative experiences to make me a better person. It means not being afraid of who I am and what I feel. It is about being able to take positive risks in life. It means not being afraid to live in the present. It is about knowing and being able to be who I am. (p. 215)

It is evident from the quotes we have seen in this chapter that the Growth stage of recovery is not an end state. It is an ongoing and dynamic way of living, in which the person continues to grow and strive for meaning, as do all psychologically healthy people. Many concepts introduced thus far reflect those championed by the positive psychology movement, and later, in Chapter 10 we will focus on the parallels and links between psychological recovery and positive psychology.

Retrospective Overview

Over the previous chapters, we have formulated a consumer-oriented definition of psychological recovery from serious mental illness, and presented a stage model of psychological recovery. The model consists of four component psychological processes: finding and maintaining hope; taking responsibility for wellness and for life; rediscovering or rebuilding a positive sense of self and identity, and finding purpose and meaning in life. These processes develop over five stages of recovery: the Moratorium stage, the Awareness stage, the Preparation stage, the Rebuilding stage, and the Growth stage. The elaboration of psychological recovery highlights the normal developmental processes that are at work in the journey of recovery from serious mental illness, and, we hope, contributes towards removing the sense of 'otherness' about people who have a mental illness. The model offers the promise of psychological well-being, or indeed, flourishing, for all who undertake this difficult journey.

Next, in Chapter 8, we will discuss some issues surrounding the stage model of psychological recovery, drawn from questions that have been raised in the recovery literature generally, or specifically in response to our work.

Summary

- The Growth stage is the culmination of the effort that has taken place in the preceding stages.
- It is an ongoing, dynamic way of living, rather than an end state.
- The Growth stage is characterized by hopefulness and a positive outlook towards the future.
- People in this stage take responsibility for their well-being and their life generally.
- The person is not afraid to risk failure or exposure of their illness in attempting new endeavours.
- Self-stigma has been replaced by a positive sense of identity that is not defined by the illness.
- The illness is incorporated as a small part of the whole person.
- The person has constructed a meaningful life for themselves, either by persevering with valued goals, or reviewing personal values and identifying new goals.
- Meaning in life is often achieved through the pursuit of self-transcendent or spiritual goals.
- Resilience in the growth stage reflects the acquisition of wisdom.
- People in the final stage of recovery can flourish, even in the presence of recurrent symptoms.

8

Common Questions Regarding the Stage Model of Psychological Recovery

Overview

The previous chapters have covered the early conceptualizations of schizo-phrenia, the four components of psychological recovery across five stages of psychological recovery before considering measurement issues informed by the model. In the process of developing, researching and training people in the stages of psychological recovery, numerous questions and challenges have arisen. This chapter provides ten common questions that are posed regarding theoretical and ethical aspects of the model. Answers are provided regarding each of the questions, however, this should be considered an ongoing dialogue rather than a final word.

Ten Questions That Have Been Raised About the Model

What is the difference between the stage model of psychological recovery and the Stages of Change Model (Transtheoretical Model of Change)?

Many practitioners in mental health and alcohol and other drug use services will be familiar with the Transtheoretical Model of Change (TTM; Prochaska and DiClemente, 1986) more commonly known as the 'stages of change model'. Given that TTM has five stages also, questions sometimes arise about how the models are different, and whether the stage model of psychological recovery was based on the

Psychological Recovery: Beyond Mental Illness, First Edition.
Retta Andresen, Lindsay G. Oades and Peter Caputi.
© 2011 John Wiley & Sons, Ltd. Published 2011 by John Wiley & Sons, Ltd.

TTM? The stage model of psychological recovery was not based on the TTM and is different to the TTM.

There are two clear differences.

1 The TTM is a cognitive and behavioural model that focuses on specific behaviours – meaning that a person can be at multiple different stages at once, for different behaviours. The stage model of psychological recovery, however, is a 'whole of experience' model, measuring the experience of living with and beyond a mental illness.
2 The TTM primarily focuses on problem behaviours, e.g. smoking cessation or reducing alcohol intake, and the relapse phase is seen as a loss of personal control. The stage model of psychological recovery, however, is growth focused, and the end state is ongoing growth rather than maintenance from loss of personal control. The two models have quite a different focus.

If the recovery process is non-linear how can there be a stage model? Don't we go back? What if you relapse?

This is an important question. Many mental health consumers experience multiple set-backs during journeys of recovery. Moreover, the individuality of the journey does not seem to lend itself to being viewed as a straight line. Much of the confusion comes from conflating the milestones along the journey, and the path taken. The paths taken are highly individualized – but if one travels north for long enough they will eventually pass a particular landmark. The logic behind the stage model of psychological recovery is based on a 'highest level reached' logic. That is, once you have made it to the Growth stage you always have made it to the Growth stage. Once you have been to New York, you have always been to New York. This doesn't mean you are currently functioning or feeling as though you are in New York. The important issue, however, is that once you have been there, you know you can – hence it is likely to be easier to go back. The stages are an abstraction, a conceptualization. Set-backs, however, may occur leading to reductions in hope, impact upon identity, motivational effects to reduce the sense of taking responsibility, or temporary loss of sense of purpose. The current empirical evidence is that there is an ordinal relationship between the stages. How people move across them, and how the return to previous stages occurs remains an empirical question for future research. Future measurement issues will aim to investigate more directly current stage and highest level attained stage, etc.

What if you relapse? This question is usually referring to symptoms of mental illness. This is a medical conceptualization, not a psychological one. A person further along the stages of psychological recovery is likely to have a broader range of resources to manage the medical relapse, and return to working towards a personal journey, if they have worked through earlier stages prior.

Isn't this just another set of standards for consumers to be measured against?

Like any tool used incorrectly, it could do harm. However, one practical purpose of the stage model of psychological recovery is to show consumers that there is a pathway towards recovery, based on previous people's experience. The approach has been developed from stories of people living with illness and refined in consultation with a range of consumers. Many consumers have provided input into this work. The measures developed to date, as outlined in Chapter 9, are rated by consumers rather than professionals.

If recovery is an individualized process, how can it be put into a model? Doesn't trying to measure it or model it lose the richness of one's personal experience?

The stage model of psychological recovery is a conceptual model with the purpose of assisting understanding and sharing of experience; and also generating fruitful research questions. It is a model, therefore it is an abstraction from a collection of experiences, and is not an experience, nor does it claim to be. Whilst the experience of recovery is an individual process, some common factors do exist in terms of the psychological process. For example, most people appear to find hope important and most people address issues regarding identity in relation to illness at some point. By creating a map of a city one does not claim to know the exact experience of the traveller. The map, however, may still be useful for the traveller. The richness of personal experience is definitely lost when one abstracts from the individual situated experience to the general – from the qualitative to the quantitative. This is a reality and not unique to the stage model of psychological recovery. The purpose, however, is not to capture the rich unique experience, but rather provide a broad framework as a reference point for multiple viewpoints and stories – not one single story.

Isn't this just another example of researchers and professionals colonizing consumers' experiences?

Many people who have lived with illness have had multiple injustices and indignities. The aim of the stage model of psychological recovery, however, is to provide a framework for people to have discussions about their personal processes. It provides a comparison point for dialogue. It also provides the opportunity for some structuring of recovery-oriented service provision and for measurement of recovery processes. If consumers were being actively exploited to use this approach or partake in research unwillingly it could be construed as colonization. Rather than colonization, a better analogy may be mutual map making. If over time the model does not fit with people's experience it will be modified in line with scientific method. The model is silent on whether the researcher has a mental illness or not.

Are there really five stages? What about the evidence that there might be only three?

The original research from the qualitative literature suggested that there were five stages. Thus far, however, some quantitative research indicates that empirically there may be three factors/clusters of experience rather than five. At the time of writing it is premature to abandon five stages when measurement continues to be developed. That is, is the model flawed or is the measurement? Interestingly, similar to the TTM, whether there are five stages is a different question to whether it is useful to work with people in terms of five stages. There is a significant amount of evidence that the five stage TTM has been useful in assisting people change their behaviour, yet there is varied evidence as to whether there are five stages. There is much more work to be done until there is a conclusive answer to this question.

The recovery process is very complex, so is this an oversimplification?

The recovery process is indeed a complex and dynamic process – which is one of the reasons it is difficult to define, understand, research and experience! The stage model of psychological recovery, is just that – a model. That is, something taken from a better known domain (i.e. a composite of multiple people's experience) and applied to a lesser known domain (i.e. the experience of an individual). The map, however, is not the territory. The model is parsimonious as feasibility of use has been considered. A four process by five stage model provides 20 possibilities on which to map experience. Any more complex and individuals, teams and systems would find it unwieldy.

If recovery is a process, does it end at the fifth stage? Does that mean you are recovered?

The lived experience of recovery is often emphasized as a process, and views of outcome or endpoint are often less favoured by mental health consumers. Researchers and managers, however, are often more interested in outcomes. Given that the stage model of psychological recovery has five stages, it could be said that reaching the Growth stage is the endpoint or the outcome. There are two issues to consider here. First, the Growth stage is a dynamic stage, that is, it involves ongoing striving for goals and purpose in line with core values – in the same way psychological well-being is indicated by purpose, growth and autonomy. It is not an endpoint, but an ongoing direction. Qualitatively, however, it is different than previous stages.

What about social inclusion, employment, stable housing, poverty, stigma? isn't the model too intrapersonal?

Stated simply, this is a model of psychological recovery for people living with and beyond mental illness. The focus of the model is intrapersonal, particularly on issues of the self and its development. Social inclusion, employment, housing and poverty are of course important to issues of mental health recovery – however, the focus of this approach is internal resources. The coherence of the model, and the fact that it is proving fertile in terms of measurement is due to the fact that it has been circumscribed about what is being measured. The claim is not that this is a comprehensive model of all things that facilitate recovery, rather, it includes ways of understanding the psychological process of that journey.

Does linking this work with positive psychology overlook the suffering that goes on for people living with illness?

This question is similar to many that are put to practitioners and researchers who identify with positive psychology. The stage model of psychological recovery, however, in no way denies suffering, and in fact the first four stages still refer back to illness, and only the final stage truly transcends it. Rather than focusing on the term positive psychology a more useful question may be: Which of the following are relevant to experiences of mental health consumers?

- Wellbeing
- Courage
- Strength
- Wisdom
- Hope
- Goals
- Values
- Resilience.

Any text on positive psychology will include a science of these ideas. In some ways this is a sensible evolution of the recovery movement, using the power of science to validate one's experience. Recovery is a debate about what constitutes progress and an outcome. Using the science of positive psychology does not deny the negative experience, rather it brings tools to develop optimal functioning in the bad times and the good. The common credo of recovery and positive psychology is to develop a life worth living.

Conclusion

The recovery movement has provided multiple challenges to mental health services, service providers, consumers, carers and researchers. This chapter is a candid attempt to address directly many of the issues and questions raised regarding the stage model of psychological recovery. It should be considered an invitation for situated dialogue, rather than a statement of reality.

Summary

- The stage model of psychological recovery is different than the Transtheoretical Model of change because it focuses on the whole experience rather than individual behaviours.
- The stage model of psychological recovery is non-linear in terms of the component processes, which may fluctuate.
- The stage model of psychological recovery is a tool, which like any other tool can be misused against consumers.
- The stage model of psychological recovery does not claim to map the richness of an individual experience. The map is not the territory.
- The stage model of psychological recovery is better described as collaborative map making rather than a colonization of experience.
- Ongoing research is investigating the validity of five stages and how the processes change across these stages.
- The stage model of psychological recovery is deliberately parsimonious in order to be useful.
- The final Growth stage is a dynamic process, that is, in order to maintain well-being one needs a purpose, values and goals.
- The stage model of psychological recovery is exactly that, a psychological model particularly focusing on issues of self and its development.
- Using tools from positive psychology to assist measurement and conceptualization does not deny suffering of consumers.

Part III

Measuring Recovery

9

Recovery-Oriented Outcome Measurement

Overview

Having developed a model of consumer-defined recovery, in this chapter we look at the measurement of recovery, and the motivation for doing so. We give a brief overview of the evolution of measurement of recovery outcomes from before the era of consumer-oriented recovery to present-day efforts to operationalize the consumer definition of recovery. We finish by introducing some measures based on the stage model of psychological recovery.

Why the Need for Measures of Recovery?

Why would one wish to measure outcomes in mental health, and in particular, why would one wish to measure recovery? Trauer (2010, p. 99) pointed out that outcome measurement can be useful for several key stakeholders: good outcome measures can provide useful information that can assist managers to evaluate their services; likewise, clinicians, and importantly, consumers and their carers can benefit from good outcome measurement – outcome measures can be used to monitor consumer progress, while consumers and their carers can engage more fully in that process. Finally, good outcome measurement can inform policy makers (Trauer, 2010).

In Chapter 1 we posited that consumers are increasingly advocating for recovery-oriented mental health services (Acuff, 2000; Crowley, 1997; Curtis, 2001). Internationally, this notion has been incorporated into mental health policy, for example, in the United States (New Freedom Commission on Mental Health, 2003a, 2003b),

Psychological Recovery: Beyond Mental Illness, First Edition.
Retta Andresen, Lindsay G. Oades and Peter Caputi.
© 2011 John Wiley & Sons, Ltd. Published 2011 by John Wiley & Sons, Ltd.

Australia (Australian Health Ministers, 2003), New Zealand (Minister of Health, 2005), Ireland (Mental Health Commission, 2005), Canada (Mental Health Commission of Canada, 2009), United Kingdom (Cross-Government Strategy: Mental Health Division, 2009) and Israel (Ramon *et al.*, 2009). In our own recovery research, we have fielded enquiries from Eastern and Western Europe, Scandinavia, Central Asia, South-East Asia and the Middle East. Although a number of countries have incorporated a recovery-orientation into policy, there is no definitive description of what this entails. Various policies highlight the need for a consumer orientation, fostering hope, meaning, fulfilment, an active sense of self, personal responsibility and resilience, and for promoting choice, social inclusion and rights (see Slade, 2009). An approach to recovery-focused practice, based on the processes of the stage model of psychological recovery, was provided by Slade (2009). The framework identifies and elucidates four tasks of mental health practitioners: to support hope by fostering relationships and social inclusion; to offer intervention options which foster self-management and personal responsibility; using the assessment process to support the person in finding meaning in their experience; and supporting identity and encouraging personal growth by promoting personal goal-planning and engendering hope (Slade, 2009).

In parallel with the movement towards recovery-oriented services, there is increasing pressure to use only evidence-based practices – those that have demonstrated positive effects on outcomes (Australian Health Ministers, 1992; New Freedom Commission on Mental Health, 2003a, 2003b; Mental Health Commission, 2005; Minister of Health, 2005; Cross-Government Strategy: Mental Health Division, 2009; Mental Health Commission of Canada, 2009). Some hold that the notion of evidence-based practice, as an outgrowth of evidence-based medicine, is incompatible with the recovery vision (Tanenbaum, 2005; Bonney and Stickley, 2008; Fisher and Happell, 2009). Often, treatment effectiveness studies have been conducted in relation to medications, and effectiveness has therefore been determined by measures of symptoms, hospitalizations and functioning. These types of outcomes may not fully represent the individual consumer's definition of recovery, and do not reflect recovery-oriented approaches to treatment. For example, a self-admission to hospital may be the result of a person's taking responsibility for his or her treatment, rather than a failure of treatment (Anthony, 2000). Tanenbaum (2005) questioned whether the elimination of symptoms without relieving suffering could be considered effective treatment, and found that consumers are likely to regard treatments – even those found to be effective in research – as merely tools to facilitate person-led recovery (Tanenbaum, 2008).

However, Torrey *et al.* (2005) and Silverstein and Bellack (2008) have countered that there are many evidence-based practices in use that are in keeping with the principles of recovery-oriented services, and that the two notions are complementary. The key, according to those authors, is to use recovery-oriented principles in service provision; for example, giving information about treatments to promote informed choice. While this is certainly in keeping with the aims of the recovery movement, much evidence-based practice research has not been conducted within a recovery framework, and has not demonstrated substantial effects on consumer-oriented outcomes (Anthony, Rogers and Farkas, 2003). The issue is with how 'effectiveness' is defined and what outcomes are measured (Tanenbaum, 2005).

There are two overarching arenas of outcome measurement: research, including investigations of the outcomes of schizophrenia and treatment effectiveness; and clinical assessment, which, in assessing individual outcomes, also informs the evaluation of services. Below we provide a brief overview of approaches to outcome measurement in these domains and how they are changing with the focus on recovery-oriented services.

Approaches to Operationalizing Recovery in Research

Early longitudinal studies of outcome, particularly of schizophrenia, employed definitions of recovery that were broader than the medical definition. As we saw in Chapter 1, most of these studies used both medical outcome measures and assessments of functioning. For example, the Vermont Longitudinal Study (Harding *et al.*, 1987a, 1987b), as well as an interview protocol determining current status on a number of functional and social dimensions, included two measures of functioning, the Global Assessment Scale (Endicott, Spitzer and Fliess, 1976), and the Strauss–Carpenter Level of Functioning Scales, which rate quantity of employment and level of intimate relationships (married/unmarried/dating) on a scale of 0 to 4. Similarly, in a longitudinal follow-up study of schizophrenia, Harrow *et al.* (2005) added at least half-time work and the absence of poor social functioning to measures of symptoms and hospitalizations. Criteria were measured using the Strauss–Carpenter Level of Functioning Scales and the Levenstein–Klein–Pollack Scale (Levenstein, Klein and Pollack, 1966), on which symptoms, hospitalizations, vocational and social functioning, life adjustment and self-support are rated on an eight-point scale. In assessing one-year outcomes of treatment for early psychosis, Whitehorn *et al.* (2002), in addition to positive and negative symptoms, used two measures of functioning: the Global Assessment of Functioning (GAF; American Psychiatric Association, 1994) and the Social and Occupational Functioning Scale (SOFAS; Goldman, Skodol and Lave, 1992). The SOFAS was derived from the GAF, and uses similar descriptions of social and occupational functioning, but omits references to symptoms. Both of these measures use a scale of 0–100, described in 10 subdivisions, and are based on clinical judgement.

Recognizing the lack of a universal definition of recovery for research, Liberman and colleagues (2002) attempted to introduce consistency by proposing dimensions that reflect the diagnostic criteria for schizophrenia, i.e., symptom remission, vocational functioning, independent living and social relationships. The criteria specified thresholds that were to be attained and maintained for two years. For example, in the case of peer relationships, the criteria specified that the person have a social interaction with a peer outside the family at least once per week. As Liberman and colleagues noted, the thresholds and durations chosen were largely arbitrary, and determined by consensus of professionals. There is a judgemental element to these definitions; assessment of recovery ought not involve moral judgements on a person's lifestyle. After all, if 'normality' is the goal of mental health services, who decides what is 'normal' (Ralph and Corrigan, 2005)? We noted earlier that Harding (1994) questioned the definition used in the Vermont study (Harding *et al.*, 1987a1987b), as they found groups of people who, while not meeting all the study criteria for recovery, were nonetheless happy with their way of life. Focus groups made up of researchers, mental health professionals and consumers showed that, although there was broad consensus on the dimensions chosen by Liberman *et al.* (2002), the operational definitions gained approval from a greater percentage of researchers than of consumers or practitioners. Consumers preferred to define recovery as an ongoing process, rather than an endpoint or goal.

While acknowledging that there are common elements to recovery, Anthony *et al.* (2003) pointed out that quantitative approaches do not allow for the diversity of recovery goals among subjects. These authors therefore urge that quantitative approaches be supplemented by the use of subjective, qualitative measures such as narrative analysis and interviews in determining best practices. However, qualitative procedures such as interviews and narratives, and multidimensional batteries such as those described above, are burdensome on consumers, staff and researchers and are often impractical for large-scale studies or routine clinical use – an area in which outcome measurement is becoming more in demand.

Assessing Outcomes in Routine Clinical Practice

The focus of the definitions of recovery presented so far has been on outcome measurement in research, including longitudinal outcome studies and studies of treatment effectiveness. However, the drive towards evidence-based practice has fuelled demand for the introduction of routine outcome measures for assessing individual outcomes and for the evaluation of services (Slade, Thornicroft and Glover, 1999; Eagar, Trauer and Mellsop, 2005; Slade *et al.*, 2006; Priebe *et al.*, 2007; Valenstein *et al.*, 2009). Outcome measures for routine use have also often failed to embrace a recovery orientation. A number of authors have proposed domains for outcome measurement. In a systematic review of this literature, Slade (2002) identified seven categories of patient-level outcome domains: wellbeing, cognition/ emotion, behaviour, physical health, interpersonal, society and satisfaction with service (Slade, 2002). The majority of authors took a medical perspective and focused the staff viewpoint on ameliorating disability. The only review that emphasized the client's subjective experience came from the consumer-oriented literature, and included domains of wellbeing, recovery (defined in terms of cognition, emotion and functioning), self-help and empowerment – representing a recovery-oriented focus (see Slade, 2002, for the full review).

In Australia, which was at the forefront of introducing mandatory routine outcome measures, a number of existing tools were selected for routine use

(Stedman *et al.*, 1997). Two clinician-rated adult mental health outcome measures have been introduced into most Australian states, the Health of a Nation Outcome Scales (HoNOS; Wing *et al.*, 1998) and the Life Skills Profile (LSP-16; Rosen, Hadzi-Pavlovic and Parker, 1989). In addition, one client-rated measure is mandatory, and varies between states. In New South Wales the Kessler-10 (K-10; Andrews and Slade, 2001) is used (Department of Health NSW, 2006). The HoNOS consists of 12 items assessing four domains: symptoms, impairment, behaviour and functioning. The LSP-16 consists of five scales: Self-Care, Non-Turbulence, Social Contact, Communication, and Responsibility. The client-rated K-10 assesses depression and anxiety symptoms.

While assessment should, ideally, contribute something to the clinical process, rather than representing a burden on clinicians and consumers, consumers found that these measures – which are typical of those used elsewhere – were not used to initiate change, and moreover do not assess those things important to them (Happell, 2008). Lakeman (2004) cautioned that, rather than informing recovery-oriented practice, such measures 'have little, if anything, [to] do with or offer to the recovery process. Indeed, they strip the person's experience of all meaning and reduce it to predetermined categories' (p. 212). A recent Australian review of outcome measures for 'chronic' mental illness has acknowledged the value of subjective assessments such as quality of life, perceived needs and recovery (Trauer, 2010).

Outcome Measurement from the Consumer Perspective

Before the rise of the recovery movement, there were few self-rated outcome measures. Possibly the earliest and most common were, and still are, measures of psychological distress, such as the Mental Health Inventory (Veit and Ware, 1983) and its derivatives, and the Kessler-10 (Andrews and Slade, 2001). Consumers use a rating scale to report levels of depression and anxiety symptoms. A more consumer-oriented approach was realized with the assessment of individual needs. The most used and tested needs measure is the Camberwell Assessment of Need Short Appraisal Schedule (CANSAS; Slade *et al.*, 1999). The CANSAS assesses the client's met and unmet needs in 22 domains, including accommodation, household skills, relationships, child care, and transport. Each domain can be rated as 'No Need', 'Met Need' or 'Unmet Need' from the perspective of the consumer, clinician and carer.

Potentially closer to a holistic recovery perspective is the assessment of quality of life (QoL). Quality of life has been conceptualized and operationalized in a variety of ways; while some measures are little more than checklists to assess the impact of a specific disease or illness, others assess satisfaction in a number of life domains, either as a questionnaire or in interview format. A number of QoL measures have been developed specifically for people with a mental illness. For example, the Quality of Life Interview (QOLI; Lehman, 1988) assesses satisfaction across eight domains: living situation, family, social relations, leisure, work, safety, finances and health; the self-rated Quality of Life Inventory (Frisch *et al.*, 1992), assessing satisfaction in 17 life domains including spirituality, creativity, civic action, and community; and the Wisconsin Quality of Life Index (W-QLI; Diamond and Becker, 1999), which assesses nine dimensions including symptoms, activities of daily living, emotional wellbeing, and personal goal attainment. The W-QLI has companion provider and caregiver versions.

Measuring Consumer-defined Recovery

Measures of consumer-oriented outcomes go only part of the way to the goal of ensuring that services promote recovery. What is required are measures of recovery as it has been defined by consumers (Davidson *et al.*, 2006). However, given that recovery is represented as a unique, personal journey, there has been a reluctance to define it as an outcome, as this is seen as prescribing what recovery should be for all consumers (Torrey *et al.*, 2005). Torrey and colleagues noted that the outcome goals identified by consumers are usually those things commonly sought by everyone, such as a home, a partner or work. While this is true, measures based on a specified set of goal domains would be contrary to the recovery movement's drive for empowerment and self-determination (Torrey *et al.*, 2005). One approach to clinical work that incorporates individualized goal setting and measurement can be found in the Collaborative Recovery Model (CRM; Oades *et al.*, 2005). The CRM enables clients to identify their personal, values-based goals, and to monitor and measure progress towards these goals (Clarke *et al.*, 2006).

In the past decade or so, researchers have been working to develop outcome measures that reflect the consumer definition of recovery. Some of these utilize existing subjective outcome measures which assess aspects of the recovery process. Writing from the perspective of psychopharmacologists wishing to work within the recovery model, Noordsy and colleagues (Noordsy *et al.*, 2000, 2002), moved towards a consumer definition of recovery by identifying three intrapersonal criteria for recovery from the literature – hope, taking responsibility and 'getting on with life' – consisting of four components: identity through life roles, relationships, work or structured activity and recreation. They offered examples of eight existing assessment tools to cover various components of these three aspects, embracing spirituality, illness management, healthy lifestyle, identity, relationships, work and recreation. Importantly, Noordsy and colleagues (2002) suggested that these quantitative measures would need to be augmented by the subjective experience of recovery, and stressed that objective measures should be coupled with measures of the value and meaningfulness of the item to the consumer.

A number of other measures of specific aspects of recovery have been used, including hope, resilience, self-efficacy, empowerment and wellbeing (Ralph, Kidder and Phillips, 2000). Resnick *et al.* (Resnick *et al.*, 2005) conducted a study aimed at identifying aspects of existing outcome measures which could be used to measure a 'recovery orientation'. Using data from the Schizophrenia Patient

Outcomes Research Team (PORT) Client Survey (Lehman *et al.*, 1998), they factor analysed items which assessed subjective aspects of recovery, and identified four aspects of a recovery orientation: Knowledge, Empowerment, Hope and Optimism, and Life Satisfaction. They suggested that, although recovery is described as a process, an empirical conceptualization could be used to assess recovery as an outcome (Resnick *et al.*, 2005). Resnick and colleagues note that a limitation of their operationalization was its dependence on items from an existing outcomes database, rather than being based in theory. The items, although subjective, focus largely on opinion about services received. For example, the first item in the *Empowerment– Self Agency* factor is: How much do your opinions and ideas count in which services you get? This does not reflect the sense of personal responsibility for one's life and wellbeing found in the consumer literature.

The first measure of recovery as a psychological construct with published psychometric properties was the Recovery Assessment Scale (RAS; Corrigan *et al.*, 1999b). Items of the RAS were based on qualitative work with consumers, and later factor analysed to reveal five factors: *Personal confidence and hope*; *Willingness to ask for help*; *Goal and success orientation*; *Reliance on others* and *No domination by symptoms* (Corrigan *et al.*, 2004). The Mental Health Recovery Measure (MHRM; Young, Ensing and Bullock, 1999), was based on Young and Ensing's conceptual model of recovery (Young and Ensing, 1999). The original version assessed the six aspects of recovery described in the model: *Overcoming Stuckness*; *Self-Empowerment*; *Learning and Self-Redefinition*; *Basic Functioning*; *Overall Well-Being*; and *New Potentials*. Later, the domains of *Spirituality* and *Advocacy/Enrichment* were added.

A collection of recovery and recovery-related measures has been compiled by Campbell-Orde *et al.* (2005). A distinction is made between measures of 'individual recovery' and 'recovery-promoting environments'. Of the eight measures of individual recovery in the volume that have been tested, only the RAS and MHRM could be considered measures of psychological recovery. The remainder incorporate 'external' factors of recovery, such as satisfaction with service or measure a single aspect such as illness management. Some were designed to evaluate a specific service or programme.

Measures Based on the Stage Model of Psychological Recovery

The model of psychological recovery we presented in Chapter 2 provides a framework for operationalizing the subjective experience of recovery. It describes the psychological process of recovery from the trauma of the illness, and focuses on positive outcomes. To recap, the model identifies four key psychological processes: finding and maintaining hope; taking responsibility for one's life; the re-establishment of a positive identity; and finding meaning and purpose in life. These processes take place over five stages of recovery: Moratorium, Awareness, Preparation,

Rebuilding and Growth (Andresen, Oades and Caputi, 2003). Due to the highly personal nature of recovery, the model is purposely flexible in terms of the means by which the person moves through this process. That is, each individual finds his or her own sources of hope, ways of finding meaning and building a positive identity. We have developed three measures based on the model. The measures are both subjective and non-prescriptive, focusing on positive psychological health.

Self-Identified Stage of Recovery

The Self-Identified Stage of Recovery (originally named the Stage of Recovery Measure) is a brief, two-part measure of recovery. Part A of the Self-identified Stage of Recovery (SISR-A) consists of five statements (each statement consisting of two sentences) that reflect the five stages of recovery. Respondents select the statement that best reflects their current experience of recovery. For example, a respondent may chose the statement 'I don't think people can recover from mental illness. I feel my life is out of control, and there is nothing I can do to help myself' reflecting the Moratorium stage.

Part B of the SISR (SISR-B) consists of four statements reflecting the four processes of recovery: Hope, Responsibility, Identity and Meaning. Respondents rate each statement on a six-point scale from 1 = 'Strongly disagree' to 6 = 'Strongly agree'. For instance, the process of Meaning is reflected in the statement 'The things I do in my life are meaningful and valuable'. A respondent would rate the extent to which he or she agrees or disagrees with this statement.

There is some evidence that the psychometric properties of the SISR are sound. Chiba, Kawakami, Miyamoto, and Andresen (2010) have developed a Japanese version of the SISR. They evaluated the psychometric properties of this version of the SISR using a sample of 223 participants with long-term mental illness drawn from both community and inpatient settings. Chiba *et al.* (2010) reported acceptable levels of internal consistency (Cronbach alpha coefficient greater than 0.70) for the total score of the SISR-B in both the community and inpatient samples. Further, Chiba *et al.* (2010) also tested the temporal stability for the SISR-A and the SISR-B, and found some evidence that these measures were stable over time. The reported statistics were modest, but acceptable, prompting the need for further research around the stability of the measure over time.

Chiba *et al.* (2010) also examined the concurrent validity of the SISR-A and SISR-B. Total scores for the SISR-A and SISR-B were significantly correlated with the RAS, the Japanese version of the Herth Hope Index (Hirano *et al.*, 2007; as cited in Chiba *et al.*, 2010), the Japanese versions of the Empowerment Scale (Yamada and Suzuki, 2007; as cited in Chiba *et al.*, 2010) and the Resilience Scale (Oshio *et al*, 2002; as cited in Chiba *et al.*, 2010). These findings provide support for the validity of the SISR-A and SISR-B.

We compared the relationship between the SISR and two other measures of recovery, the Recovery Assessment Scale (RAS: Corrigan *et al.*, 1999b) and the Mental Health Recovery Measure (MHRM; Young and Ensing, 1999; Ralph, Kidder and Phillips, 2000) in a sample of adults with a diagnosis of a psychiatric disorder and high support needs (Andresen, Caputi and Oades, 2010). We found high correlations between the SISR-B and the MHRM and RAS, and lower correlations between the SISR-A and the other recovery measures. We then compared the SISR-A and the individual SISR-B items of Hope, Identity, Meaning and Responsibility to the subscales of the RAS and MHRM, and found low to moderate correlations. The findings not only provided further support for the validity of these measures, but they highlighted that the SISR-A, being a stage measure, is assessing unique aspects of recovery not assessed by contunuous recovery measures.

We also looked at whether the RAS and MHRM scores differed across stages assessed by the SISR-A (Andresen, Caputi and Oades, 2010). One would anticipate lower scores on the RAS and MHRM in the Moratorium stage than at later stages, and highest scores in the Growth stage. Standardized total scores for the RAS and MHRM differed significantly across stages, and as anticipated, scores increased steadily across the stages of recovery. Significant differences were also observed in some of the subscales of the RAS (*Personal confidence and hope, Goal success orientation* and *Not dominated by symptoms*) and all subscales of the MHRM except *Overcoming stuckness*. These findings provide useful insight into what might be important in recovery, and demonstrate the theoretical utility of the SISR. For example, we found that scores on *Reliance on others* and *Willingness to ask for help* (subscales of the RAS) were higher at Moratorium than at Awareness. Given the conceptual association between these two subscales, this result suggests that, while asking for help is important in recovery, it may not be sufficient for higher levels of recovery (Andresen, Caputi and Oades, 2010, p. 315).

Notably, we also found evidence that recovery measures such as the RAS, MHRM and SISR assess aspects of recovery that are not detected by traditional clinical measures (Andresen, Caputi and Oades, 2010). We examined the relationship between four clinical measures, the Health of the Nation Outcome Scales (Wing *et al.*, 1998), the Life Skills Profile-16 (Rosen, Hadzi-Pavlovic and Parker, 1989), the Global Assessment of Functioning (American Psychiatric Association, 1994) and the Kessler-10 (Andrews and Slade, 2001), and the RAS, MHRM, SISR-A and SISR-B. There was little relationship between recovery and clinical measures. Only the Kessler-10 was found to be correlated with the recovery measures. These findings support the position held by consumers that traditional approaches to outcome measurement overlook things that are important to them in their recovery process.

Short Interview to Assess Stages of Recovery

The Short Interview to assess Stages of Recovery (SIST-R: Wolstencroft *et al.*, 2010) is a brief interview-based measure that identifies an individuals' stage of recovery from mental illness. Our motivation for developing the SIST-R was twofold: We wanted to develop a recovery measure that would (i) be feasible and acceptable for clinicians to use in various service settings, and (ii) facilitate collaborative discussion between consumer and clinician, therefore allowing the possibility to explore 'something more' in terms of understanding the process of recovery. The SIST-R encompasses the elements of feasibility espoused by Slade, Thornicroft and Glover (1999). Consequently, the SIST-R is brief, easy to use, adopts language that is relevant, and seen as a valuable tool in supporting consumers and practitioners within recovery-oriented services.

The interview schedule consists of five questions. Each question is read out to the respondent who is then asked to make a choice between two options, A or B in each question. If the respondent chooses option A then his or her stage is identified at that point. If option B is chosen then the respondent proceeds to the next question with options A or B. To illustrate, consider the first question from the interview schedule:

> *A) Do you find it difficult to feel hopeful about your future or in control of what is happening to you?*
> *OR*
> *B) Do you think that there are things that you could possibly do, or will be doing in the future, that will help you to recover and take you beyond how you feel today?*

Choosing option A would suggest the respondent is in the Moratorium stage of recovery, while choosing B would suggest the respondent may be in the Awareness stage of recovery. The interview continues through the questions until the respondent chooses option A. If the respondent arrives at question 5, he or she will finish by choosing option A, which will indicate the stage of Growth.

A description of the development of the SIST-R is provided by Wolstencroft *et al* (2010). We report some preliminary psychometric findings for the SIST-R, although some caution is needed in interpreting these findings given they are based on a sample of 18 consumers (Wolstencroft *et al.*, 2010). Initially, the concordance in the stage of recovery as identified by the SIST-R and the Stages of Recovery Instrument (STORI – see the next section for a description; Andresen, Caputi and Oades, 2006) was assessed. We found substantial concordance between the two measures, thus providing preliminary evidence for the validity of the SIST-R as a measure of recovery (Wolstencroft *et al.*, 2010).

We also examined the construct validity of the SIST-R. Participants' scores on the Kessler-10 and the subscales of the RAS were correlated with those of the SIST-R (Wolstencroft *et al.*, 2010). Low to moderate correlations were observed between the RAS subscales and the SIST-R. A small negative correlation was observed between the Kessler-10 and the SIST-R. However, given the small sample size there is a need for further research to examine whether these relationships are present in a larger sample.

Stages of Recovery Instrument

The final consumer-oriented measure of recovery described in this section is the Stages of Recovery Instrument (STORI: Andresen, Caputi and Oades, 2006).

The STORI is a 50-item self-report measure that yields five subscales corresponding to the five stages of recovery, Moratorium, Awareness, Preparation, Rebuilding and Growth. The development of the STORI is grounded in the stage model of recovery (Andresen, Caputi and Oades, 2003). As outlined in Andresen, Caputi and Oades (2006), item generation was significantly influenced by five key studies that identified stages or phases of recovery (Davidson and Strauss, 1992; Baxter and Diehl, 1998; Pettie and Triolo, 1999; Young and Ensing, 1999; Spaniol *et al*, 2002). In particular, these studies provided evidence for the four component processes associated with recovery – finding and maintaining hope, re-establishing a positive identity, finding meaning in life and taking responsibility for one's life (Andresen, Caputi and Oades, 2006, p. 974). Conceptually, the STORI has a complex structure reflecting the four component processes that are assumed to vary across five stages of recovery.

Recently, the STORI has received growing attention in the psychological and psychiatric literature. For instance, Deane and Andresen (2006) have used the STORI in a review of a volunteer programme to increase and support social contact and friendships with people with mental illness. Puschner *et al.* (2010) have included a 30 item version of the STORI in an international study of the outcomes of clinical decision making with individuals with serious mental illness. Given its increased use in research and practice, what can be said about the psychometric properties of the STORI? We provided initial support for the internal consistency of the subscales representing the stages of recovery with alpha coefficients ranging from 0.88 to 0.94 (Andresen, Caputi and Oades, 2006). Weeks, Slade and Hayward (2010) also reported strong alpha coefficients for these subscales with Cronbach's alpha coefficients between 0.81 and 0.87. They also found strong evidence for the temporal stability of the subscales with re-test reliability coefficients of at least 0.90 for each stage subscale.

There is also evidence for the concurrent validity of the STORI. In our original paper (Andresen, Caputi and Oades, 2006) we correlated the STORI subscales with a set of measures that included the Mental Health Inventory – five item version (Stewart, Hays and Ware, 1988) – the RAS, the Psychological Well-Being Scales (Ryff and Keyes, 1995), the Adult State Hope Scale (Snyder *et al.*, 1996) and the Connor–Davidson Resilience Scale (Connor and Davidson, 2003). A distinct pattern of relationships emerged from this analysis. We found negative correlations between the subscale for Moratorium (stage 1) and the other measures (ranging from − 0.44 to − 0.68); on the other hand significant positive associations were observed between the subscale for Growth (stage 5) and the other measures (ranging from 0.53 to 0.79) (Andresen, Caputi and Oades, 2006). There were no significant associations observed between stage 3 subscale and the other measures. There were only some negative associations found for the stage 2 subscale, and some significant positive correlations between the stage 4 subscale and the other measures. The pattern of correlations, increasing from negative in stage 1 through to highly positive at stage 5, lend some support to the ordinal nature of the stages of the model. Moreover, we concluded that these patterns of findings suggest that stages 2, 3 and 4 subscales may be measuring variables not detectable by the other measures used in their study (Andresen, Caputi and Oades, 2006).

Weeks, Slade and Hayward (2010) observed a similar pattern of relationships between the subscales of the STORI and the RAS, finding a strong negative association between the RAS and the Stage 1 subscale and moderate to strong positive associations between the RAS and the subscales of Stages 3, 4 and 5, with the correlations in increasing size from Stage 3 ($r = .458$) to Stage 5 ($r = .735$). Weeks, Slade and Hayward (2010) argued that these findings suggest the sequential or ordinal nature of stages. We also found evidence for ordinality when examining the inter-correlation of stage subscales (Andresen, Caputi and Oades, 2006). Stage 1 scores were positively correlated with stage 2 and 3 scores ($r = .33$ and .22, respectively), but negatively correlated with stage 5 scores ($r = -.05$). There was no correlation between stage 1 and stage 4 scores. Stage 2 scores were positively correlated with stage 3 and 4 scores ($r = .88$ and .66, respectively), and stage 3 scores were positively correlated with stage 4 and 5 scores ($r = .82$ and .29, respectively). Stage 4 and 5 scores were also correlated ($r = .52$). We argued that this pattern of correlations provided support for the validity of the subscales of the STORI – proximal stages were positively correlated, while distal stages had weak association, with the most distal stages being negatively correlated.

In our original investigation, we conducted a cluster analysis of the items of the STORI to determine whether they clustered into the five theoretically determined stages of recovery (Andresen, Caputi and Oades, 2006). Interestingly, the most interpretable solution contained only three clusters. The first cluster comprised stage 1 items; the second cluster consisted of stage 2 and 3 items as well as four stage 4 items; the third cluster consisted of the stage 5 items and six stage 4 items. Similarly, Weeks, Slade and Hayward (2010) also found a three-cluster solution for the items of STORI. These findings point to further research focusing on whether the STORI items discriminate between the stages (Andresen, Caputi and Oades, 2006). However, at a more fundamental level it does raise the question (as noted by Weeks, Slade and Hayward, 2010) of whether recovery is best described by a three or five stage model. Conceptually, we have argued for a five-stage model of recovery (Andresen, Caputi and Oades, 2003). However, empirically, the evidence points to a three-stage model. We addressed this anomaly by considering a general issue with psychological change models (Andresen, Caputi and Oades, 2006) and drew on Smedslund (1997), who argued the stage models of change, such as the Transtheoretical Model, would describe the behavioural outcome for smoking cessation as either smoking or non-smoking. However, there are processes that described the intermediate stages between smoking and non-smoking. Similarly, a three-stage model of recovery may represent a distinction between stages hope-lessness, loss of identity and meaning in life; transition; and finally growth. However, such a conceptualization may not explain the complex nature of recovery from serious mental illness. Perhaps further effort should be directed to testing the ability of the STORI to discriminate between the five stages of the model.

The absence of empirical evidence for a five-stage model may be a measurement issue rather than a conceptual one.

Concluding Comment

In this chapter we argued for the relevance of recovery measurement. In particular, we noted the importance of consumer-based measures of recovery. There is a growing interest in this class of measures. In this chapter, we have introduced and discussed three measures that fall within this framework. To date, the research findings show that these measures, the SISR, SIST-R and the STORI, are reliable and valid measures of consumer-based psychological recovery. The empirical evidence also points to the theoretical underpinning of a stage model of psychological recovery, as depicted, for instance, in the evidence for the ordinal or sequential nature of stages of recovery. However, the process of validating these measures is still in its infancy – more empirical and theoretical work is warranted, as we have raised in this chapter. It is our hope that this chapter will encourage the reader to consider using these measures in their own research and practice.

Summary

- Consumer-oriented measures of recovery can make important contributions to research and practice.
- The Stage Model of Recovery has initiated the development of three consumer-based measures of recovery: Self-Identified Stage of Recovery, Short Interview to identify Stages of Recovery and the Stages of Recovery Instrument.
- There is growing empirical support for the reliability and validity of these measures.
- Empirical research supports the inclusion of recovery measures in outcome assessment and evaluation.

Part IV

Towards a Positive Future

10

Psychological Recovery and Positive Psychology

Overview

In this chapter we explore the convergence of psychological recovery and positive psychology. We examine how key concepts of the stage model of psychological recovery link to the established research, scholarship and measurement within the science of positive psychology. It will be argued that the science of positive psychology provides a 'bridge' between lived experience and scientific discourse. In many ways, the recovery movement is a debate about what and who defines and outcome, and positive psychology also offers approaches to outcome measurement within mental health service provision.

A Scientific Approach to Recovery

The stage model of psychological recovery brings to the fore the necessity of a positive psychological approach in recovery. The positive psychology movement arose in response to a perceived emphasis in psychology on repairing damage within a disease model of human functioning (Seligman and Csikszentmihalyi, 2000). It advocates shifting focus away from pathology and towards building positive qualities (Seligman and Csikszentmihalyi, 2000). Resnick and Rosenheck (2006) highlighted the parallel themes and potential synergies between positive psychology and personal recovery, with the particular example of strengths. Our discussion of each of the processes of recovery at each stage has incorporated many concepts from the positive psychology literature, and these are highlighted in the following discussion.

Psychological Recovery: Beyond Mental Illness, First Edition.
Retta Andresen, Lindsay G. Oades and Peter Caputi.
© 2011 John Wiley & Sons, Ltd. Published 2011 by John Wiley & Sons, Ltd.

In our view, the science of positive psychology provides a 'bridge' between lived experience and scientific discourse, including outcome measurement within mental health service provision. In many ways, the recovery movement is a debate about what and who defines and outcome. The humanistic movement in psychology did not gain lasting support in the discipline of psychology because it relied almost exclusively on qualitative methods. While qualitative methods are immensely important in understanding and communicating the richness of personal experience, to rely solely on these methods may prove detrimental to the original cause of the recovery movement. Developing and linking with appropriately chosen quantitative approaches can only strengthen the impact and reach of the recovery movement. Table 10.1 illustrates potential linkages between recovery experiences, positive psychology concepts and measurement.

Abraham Maslow first coined the term positive psychology (Seligman and Csikszentmihalyi, 2000) and in one sense, modern day positive psychology is a form of quantitative humanistic psychology, a not incompatible bed-fellow with recovery approaches.

Hope

The twin elements of hope theory – agency and pathways (Snyder, 2000b; Snyder, Irving and Anderson, 1991) – have been demonstrated in the discussion of the recovery process. Hope, as defined in hope theory, has been empirically associated with recovery from loss and trauma (Elliott *et al.*, 1991) and in finding meaning in life (Feldman and Snyder, 2005). Elliott (2002) and Snyder (2000a) have urged psychologists to take heed of hopeful thinking, personal resources and positive attributes in patients with severe disabilities, and to promote strengths in the pursuit of meaningful goals.

Meaning and Purpose

The search for meaning is another area of positive psychology relevant to recovery. The drive to find meaning in suffering (Davis, Nolen-Hoeksema and Larson, 1998) and to find purpose in life in spite of loss or trauma (Jaffe, 1985) appears to be an innate human condition (Frankl, 1984). Baumeister and Vohs (2002) described four requirements for a meaningful life. These are: a purpose in life, such as a goal or future fulfilment; values, by which one shapes one's actions; a sense of efficacy, or the ability to pursue those values and goals; and self-worth, a basis for believing oneself to be a worthy person. Meaning has been empirically linked to one's valued roles and goals in life (e.g. Little, 1998; Lukas, 1998; Emmons, 1999a, 1999b), and thus, with loss, a person is often compelled to re-evaluate his or her goals in order to restore meaning to life.

Table 10.1 Psychological recovery concepts related to positive psychology research and measurement.

Psychological recovery concept	Positive Psychology Research and relevant constructs	Relevant measures predominantly used in non clinical populations
Hope	Hope Theory	State and Trait Hope (Snyder, 2000b)
Meaning and Purpose	Purpose in Life	Purpose in Life Scale (A. Marsh *et al.*, 2003)
Responsibility	Self Determination Theory Self Regulation	Self Regulation Questionnaires (Brown and Lawendowski, 1999) Self Determination Scale (Deci and Ryan, 2002)
Identity	Best Possible Self	Narrative description of Best Possible Self (Sheldon, and Lyubomirsky, 2006)
Resilience	Dual Process Model	Goal Appraisal Measures (Brandtstadter and Rothermund, 2002)
Strengths	Strengths Coaching	VIA strengths survey (Petersen and Seligman, 2004) Strengths Use survey Realise2 (Linley, 2008) Camera (Oades and Crowe, 2008)
Values	Values Clarification	Survey of Life Principles (Ciarrochi and Bailey, 2008) VIA strengths survey (Petersen and Seligman, 2004) Camera (Oades and Crowe, 2008)
Autonomous Goals	Self Determination Theory	Perceived Locus of Causation Sheldon and Kasser (2001)
Growth	Post traumatic growth	Changes in Outlook Questionnaire, Stress Related Growth Scale, Posttraumatic Growth Inventory, Perceived Benefit Scale, Thriving Scale (Joseph and Linley, 2008)
Wellbeing	Psychological Well-Being	Psychological Well-Being Scale (Ryff and Keyes, 1995)
Living with illness	Flourishing	Mental Health Continuum (Keyes, 2002)

Responsibility

Self Determination Theory is centred on the pursuit of personal goals. This theory of human motivation, founded on humanistic principles, is based on the assumption that people have an innate tendency towards psychological growth, a unified self, and autonomous, responsible behaviour (Deci and Ryan, 2002). This overlaps very closely with narratives from consumers regarding their psychological recovery, and the need to take charge of their lives. Below we discuss the importance of autonomous motivation, exemplified by the pursuit of autonomous goals, in wellbeing.

Identity

The importance of sense of self and identity is well established in the literatures related to enduring mental illness and recovery (Davidson and Strauss, 1992; Buckley-Walker, Crowe and Caputi, 2010). Within positive psychology, the use of the 'best possible self' exercise has demonstrated benefits. Markus and Nurius (1986) defined possible selves as idiographic representations of goals, which encompass all of the futures a person can imagine. Sheldon and Lyubomirsky (2006) investigated the benefits of the best possible self, which involves writing about oneself into the future. This is seen has having benefits because it encourages self-regulation, allows self-learning and is likely to assist a person to readjust their priorities. They used the following exercise:

> 'Think about your best possible self' means that you imagine yourself in the future, after everything has gone as well as it possibly could. You have worked hard and succeeded at accomplishing all of your life goals. Think of this as the realization of your life dreams, and of your own best potentials. In all of these cases you are identifying the best possible way that things might turn out in your life, in order to help guide your decisions now. You may not have thought about yourself in this way before, but research suggests that doing so can have a strong positive effect on your mood and life satisfaction. So, we'd like to ask you to continue thinking in this way over the next few weeks, following up on the initial writing that you're about to do.

Sheldon and Lyubomirsky (2006) demonstrated immediate gains in positive emotion, and more self-concordant motivation from this exercise. While this is an early study with a population without mental illness, it is described here to demonstrate the potential linkages between mental health recovery and the science of positive psychology.

Resilience

Recovery research can also be informed by the literature on resilience and thriving. These concepts have been explored in the context of post-traumatic growth. Self-described personal attributes contributing to resilience are: the ability to control the course of life; an inner drive; a constructive orientation, and a strong sense of self-worth (Watt *et al.*, 1995; cited in Rutter, 2000). Resilience represents the ability to 'bounce back' or 'bounce forward' from adversity, and also, therefore, to be willing to take risks.

Brandtstädter (1989, 1992, 2006, 2009) views resilience as a complex process, in which people experience a dual process of accommodation and assimilation (e.g. adjusting goals and striving for goals) in the face of adversity. In this model, resilience enables one to maintain or even improve along their expected developmental trajectories. In this model resilience is not a trait, but a dynamic process. The complexity and dynamic nature of this model is similar in nature to the stage model of psychological recovery and current research of the authors is investigating the dual process of approach goals and avoidance goals across the stages of psychological recovery.

Strengths

While mental health consumers may not often feel strong, narratives of recovery refer to strengths used under adversity. Within the positive psychology literature there has been a recent proliferation of research on personal strengths and the benefits of employing these strengths. Within this literature there are different definitions of strengths, and consequently different measures derived from these definitions. Peterson and Seligman (2004), based on a virtue ethics position, refer to strengths as 'distinguishable routes to displaying one or another of the virtues.' In this way, strengths are character strengths, values put into action, morally imbued towards living the good life. As illustrated in Table 10.1, the VIA Strengths Survey is one way of assessing strengths.

Linley and Harrington (2002) define strength as 'a natural capacity for behaving, thinking or feeling in a way that allows optimal functioning and performance in the pursuit of valued outcomes.' Linley's more recent work has led to the development of the Realise2 instrument, which includes realized strengths, unrealized strengths, weakness and learned behaviours. This approach lends itself to strengths coaching, which Oades, Crowe and Nguyen (2009) have used to underpin recovery-oriented service provision. Strengths and values are relevant throughout the stages of psychological recovery, and underpin the development of a preferred identity.

Values

Values have been defined as conceptual representations of desired life-outcomes (Bardi and Schwartz, 2003). Rather than being linked explicitly to the achievement of specific outcomes, values relate more to the quality of action brought to bear in a particular situation. This definition of values relates to the notion of moving towards one's 'preferred identity'. In determining purpose and meaning in life, values are important in guiding the direction of each individual's journey, but not the specific steps. Values are pervasive across time, and can provide a cohesive structure to guide our behaviour as individuals. Relevant to mental health recovery, values can provide a powerful motivational force in directing purposeful action during times of adversity. Research indicates that individuals who engage in more value-consistent behaviour experience higher quality of life and reduced physical and psychological pain than other individuals (Twohig, Hayes and Akihiko, 2006; Gregg *et al.*, 2007).

Autonomous Goals

Much literature that adopts a positive approach to psychology is centred on the pursuit of personal goals (e.g. Diener, 2000; Ryan and Deci, 2000b; Seligman and Csikszentmihalyi, 2000), and hope has been shown to be predicted by the pursuit of autonomous personal goals (e.g. McGregor and Little, 1998; Emmons, 1999c; Ryan and Deci, 2000b).

Lunt (2002), a consumer, demonstrated how personal goals are interwoven into all aspects of recovery in his description of the process. Lunt described recovery as the redefinition of identity by moving from hopelessness to taking action with new meaning and purpose. By owning and sustaining a goal in life, the meaning of that goal becomes integrated into the individual's sense of self (Lunt, 2002). Lunt's description illustrates the importance of goal ownership, or autonomy, in finding meaning and establishing a positive identity.

Self Determination Theory research has identified the importance of autonomous goals in motivation (e.g. Deci and Ryan, 1991; Ryan *et al.*, 1996), goal attainment and wellbeing. In Self Determination Theory, autonomous goals are those which are intrinsically motivating to the person, that is, they represent things the person enjoys, or those goals that reflect the person's core values and therefore represent the self (Sheldon and Kasser, 2001). The pursuit of autonomous goals has been linked to a sense of identity, for example, Deci and Ryan (1991), King (1998) and Elliott *et al.* (2000). Emmons (1999a, 1999b), McGregor and Little (1998), Sheldon and Kasser (1998) and others have shown that the successful pursuit of meaningful personal goals can lead to psychological well-being as described by Ryff (1989).

The power of seemingly small autonomous goals to engender agency and hope in the recovery process is illustrated by one of Davidson's (1993) subjects. The client wanted to buy the materials to take up sewing, but had been told by her mother that they had sufficient sewing materials already:

> Nancy arrived one morning and announced proudly to the staff and patients that she had been successful . . . in purchasing her first, very own, spool of thread . . .. Following this purchase of thread, Nancy's mood seemed to change from that of anxious despair to eager exploration, as she became active in investigating a psychosocial club and vocational program she could attend following discharge from our day program . . ..
> (Davidson, 1993, p. 203)

Growth

The concepts of thriving and post-traumatic growth emphasize growth following loss or trauma, through meeting the challenge of the loss and using it is a stimulus for growth (O'Leary, 1998; Tedeschi, Park and Calhoun, 1998). Post-traumatic growth may entail a changed sense of self, changed relationships and existential spiritual growth (Calhoun and Tedeschi, 2001). Once more, these concepts resonate with the recovery literature. The concept of growth mindset described by Dweck (2006) also relates closely to consumers' descriptions of the process of believing that personal change is possible.

Wellbeing

The components of the process and outcome of psychological recovery evoke the qualities of psychological well-being as described by Ryff and Keyes (Ryff, 1989; Ryff and Keyes, 1995). Dissatisfied with extant measures of wellbeing, Ryff reviewed the literature on the philosophy of optimal human functioning, including Roger's concept of self-actualization, Jung's individuation, Allport's definition of maturity, and Buhler's examination of fulfilment of life, amongst others. From this literature, Ryff identified six major aspects of psychological well-being. These were: self-acceptance – holding a positive attitude towards oneself, including acceptance of self and one's past life; positive relations with others – empathy and affection for all human beings and the ability to love; autonomy – independence and self-regulation of behaviour, and an internal locus of evaluation; environmental mastery – the ability to choose or create environments beneficial to one's mental health, and the ability to advance in the world and change it creatively; purpose in life – belief that there is a meaning and purpose to life, and a sense of intentionality and directedness, which may change over the life span; and personal growth – continuing to grow as a person, developing one's potential, and confronting new challenges at different stages of life (Ryff, 1989). These elements of psychological well-being, then, are clearly represented in the concept of recovery.

Living with Illness and Flourishing

The links between the concepts of psychological recovery and the dimensions of optimal human functioning highlight the need for a positive psychological approach to the understanding of mental illness and recovery. The fifth stage of psychological recovery, Growth, reflects Keyes' (2003) concept of 'flourishing'. Aspects of flourishing include the experience of high levels of psychological well-being, self-worth, self-determination, continued personal growth, positive relationships and meaning in life (Keyes, 2003). According to Keyes, the absence of mental illness symptoms is neither necessary nor sufficient for flourishing. That normal healthy development can take place in the absence of psychological or environmental obstructions is in keeping with central tenets of the consumer recovery movement – a need to move away from the medical or rehabilitation model of recovery, and to focus instead on what helps people to grow and thrive (e.g. Fisher, 1994; Deegan, 1996b; Schmook, 1996; Bassman, 2000).

Summary

- The science of positive psychology can provide an 'empirical bridge' between the lived experience of recovery and the need for services to measure outputs and outcomes.
- Hope, Meaning and Purpose, Responsibility and Identity, which constitute the four component processes of psychological recovery, have well established literatures and related quantitative measures in the science of positive psychology.
- Resilience (when defined as a developmental process), Strengths and Values have increasing scientific investigation and relate closely to the lived experience of recovery.
- Self Determination Theory is relevant to psychological recovery due to its focus on autonomy, relating to others and the need to feel competent.
- Post-traumatic growth has relevance to understanding the experience of psychological recovery.
- Psychological well-being and flourishing are concepts with measures that directly parallel many of the issues described by consumers in their experience of psychological recovery (e.g. living a meaningful life having symptoms).

11

Reflections and Future Directions

From Wellness to Wellbeing

Psychological recovery is characterized by living a flourishing life, regardless of the presence of recurring symptoms: a person may have 'clinically' recovered, or may not. Two streams of literature, which developed in parallel, converged to overturn the spectre of the course of schizophrenia as a life-long downward spiral. Empirical longitudinal evidence has shown that many people who were diagnosed with schizophrenia were later found to be living normal lives, with no signs of the illness. At the same time, people who had experienced schizophrenia and were living productive lives – sometimes in a professional capacity – were writing their personal stories of recovery. The definition of recovery used in the empirical research was centred on measures of symptoms and functioning, and was at times so stringent that some people who have never had a mental illness may not have met the criteria. On the other hand, the consumer literature for the most part does not adhere to these traditional 'clinical' definitions of recovery.

The consumer meaning of recovery goes beyond definitions of illness, emphasizing instead wellbeing – or 'living the good life'. Consumer-oriented literature highlights factors contributing to poor outcome that are not due to the illness or the effectiveness of medications, including: hopelessness, community attitudes towards mental illness, social exclusion and the iatrogenic effects of medication and treatment. Cultures and service approaches that do not devalue the person who has a mental illness, and which encourage a meaningful role in society, facilitate recovery. Consumers have called for recovery-oriented services, that move away from the disability-rehabilitation paradigm and focus on a positive outlook,

Psychological Recovery: Beyond Mental Illness, First Edition.
Retta Andresen, Lindsay G. Oades and Peter Caputi.
© 2011 John Wiley & Sons, Ltd. Published 2011 by John Wiley & Sons, Ltd.

personal values, building on strengths, self-determination, finding meaning in life and optimal psychological health.

We have taken the liberty of extending the possibility of recovery from schizophrenia to apply to all enduring mental illnesses. There are two bases for this: first, schizophrenia is a complex and very impactful mental illness, with the most pessimistic prognosis; and second, some of the participants in the qualitative studies had diagnoses other than schizophrenia. Our assumption is that if a person with schizophrenia, who has been given no hope of recovery, can harness their psychological resources to build a good life for themselves, then there is little reason to believe that the same is not possible for people with other mental illnesses. And this is evident in the consumer literature; hope is the key.

The real-life accounts of people who have been diagnosed with a mental illness reveal that, not only can people with ongoing or recurring symptoms consider themselves recovered, conversely, some people with no signs or symptoms do *not* consider themselves recovered – a legacy of the long-held belief that schizophrenia has a lifelong deteriorating course. The concept of *psychological* recovery can be applied in many scenarios: the person who feels life is 'over' because they have received a diagnosis of serious mental illness; the person who is struggling and battling symptoms; the person who is receiving adequate medical treatment, and yet feels that life has stagnated; and the person who is clinically well, but does not believe they can recover. This is reflected in the concept of flourishing, which holds that mental illness symptoms and Wellbeing are not on a continuum, but can coexist or alternatively, be simultaneously absent. We found that the processes of recovery from mental illness are no more mysterious or different from the processes of growth and human development. They are reflected in the literature on living with loss, acquired disability and psychological trauma, and this literature is one of personal development. Recovery themes such as autonomy, core values, intrinsically valued goals, transcendent goals, courage, resilience and wisdom are reflected in the positive psychology tenets of 'flourishing'. Harry Stack Sullivan is famously quoted as saying that we are all 'much more simply human than otherwise' (1953, pp. 32–33), and the stage model of psychological recovery reflects this. Lessons learned from people struggling with and recovering from mental illness are valuable lessons that can be applied by people from all walks of life.

Applications of the Model

As recovery is becoming more widely accepted, mental health policies internationally are increasingly recognizing the role of mental health services in promoting recovery, rather than merely monitoring treatment and social welfare. In Australia, the National Standards for Mental Health Services 2010 (Department of Health and Aging, 2010), employs the language of psychological recovery in its principles of recovery-oriented practice, including: honouring the uniqueness of the individual, supporting responsibility and empowerment, maintaining hope for a meaningful life, respect for personal values, collaboration on recovery goals and recognizing wellbeing as an important outcome. These principles echo the overarching processes of recovery – hope, personal responsibility, positive identity and meaning in life that we have discussed throughout this book.

How then, should mental health practitioners proceed to use a recovery orientation in the delivery of services? The model of psychological recovery highlights the need for positive approaches to treatment that recognize the individual as goal-directed and growth-oriented, rather than as a passive recipient of treatment (Seligman and Csikszentmihalyi, 2000). Approaches that do not recognize the inner tendency towards self-determination can become controlling, thereby exacerbating helplessness and hindering recovery. 'Even though schizophrenia may be the result of a broken brain, . . . treatment needs to address the meaning or purpose of life. A person's belief system can instil hope' (Murphy, 1998, p. 188). The five-stage, four-process model of recovery represents a 'ladder of hope' for mental health professionals, who can in turn utilize the model to teach clients and their families about recovery. The quotations in the book have the potential to validate consumers' experience, and help lead loved ones to a deeper understanding. The model provides a potential pathway, and the illustrative examples are rich with material that may be used as seeds for recovery work and the development of recovery programmes.

The elements of the model, as they have been elaborated in the book, can provide a basis for recovery-oriented service provision. If we look at each process in turn, we can find clues to helping a person to be the best they can be and to achieve personal growth. First, promoting hope can be achieved by showing the person that recovery is possible – the longitudinal research we have presented gives the 'hard facts', while the recovery stories can provide inspiration. This initial hope can be furthered by following the guidelines of hope theory: encouraging the person to identify goals, consider pathways to the goal, and to take challenging, but achievable, steps. Responsibility can be promoted by educating the person on the limits of medications to provide a meaningful life, and demonstrating that recovery requires personal action, as described by other consumers. Again, the person's personal aspirations will form the basis of this work. Motivational techniques can help people to overcome barriers to their sense of agency regarding taking personal responsibility. Risk-taking is another feature of taking responsibility, and this can be achieved by encouraging activities that will enhance the person's personal growth, even though there is a risk of failure. The key to success will be that the risks and benefits of the activity have been considered and discussed, and the activity is an autonomous choice of the client. Trying and succeeding promotes a sense of agency and increases hope, while failure can be utilized as a learning mechanism and to build resilience. A positive identity is promoted in different ways. First, identifying one's core personal values can lead a person back to his or her 'true self' that may have been lost in the experience of mental illness and treatment. Once back in touch with 'who they are', the person can identify and pursue goals in keeping with this still-intact self. Sometimes, as we have seen, they may reassess previously held values and take a different direction in life. The important thing is that the person ceases to identify themselves in terms of illness. Related to the re-establishment of a positive identity is the search for meaning. Pursuing goals and activities that reflect deeply held values gives life meaning. In the process of building hope, taking responsibility and reconnecting with a positive identity, therefore, the person will be pursuing valued autonomous goals, and this is a path to a meaningful life. Goals that provide meaning are frequently in the domains of improved personal relationships, creativity or altruism. As the person identifies their core values, pursues their valued goals, takes personal responsibility for their wellbeing, succeeds in some endeavours and fails in others and pursues a meaningful life, they may achieve resilience, wellbeing, personal growth and wisdom.

This brief overview describes how the four processes can provide content for recovery work, and these should be used with sensitivity to the person's stage of recovery: Moratorium, Awareness, Preparation, Rebuilding or Growth. Some structure for working towards psychological recovery can be found in the Collaborative Recovery Model (CRM; Oades *et al.*, 2005), which we have developed with our colleagues at the University of Wollongong. The CRM draws on positive psychology and coaching principles to promote psychological recovery (Oades, Crowe and Nguyen, 2009). The CRM combines Snyder's model of hope with Self Determination Theory to engender hope in clients. Utilizing positive psychological approaches of values clarification and strengths identification, clinicians work collaboratively with clients to help them build a meaningful life in keeping with a positive identity. The focus is always on autonomous approach goals, rather than on disability and weakness, with sensitivity to the client's stage of recovery. Training in this model was found to promote positive attitudes towards recovery (Crowe *et al.*, 2006) and improve the quality and consistency with which clinicians set autonomous goals with clients (Clarke *et al.*, 2009a). The CRM offers a way of changing the culture of mental health services, as urged by the consumer movement, by training those at the coalface to work collaboratively in a values-based, recovery-oriented manner (Oades, Crowe and Nguyen, 2009).

A similar approach to the CRM has been applied in a self-development programme, *Flourish*, for people with long-term mental illness (Oades *et al.*, 2008). Flourish is a positive psychology intervention developed by a team of researchers and consumers, and utilizes similar approaches and tools as the CRM. It centres on a handbook and set of audio recordings, which participants in the programme use at home. They are supported in the programme by telephone coaching and peer-led discussion meetings. People who completed a pilot of the 12-week Flourish programme demonstrated increases in several aspects of Psychological Well-Being (Oades *et al.*, 2009). Structured applications, such as the CRM and Flourish, lend themselves to adaption for independent self-development programmes, and computerized and internet-based delivery. Such applications would be invaluable in providing clinical or self-help programmes to people who are isolated, whether by geography or by physical or mental disability. Such approaches promise to empower consumers in accessing recovery-oriented services.

Recovery Measures in Clinical Work, Evaluation and Research

There has been a call in recent years to bring evidence-based practice into line with recovery-oriented values, but the notion of measuring recovery outcomes has met with scepticism from both the consumer and the scientific camps (Solomon and Stanhope, 2004; Bellack, 2006). It has been suggested that any type of evidence-based practice can be delivered within a philosophy of recovery-oriented practice, and that evaluation can be based on the assessment of a service's commitment to these values (e.g. Farkas *et al.*, 2005). However, Solomon and Stanhope (2004) have pointed out that measures traditionally used as a basis for evidence of effectiveness do not address a person's quality of life or other subjective aspects of recovery. Consumers, too, have questioned the value of outcome measurement, and want to see a purpose to measurement that will benefit the consumer (Happell, 2008). Although there is still much work to be done, we have demonstrated that there is strong agreement amongst researchers on what consumer-defined recovery is, and how it should be measured. The measures we have presented in this book have generated a great deal of interest from around the world, highlighting the demand for recovery-oriented outcome and evaluation measures.

In the clinic, subjective recovery measures could be used as a catalyst for discussion about the concept of psychological recovery, about the pathways to recovery and about where the client places him or herself on the recovery journey. Anecdotal feedback from consumers piloting the STORI indicated that self-completion of the measure gave them an understanding of the process of recovery, engendered hope and helped them identify aspects of life on which they could work to promote their own wellbeing. Some felt they could use the measure to monitor their own change and progress. Capturing such an effect in a clinical situation could prove very fruitful, and it was with this in mind that the SIST-R was developed. Administering a measure as an interview-based assessment opens the way for dialogue between the clinician and client that is not readily achievable with a self-completed measure that is filed away without feedback. The use of measures to simultaneously provide material for collaborative work and an indication of progress promises to be a way of satisfying consumer demands for meaningful assessments, while also meeting the requirements of evidence-based practice.

While recognizing subjective experiences described by consumers as processes of recovery, Liberman and Kopelowicz (2002) suggested that these may be a result of the treatment environment, and as such are not viable measures of outcome. On the contrary, we contend that practices which result in hope, self-responsibility, a positive sense of self and meaning in life are providing legitimate recovery outcomes which are measurable. Our research has shown that recovery-oriented measures offer unique information about consumer outcomes and offer a way forward in marrying evidence-based practice with recovery-oriented consumer outcomes. While empirical research has shown us the extent of clinical recovery, Bellack (2006) has stressed the need for similar research into the prevalence of consumer-defined recovery, and into the factors that promote recovery. The measures that we and other researchers have developed go some way towards meeting this need.

Current and Future Research Directions

Current research developments

The model has proven fruitful in generating testable research hypotheses surrounding the stages and processes of recovery. Currently, colleagues at the University of Wollongong are investigating such areas as the relationship between hope and identity during recovery, using personal construct methodology (Buckley-Walker, Crowe and Caputi, 2010); the function of metaphor in consolidating identity and meaning during the stages of recovery (Mould, Oades and Crowe, 2010); approach and avoidance goals across stages of recovery; the meaning of the illness, hope and responsibility in self-management of wellness; the language used in recovery stories and therapeutic writing across stages of recovery, and its relationship with wellbeing; and the relationship between hope and the alliance between clinicians and clients.

Exploration of the potential for expanding the model into other areas is also ongoing. For example, research is investigating the stages of identity in carers of people with a mental illness; comparing consumers' perceived stage of recovery and perceptions of their carers, and the relationship of perceived stage of recovery with carers' hope; comparing perceptions of risk taking between clinicians and their clients; increasing the 'real relationship' between clinician and client by using parallel processes in training (Oades, Crowe and Nguyen, 2009); and examining the processes of recovery in people with co-occurring substance use and mental health disorders. The foregoing examples demonstrate how relationships between the various elements of the model can be teased out with empirical research to provide insights which may be applied in clinical practice, mental health support services, self-help programs, carer support and clinical training.

The model provides a framework that has already proven a useful heuristic for education in clinical psychology, mental health staff training, service development and consumer and carer education, promoting flourishing in people with serious mental illness.

Future research directions

People who have recovered from mental illness are adamant that it is a deeply personal journey. In a review of studies on thriving in the presence of terminal illness, Massey *et al.* (1998) asked, 'Who determines if and when a person is thriving?' (p. 7) and warned against imposing our own values in answering this question. To avoid imposing external values on recovery, we have endeavoured to distil the core components of consumer-defined recovery into a model that is inherently flexible. No particular behaviours are specified, as it is for the individual to define his or her goals in life. The model offers a framework for measurable constructs, while respecting consumer views that recovery is an individual process. In contrast to traditional measures of recovery, measures based on psychological recovery assess the development of positive aspects of psychological health and growth from the perspective of the individual. Future research directions include longitudinal validation of the stage model of psychological recovery, including prospective studies, to determine the number of stages; further validation of the measures, including comparison with recovery-oriented, yet objective measures; further research on the relationship between the stages and of the processes across the stages; and the development and evaluation of interventions targeting the component processes of recovery. These undertakings will further scientific exploration of the process of psychological recovery and promote the application of evidence-based practices that are truly recovery-oriented.

A Word About Words

There have been a number of efforts to distinguish between the two meanings of recovery, including the distinction between clinical versus consumer models of recovery (Bellack, 2006), 'recovery *from*' as opposed to 'recovery *in*' mental illness (Davidson and Roe, 2007) and 'clinical' versus 'personal' recovery (Slade, Amering and Oades, 2008). These are useful distinctions, and help clarify the different meanings of the term in common use and in the scholarly literature. We now know that people can recover in the clinical sense from serious mental illness – that is, in terms of objective measures of symptoms and functioning. We also know that people can recover psychologically from the impact of mental illness, while still experiencing recurring symptoms. However, it is important that we take care in the way recovery is conceptualized in practice. The notions 'recovery from mental illness' and 'recovery in mental illness' are not mutually exclusive, as we have discussed. We must take care not to assume that consumer-oriented recovery *always* means non-clinical recovery. It would be a simple matter to slip from such a belief into 'lowering the bar' of recovery, implicitly limiting the heights to which a person can aspire. Further, some favour the use of borrowed terms such as 'in recovery' and 'recovering' to describe a person living well in the presence of recurring symptoms. Are these terms denying the person an identity not defined by the illness? While living a fulfilling life 'within the limits of disability' is one way of conceptualizing recovery, it is important that professionals and practitioners do not implicitly impose those limits, inadvertently returning consumers to square one in their battle for hope. While understanding that recovery does not necessarily mean clinical recovery, and that recovery should not be judged by imposed cultural values, we should beware of sliding into lowered expectations. While it may be too early to claim unequivocally that everyone *can* recover from serious mental illness, there is no way of determining that any individual can *not* recover. The hope and the opportunity to live *beyond* mental illness must be there for everyone. Recovery should be the expectation (Tenney, 2000).

Afterword

We have strived to honour the stories of people who have lived, or are living, with a mental illness. We hope that, in quoting them, we have been faithful to their meanings. There has been some concern aired in the literature that in researching recovery, attempting to define recovery, or describing services as recovery-oriented, professionals are appropriating the language of recovery and 'colonizing' the experience. It is our sincere hope that our work is not seen in that light. Rather than colonizing experiences, we would hope that a model can act as an interpreting device, in which people can share a range of experiences and stories. We were, and still are, moved by the stories of consumers, and hope that by applying our resources to distilling the essence of their words into a usable model of recovery, we will advance the drive towards recovery-oriented service. Our deepest gratitude extends to those people who have shared their experiences of mental illness and recovery in research or in published works, in the hope of leading others to a greater understanding. We hope we have learned the lessons that they have offered, and trust that in conveying them in this form, we will further the recovery cause.

Psychological Recovery: Beyond Mental Illness, First Edition.
Retta Andresen, Lindsay G. Oades and Peter Caputi.
© 2011 John Wiley & Sons, Ltd. Published 2011 by John Wiley & Sons, Ltd.

References

Abramson, L.Y., Metalsky, G.I. and Alloy, L.B. (1989) Hopelessness depression: A theory-based subtype of depression. *Psychological Review*, 96 (2), 358–372.

Acuff, C. (2000) Commentary: Listening to the message. *Journal of Clinical Psychology*, 56 (11), 1459–1465.

Adams, S.M. and Partee, D.J. (1998) Hope: The critical factor in recovery. *Journal of Psychosocial Nursing and Mental Health Services*, 36 (4), 29–32.

Ahern, L. and Fisher, D. (2001) Recovery at your own PACE (Personal Assistance in Community Existence). *Journal of Psychosocial Nursing and Mental Health Services*, 39 (4), 22–32, 50–51.

Alexander, D. (1994) A death-rebirth experience, in *The Experience of Recovery* (eds L. Spaniol and M. Koehler), Center for Psychiatric Rehabilitation, Boston, pp. 36–39.

American Psychiatric Association (1952) *Diagnostic and Statistical Manual of Mental Disorders*, American Psychiatric Association, Washington, DC.

American Psychiatric Association (1980) *Diagnostic and Statistical Manual of Mental Disorders: DSM-III*, American Psychiatric Association, Washington, DC.

American Psychiatric Association (1994) *Diagnostic and Statistical Manual of Mental Disorders: DSM-IV*, American Psychiatric Association, Washington, DC.

Andreasen, N.C., Carpenter, W.T., Kane, J.M., *et al.* (2005) Remission in schizophrenia: Proposed criteria and rationale for consensus. *American Journal of Psychiatry*, 162 (3), 441–449.

Andresen, R., Oades, L. and Caputi, P. (2003) The experience of recovery from schizophrenia: towards an empirically-validated stage model. *Australian and New Zealand Journal of Psychiatry*, 37, 586–594.

Andresen, R., Caputi, P. and Oades, L. (2006) The Stages of Recovery Instrument: Development of a measure of recovery from serious mental illness. *Australian and New Zealand Journal of Psychiatry*, 40, 972–980.

Andresen, R., Caputi, P and Oades, L.G. (2010) Do clinical outcome measures assess consumer-defined recovery? *Psychiatry Research*, 177, 309–317.

Andrews, G. and Slade, T. (2001) Interpreting scores on the Kessler population. Australian and New Zealand Journal of Psychiatry Psychological Distress Scale (K10). *Australian and New Zealand Journal of Public Health*, 25, 494–497.

Angermeyer, M.C. and Matschinger, H. (2003) The stigma of mental illness: Effects of labelling on public attitudes towards people with mental disorder. *Acta Psychiatrica Scandinavica*, 108 (4), 304–309.

Anonymous (1989) First person account: A delicate balance. *Schizophrenia Bulletin*, 15 (2), 345–346.

Anonymous (1994a) The challenge of recovery, in *The Experience of Recovery* (eds L. Spaniol and M. Koehler), Center for Psychiatric Rehabilitation, Boston, 13–17.

Anonymous (1994b) Coping and recovery, in *The Experience of Recovery* (eds L. Spaniol and M. Koehler), Center for Psychiatric Rehabilitation, Boston, p. 25.

Anthony, W.A. (1993) Recovery from mental illness: The guiding vision of the mental health service system in the 1990s. *Psychosocial Rehabilitation Journal*, 16 (4), 12–23.

Anthony, W.A. (2000) A recovery-oriented service system: Setting some system level standards. *Psychiatric Rehabilitation Journal*, 24 (2), 159–168.

Anthony, W.A. (2001) A vision for psychiatric rehabilitation research. *Psychiatric Rehabilitation Journal*, 25 (1), 1–2.

Anthony, W.A. and Liberman, R.P. (1992) Principles and practice of psychiatric rehabilitation, in *Handbook of Psychiatric Rehabilitation*, (ed. R.P. Liberman), Macmillan, New York, pp. 1–29.

Anthony, W.A., Cohen, M.R. and Farkas, M. (1990) *Psychiatric Rehabilitation*, Boston University Center for Psychiatric Rehabilitation, Boston.

Anthony, W.A., Rogers, E.S. and Farkas, M. (2003) Research on evidence-based practices: Future directions in an era of recovery. *Community Mental Health Journal*, 39 (2), 101–114.

Arboleda-Florez, J. (2003) Considerations on the stigma of mental illness. *Canadian Journal of Psychiatry*, 48 (10), 645–650.

Armstrong, M. (1994) What happened and how 'What Happened' got better, in *The Experience of Recovery* (eds L. Spaniol and M. Koehler), Center for Psychiatric Rehabilitation, Boston, pp. 52–53.

Austin, J.T. and Vancouver, J.B. (1996) Goal constructs in psychology: Structure, process, and content. *Psychological Bulletin*, 120 (3), 338–375.

Australian Health Ministers (1992) *National Mental Health Policy*, Australian Government, Canberra.

Australian Health Ministers (2003) *National Mental Health Plan 2003-2008*, Australian Government, Canberra.

Bachrach, L.L. (1992) Psychosocial rehabilitation and psychiatry in the care of long-term patients. *American Journal of Psychiatry*, 149 (11), 1455–1463.

Bardi, A. and Schwartz, S.H. (2003) Values and behavior: Strength and structure of relations. *Personality and Social Psychology Bulletin*, 29, 1207–1220.

Barker, P. (2001) The Tidal Model: developing an empowering, person-centred approach to recovery within psychiatric and mental health nursing. *Journal of Psychiatric and Mental Health Nursing*, 8 (3), 233–240.

Barker, P. (2003) The Tidal Model: Psychiatric colonization, recovery and the paradigm shift in mental health care. *International Journal of Mental Health Nursing*, 12 (2), 96–102.

Barlow, D.H. and Durand, V.M. (eds) (1995) *Abnormal Psychology: An Integrative Approach*, Brooks/Cole, Pacific Grove, CA.

Barton, R. (1998) The rehabilitation-recovery paradigm: A statement of philosophy for a public mental health system. *Psychiatric Rehabilitation Skills*, 2 (2), 171–187.

Bassman, R. (2000) Agents, not objects: Our fights to be. *Journal of Clinical Psychiatry, In Session*, 56 (11), 1395–1411.

Bassman, R. (2001) Overcoming the impossible: My journey through schizophrenia. *Psychology Today*, 34 (1), 34–40.

Baumeister, R.F. and Vohs, K.D. (2002) The pursuit of meaningfulness in life, in *Handbook of Positive Psychology* (eds C. Snyder and S.J. Lopez), Oxford University Press, New York, pp. 608–618.

Baxter, E.A. and Diehl, S. (1998) Emotional stages: Consumers and family members recovering from the trauma of mental illness. *Psychiatric Rehabilitation Journal*, 21 (4), 349–355.

Bell, M., Lysaker, P. and Milstein, R. (1996) Clinical benefits of paid work activity in schizophrenia. *Schizophrenia Bulletin*, 22 (1), 51–67.

Bellack, A.S. (2006) Scientific and consumer models of recovery in schizophrenia: Concordance, contrasts, and implications. *Schizophrenia Bulletin*, 32 (3), 432–442.

Berman, R. (1994) Lithium's other face, in *The Experience of Recovery* (eds L. Spaniol and M. Koehler), Center for Psychiatric Rehabilitation, Boston, pp. 40–45.

Bertelsen, A. (2002) Schizophrenia and related disorders: Experience with current diagnostic systems. *Psychopathology*, 35, 89–93.

Bjorklund, R. (1998) First person account: Psychosocial implications of stigma caused by misdiagnosis. *Schizophrenia Bulletin*, 24 (4), 653–655.

Bleuler, E. (1911/1950) *Dementia Praecox or the Group of Schizophrenias* (J. Zinkin, translator), International Universities Press, Oxford.

Bleuler, M. (1972/1978) *The schizophrenic disorders: Long-term patient and family studies* (S.M. Clemens, translator), Yale University Press, New Haven, CT.

Bluck, S. and Glueck, J. (2004) Making things better and learning a lesson: Experiencing wisdom across the lifespan. *Journal of Personality*, 72 (3), 543–572.

Bonney, S. and Stickley, T. (2008) Recovery and mental health: a review of the British literature. *Journal of Psychiatric and Mental Health Nursing*, 15 (2), 140–153.

Brandtstädter, J. (1989) Personal self-regulation of development: Cross-sequential analyses of development-related control beliefs and emotions. *Developmental Psychology*, 25, 96–108.

Brandtstädter, J. (1992) Personal control over development: Some developmental implications of self-efficacy, in *Self-efficacy: Thought Control of Action* (ed. R. Schwarzer), Hemisphere, New York, pp. 127–145.

Brandtstädter, J. (2006) Action perspectives on human development, in *Handbook of Child Psychology*, 6th edn, Vol. 1 (eds R. M. Lerner and W. Damon), John Wiley & Sons, Inc, Hoboken, NJ, pp. 516–568.

Brandtstädter, J. (2009) Goal pursuit and goal adjustment: Self-regulation and intentional self-development in changing developmental contexts. *Advances in Life Course Research*, 14 (1–2), 52–62.

Brandtstädter, J. and Rothermund, K. (2002) The life-course dynamics of goal pursuit and goal adjustment: A two-process framework. *Developmental Review*, 22 (1), 117–150.

Bresnahan, M., Menezes, P., Varma, V. and Susser, E. (2003) Geographical variation in incidence, course and outcome of schizophrenia: A comparison of developing and developed countries, in *The Epidemiology of Schizophrenia* (eds R.M. Murray, P.B. Jones, E. Susser, J. van Os and M. Cannon), Cambridge University Press, New York, pp. 18–33.

Brown, J. M., Miller, W. R. and Lawendowski, L. A. (1999). The Self-Regulation Questionnaire. In L. VandeCreek and T. L. Jackson (Eds.), *Innovations in clinical practice: A source book* (Vol. 17, pp. 281–289). Sarasota, FL: Professional Resource Press.

Brown, L.D., Wituk, S. and Lucksted, A. (2010) *Theoretical Foundations of Mental Health Self-Help Mental Health Self-Help*, Springer-Verlag, New York, pp. 19–38.

Brown, P.C. and Tucker, W.M. (2005) Overstating the case about recovery (comment). *Psychiatric Services*, 56 (8), 1022.

Brunstein, J.C. (1993) Personal goals and subjective well-being: A longitudinal study. *Journal of Personality and Social Psychology*, 65 (5), 1061–1070.

Brunstein, J.C., Schultheiss, O.C. and Maier, G.W. (1999) The pursuit of personal goals: A motivational approach to well-being and life adjustment, in *Action and Self-development: Theory and Research Through the Life Span* (eds J. Brandtstaedter and R.M. Lerner), Sage Publications, Thousand Oaks, CA, pp. 169–196.

Buckley-Walker, K., Crowe, T. and Caputi, P. (2010) Exploring identity within the recovery process of people with serious mental illnesses. *Psychiatric Rehabilitation Journal*, 33 (3), 219–227.

Byrne, C.M., Woodside, H., Landeen, J., *et al.* (1994) The importance of relationships in fostering hope. *Journal of Psychosocial Nursing and Mental Health Services*, 32 (9), 31–34.

Calhoun, L.G. and Tedeschi, R.G. (2001) Posttraumatic growth: The positive lessons of loss. In R.A. Neimeyer (ed.), Meaning reconstruction & the experience of loss (pp. 157–172). Washington, DC: American Psychological Association.

Campbell-Orde, T., Chamberlin, J., Carpenter, J. and Leff, H.S. (eds) (2005) *Measuring the Promise: A Compendium of Recovery Measures*, Volume II – 10/2005, The Evaluation Centre@HSRI, Cambridge, MA.

Carpenter, W.T. and Buchanan, R.W. (1994) Medical progress: Schizophrenia. *New England Journal of Medicine*, 220 (10), 681–690.

Carver, C.S. (1998) Resilience and thriving: issues, models and linkages. *Journal of Social Issues*, 54 (2), 245.

Chadwick, P.K. (1997) Recovery from psychosis: learning more from patients. *Journal of Mental Health*, 6 (6), 577–588.

Chamberlin, J. (1990) The ex-patients' movement: Where we've been and where we're going. *The Journal of Mind and Behavior*, 11 (3), 323–336.

Chamberlin, J. (1996) Citizenship rights and psychiatric disability. World Mental Health Day Conference in Stockholm, Sweden, October 10. http://www.power2u.org/articles/empower/citizenship.html (retrieved 19 October 2002).

Chamberlin, J. and Rogers, J.A. (1990) Planning a community-based mental health system. Perspective of service recipients. *American Psychologist*, 45 (11), 1241–1244.

Chaplin, R. (2000) Psychiatrists can cause stigma too. *British Journal of Psychiatry*, 177, 467.

Charmaz, K. (1983) Loss of self: A fundamental form of suffering in the chronically ill. *Sociology of Health and Illness*, 5 (2), 168–195.

Charmaz, K. (1999) From the 'sick role' to stories of self: Understanding the self in illness, in *Self, Social Identity, and Physical Health: Interdisciplinary Explorations* (eds R.J. Contrada and R.D. Ashmore), Oxford University Press, New York, pp. 209–239.

Chiba, R., Kawakami, N., Miyamoto, Y. and Andresen, R. (2010) Reliability and validity of the Japanese version of the Self-Identified Stage of Recovery for people with long term mental illness. *International Journal of Mental Health Nursing*, 19 (3), 195–202.

Chovil, I. (2000) First person account: I and I, dancing fool, challenge you the world to a duel. *Schizophrenia Bulletin*, 26 (3), 745–747.

Chovil, I. (2005) Reflections on schizophrenia, learned helplessness/dependence, and recovery. *Psychiatric Rehabilitation Journal*, 29 (1), 69–71.

Ciarrochi, J. and Bailey, A. (2008) *A CBT-Practicioner's Guide to ACT: How to Bridge the Gap Between Cognitive Behavioral Therapy and Acceptance and Commitment Therapy*, New Harbinger Publications, Oakland, CA.

Ciompi, L. (1980/2005) The natural history of schizophrenia in the long term, in *Recovery from Severe Mental Illnesses: Research Evidence and Implications for Practice*, Vol. 1 (eds L.

Davidson, C. Harding and L. Spaniol), Center for Psychiatric Rehabilitation, Boston, pp. 224–235.

Ciompi, L. and Muller, C. (1976) *The Life Course and Aging in Schizophrenia: A Catamnestic Longitudinal Study into Advanced Age* (E. Forsberg, translator), Springer Verlag, Berlin.

Clare, A.W. (1980) *Psychiatry in Dissent*, Routledge, London.

Clarke Institute of Psychiatry (1998) Review of best practices in mental health reform. Prepared for the Advisory Unit on Mental Health. *Catalogue number H39-441/1997E*, Health Canada, Ottawa, Ontario.

Clarke, S.P., Oades, L.G., Crowe, T.P. and Deane, F.P. (2006) Collaborative Goal Technology: Theory and Practice. *Psychiatric Rehabilitation Journal*, 30 (2), 129–136.

Clarke, S.P., Crowe, T.P., Oades, L.G. and Deane, F.P. (2009a) Do goal-setting interventions improve the quality of goals in mental health services? *Psychiatric Rehabilitation Journal*, 32 (4), 292–299.

Clarke, S., Oades, L., Crowe, T., *et al.* (2009b) The role of symptom distress and goal attainment in promoting aspects of psychological recovery for consumers with enduring mental illness. *Journal of Mental Health* 18 (5), 389–397.

Cloutier, G.R. (1994) Overcoming the black garden, in *The Experience of Recovery* (eds L. Spaniol and M. Koehler), Center for Psychiatric Rehabilitation, Boston, pp. 29–34.

Connor, K.M. and Davidson, J.R.T. (2003) Development of a new resilience scale: the Connor–Davidson Resilience Scale (CD-RISC). *Depression and Anxiety*, 18 (2), 76–82.

Cooper, J.E., Kendell, R.E., Gurland, B.J., *et al.* (1972) *Psychiatric Diagnosis in New York and London*, Oxford University Press, London.

Corrigan, P.W. and Watson, A.C. (2002) The paradox of self-stigma and mental illness. *Clinical Psychology: Science and Practice*, 9 (1), 35–53.

Corrigan, P.W., Faber, D., Rashid, F. and Leary, M. (1999a) The construct validity of empowerment among consumers of mental health services. *Schizophrenia Research*, 38 (1), 77–84.

Corrigan, P.W., Giffort, D., Rashid, F., *et al.* (1999b) Recovery as a psychological construct. *Community Mental Health Journal*, 35 (3), 231–239.

Corrigan, P.W., Salzer, M., Ralph, R.O., Sangster, Y. and Keck, L. (2004) Examining the factor structure of the Recovery Assessment Scale. *Schizophrenia Bulletin*, 30 (4), 1035–1041.

Coursey, R.D., Gearon, J., Bradmiller, M.A., *et al.* (2000) A psychological view of people with serious mental illness. *New Directions for Mental Health Services*, 88, 61–72.

Couture, S.M. and Penn, D.L. (2003) Interpersonal contact and the stigma of mental illness: A review of the literature. *Journal of Mental Health (UK)*, 12 (3), 291–305.

Craig, T.J., Siegel, C., Hopper, K., *et al.* (1997) Outcome in schizophrenia and related disorders compared between developing and developed countries: A recursive partitioning re-analysis of the WHO. *British Journal of Psychiatry*, 170 (3), 229–233.

Cross-Government Strategy: Mental Health Division (2009) New Horizons: A Shared Vision for Mental Health. http://www.dh.gov.uk/prod_consum_dh/groups/dh_digitalassets/@dh/@en/documents/digitalasset/dh_109708.pdf (retrieved 13 April 2010).

Crowe, T.P., Deane, F.P., Oades, L.G., *et al.* (2006) Effectiveness of a collaborative recovery training program in Australia in promoting positive views about recovery. *Psychiatric Services*, 57 (10), 1497–1500.

Crowley, K. (1997). Implementing the concept of recovery, *Final report: Blue Ribbon Commission on Mental Health*, Wisconsin Department of Health Services, Madison.

Crowley, K. (2000) *The Power of Procovery in Healing Mental Illness*. Kennedy Carlisle, Los Angeles.

Curtis, L.C. (2000) Moving beyond disability: Recovery from psychiatric disorders: One person's perspective. *The Capstone*, 17 (2), 4–5.

Curtis, L.C. (2001) A Vision of Recovery: A Framework for Psychiatric Rehabilitation Services: Discussion paper prepared for Northern Sydney Area Mental Health Service. North Sydney Area Health Service, North Ryde, NSW.

Davidson, L. (1993) Story telling and schizophrenia: Using narrative structure in phenomenological research. *The Humanistic Psychologist*, 21, 200–220.

Davidson, L. (1994) Phenomenological research in schizophrenia: From philosophical anthropology to empirical science. *Journal of Phenomenological Psychology*, 25 (1), 104–130.

Davidson, L. (2002) Intentionality, identity and delusions of control in schizophrenia: A Husserlian perspective. *Journal of Phenomenological Psychology*, 33 (1), 40–58.

Davidson, L. and McGlashan, T.H. (1997) The varied outcomes of schizophrenia. *Canadian Journal of Psychiatry*, 42 (1), 34–43.

Davidson, L. and Roe, D. (2007) Recovery from versus recovery in serious mental illness: One strategy for lessening confusion plaguing recovery. *Journal of Mental Health*, 16 (4), 459–470.

Davidson, L. and Stayner, D.A. (1997) Loss, loneliness and the desire for love: Perspectives on the social lives of people with schizophrenia. *Psychiatric Rehabilitation Journal*, 20 (3), 3–12.

Davidson, L. and Strauss, J.S. (1992) Sense of self in recovery from severe mental illness. *British Journal of Medical Psychology*, 65, 131–145.

Davidson, L. and Strauss, J.S. (1995) Beyond the biopsychosocial model: Integrating disorder, health and recovery. *Psychiatry*, 58 (1), 44.

Davidson, L., O'Connell, M.J., Tondora, J., *et al.* (2005) Recovery in serious mental illness: A new wine or just a new bottle? *Professional Psychology, Research and Practice*, 36 (5), 480–487.

Davidson, L., O'Connell, M., Tondora, J., *et al.* (2006) The top ten concerns about recovery encountered in mental health system transformation. *Psychiatric Services*, 57 (5), 640–645.

Davidson, L., Schmutte, T., Dinzeo, T. and Andres-Hyman, R. (2008) Remission and recovery in schizophrenia: Practitioner and patient perspectives. *Schizophrenia Bulletin*, 34 (1), 5–8.

Davis, C.G., Nolen-Hoeksema, S. and Larson, J. (1998) Making sense of loss and benefiting from the experience: Two construals of meaning. *Journal of Personality and Social Psychology*, 75 (2), 561–574.

Deane, F. and Andresen, R. (2006) Evolution and sustainability of the Helping Hands Volunteer Program: Consumer recovery and mental health comparisons six years on. *Australian Journal of Rehabilitation Counselling*, 12 (2), 88–103.

Deci, E.L. and Ryan, R.M. (1991) A motivational approach to self: Integration in personality, in *Nebraska Symposium on Motivation. Current Theory and Research in Motivation*, Vol. 38, (ed. R. Dienstbier), University of Nebraska Press, Lincoln, NE, pp. 237–288.

Deci, E.L. and Ryan, R.M. (2000) The 'what' and 'why' of goal pursuits: Human needs and the self-determination of behavior. *Psychological Inquiry*, 11 (4), 227–268.

Deci, E.L. and Ryan, R.M. (eds) (2002) *Handbook of Self-Determination Research*, University of Rochester Press, Rochester, NY.

Deegan, P. (1988) Recovery: The lived experience of rehabilitation. *Psychosocial Rehabilitation Journal*, 11 (4), 11–19.

Deegan, P. (1990) Spirit breaking: When the helping professions hurt. *The Humanistic Psychologist*, 18 (3), 301–313.

Deegan, P. (1994) Recovery: The lived experience of rehabilitation, in *The Experience of Recovery* (eds L. Spaniol and M. Koehler), Center for Psychiatric Rehabilitation, Boston, pp. 54–59.

Deegan, P. (1996a) Recovery and the conspiracy of hope. Sixth Annual Mental Health Services Conference of Australia and New Zealand, Brisbane, Australia.

Deegan, P. (1996b) Recovery as a journey of the heart. *Psychiatric Rehabilitation Journal*, 19 (3), 91–97.

Deegan, P. (1997) Recovery and empowerment for people with psychiatric disabilities. *Social Work in Health Care*, 25 (3), 11–24.

Department of Health (1999) National Service Framework for Mental Health: Modern Standards and Service Models, Department of Health, London.

Department of Health (2001) The Journey to Recovery: the Government's Vision for Mental Health Care, Department of Health, London.

Department of Health and Aging (2010) National Standards for Mental Health Services, http://www.health.gov.au/internet/main/publishing.nsf/content/mental-pubs-n-servst102010 (retrieved 30 October 2010).

Department of Health NSW (2006) Mental Health Outcomes and Assessment Tools (MH-OAT) Data Collection Reporting Requirement 1 July 2006. http://www.health.nsw.gov.au (retrieved 26 March 2007).

DeSisto, M., Harding, C.M., McCormick, R.V., *et al.* (1995a) The Maine and Vermont three-decade studies of serious mental illness. I. Matched comparison of cross-sectional outcome. *British Journal of Psychiatry*, 167 (3), 331–338.

DeSisto, M., Harding, C.M., McCormick, R.V., *et al.* (1995b) The Maine and Vermont three-decade studies of serious mental illness. II. Longitudinal course comparisons. *British Journal of Psychiatry*, 167 (3), 338–342.

Diamond, R. and Becker, M. (1999) The Wisconsin Quality of Life Index: a multidimensional model for measuring quality of life. *Journal of Clinical Psychiatry*, 60 (3), 29–31.

Dickerson, F.B. (2000) Cognitive behavioural therapy for schizophrenia: A review of recent empirical studies. *Schizophrenia Research*, 43 (2–3), 71–90.

Dickerson, G. (1994) Keeping time in chaos, in *The Experience of Recovery* (eds L. Spaniol and M. Koehler), Center for Psychiatric Rehabilitation, Boston, pp. 26–28.

Diener, E. (2000) Subjective well-being: The science of happiness and a proposal for a national index. *American Psychologist*, 55 (1), 34–43.

Diener, E., Suh, E.M., Lucas, R.L. and Smith, H.L. (1999) Subjective well-being: Three decades of progress. *Psychological Bulletin*, 125 (2), 276–302.

Duckworth, K., Nair, V., Patel, J.K. and Goldfinger, S.M. (1997) Lost time, found hope and sorrow: The search for self, connection and purpose during 'awakenings' on the new antipsychotics. *Harvard Review of Psychiatry*, 5 (4), 227–233.

Dunn, D.S. (1996) Well-being following amputation: Salutary effects of positive meaning, optimism and control. *Rehabilitation Psychology*, 41 (4), 285–302.

Dweck, C.S. (2006) *Mindset: The New Psychology of Success*, Random House, New York.

Eagar, K., Trauer, T. and Mellsop, G. (2005) Performance of routine outcome measures in adult mental health care. *Australian and New Zealand Journal of Psychiatry*, 39 (8), 713–718.

Elliot, A.J. and Church, M.A. (1997) A hierarchical model of approach and avoidance achievement motivation. *Journal of Personality and Social Psychology*, 72 (1), 218–232.

Elliot, A.J. and Sheldon, K.M. (1998) Avoidance personal goals and the personality-illness relationship. *Journal of Personality and Social Psychology*, 75 (5), 1282–1299.

Elliot, A.J., Sheldon, K.M. and Church, M.A. (1997) Avoidance personal goals and subjective well-being. *Personality and Social Psychology Bulletin*, 23 (9), 915–927.

Elliott, T.R. (2002) Psychological explanations of personal journeys: Hope for a positive psychology in theory and practice, and policy. *Psychological Inquiry*, 13 (4), 295–298.

Elliott, T.R. and Kurylo, M. (2000) Hope over acquired disability: Lessons of a young woman's triumph, in *Handbook of Hope: Theory, Measures and Applications* (ed. C.R. Snyder), Academic Press, San Diego, CA, pp. 373–386.

Elliott, T.R., Kurylo, M. and Rivera, P. (2002) Positive growth following acquired physical disability, in *Handbook of Positive Psychology* (eds C. Snyder and S.J. Lopez), Oxford University Press, New York, pp. 687–698.

Elliott, T.R., Witty, T.E., Herrick, S. and Hoffman, J.T. (1991) Negotiating reality after physical loss: Hope, depression, and disability. *Journal of Personality and Social Psychology*, 61 (4), 608–613.

Elliott, T.R., Uswatte, G., Lewis, L. and Palmatier, A. (2000) Goal instability and adjustment to physical disability. *Journal of Counseling Psychology*, 47 (2), 251–265.

Emmons, R.A. (1986) Personal strivings: an approach to personality and subjective well-being. *Journal of Personality and Social Psychology*, 51 (5), 1058–1068.

Emmons, R.A. (1999a) Personal goals and life meaning, in *The Psychology of Ultimate Concerns*, Guildford Press, New York, pp. 137–156.

Emmons, R.A. (1999b) Personal goals and subjective well-being, in *The Psychology of Ultimate Concerns*, Guildford Press, New York, pp. 137–156.

Emmons, R.A. (1999c) *The Psychology of Ultimate Concerns*, Guildford Press, New York.

Emmons, R.A., Colby, P. and Kaiser, H.A. (1998) When losses lead to gains: Personal goals and the recovery of meaning, in *The Human Quest for Meaning: A Handbook of Psychological Research and Clinical Applications* (eds P.T.P. Wong and P.S. Fry), Lawrence Erlbaum Associates, Mahwah, NJ, pp. 163–178.

Endicott, J., Spitzer, R.L. and Fliess, J.L. (1976) The Global Assessment Scale: A procedure for measuring overall severity of psychiatric disturbance. *Archives of General Psychiatry*, 33, 766–771.

Epstein, M. and Olsen, A. (1998) An introduction to consumer politics. *Journal of Psychosocial Nursing and Mental Health Services*, 36 (8), 40–49.

Erikson, E.H. (1963) *Childhood and Society*, Norton, New York.

Erikson, E.H. (1968) *Identity: Youth and Crisis*, Norton, New York.

Erikson, E.H. (1975) Identity crisis in perspective, in *Life History and the Historical Moment* (ed. E.H. Erikson), Norton, New York, pp. 17–47.

Estroff, S. (1989) Self, identity, and subjective experiences of schizophrenia: In search of the subject. *Schizophrenia Bulletin*, 15 (2), 189–196.

Everett, B. (1994) Something is happening: The contemporary consumer and psychiatric survivor movement in historical context. *The Journal of Mind and Behavior*, 15 (1–2), 55–70.

Farkas, M., Gagne, C., Anthony, W.A. and Chamberlin, J. (2005) Implementing recovery-oriented evidence-based programs: Identifying the critical dimensions. *Community Mental Health Journal*, 41 (2), 141–158.

Fekete, D.J. (2004) How I quit being a 'mental patient' and became a whole person with a neuro-chemical imbalance: Conceptual and functional recovery from psychosis. *Psychiatric Rehabilitation Journal*, 28 (2), 189–194.

Feldman, D.B. and Snyder, C.R. (2005) Hope and the meaningful life: Theoretical and empirical associations between goal-directed thinking and life meaning. *Journal of Social and Clinical Psychology*, 24 (3), 401–421.

Fisher, D.B. (1994) Health care reform based on an empowerment model of recovery by people with psychiatric disabilities. *Hospital and Community Psychiatry*, 45 (9), 913–915.

Fisher, D.B. (2003) People are more important than pills in recovery from mental disorder. *Journal of Humanistic Psychology*, 43 (2), 65–68.

Fisher, D.B. and Ahern, L. (2002) Evidence-based practices and recovery. *Psychiatric Services*, 53 (5), 632–633.

Fisher, J.E. and Happell, B. (2009) Implications of evidence-based practice for mental health nursing. International Journal of Mental Health Nursing, 18 (3), 179–185.

Fitzpatrick, C. (2002) A new word in serious mental illness: Recovery. *Behavioral Healthcare Tomorrow*, 11 (4), 16–21, 33, 44.

Fox, V. (2002) First person account: A glimpse of schizophrenia. *Schizophrenia Bulletin*, 28 (2), 363–365.

Frankl, V.E. (1984) *Man's Search for Meaning*, Updated and Revised edition, Simon & Schuster, New York.

Frese, F.J. (1997) The consumer-survivor movement, recovery, and consumer professionals. *Professional Psychology, Research and Practice*, 28 (3), 243–245.

Frese, F.J. (2000) Psychology practitioners and schizophrenia: A view from both sides. *Journal of Clinical Psychology, In Session*, 56 (11), 1413–1426.

Frese, F.J., Stanley, J., Kress, K. and Vogel-Scibilia, S. (2001) Integrating evidence-based practices and the recovery model. *Psychiatric Services*, 52 (11), 1462–1468.

Frisch, M.B., Cornell, J., Villanueva, M. and Retzlaff, P.J. (1992) Clinical validation of the Quality of Life Inventory: A measure of life satisfaction for use in treatment planning and outcome assessment. *Psychological Assessment*, 4 (1), 92–101.

Gara, M.A., Rosenberg, S. and Mueller, D.R. (1989) Perception of self and other in schizophrenia. *International Journal of Personal Construct Psychology*, 2 (3), 253–270.

Gerlach, J. and Larsen, E.B. (1999) Subjective experience and mental side-effects of antipsychotic treatment. *Acta Psychiatrica Scandinavica*, 99, (Supplement 395), 113–117.

Glass, C.R. and Arnkoff, D.B. (2000) Consumers' perspectives on helpful and hindering factors in mental health treatment. *Journal of Clinical Psychology*, 56 (11), 1467–1480.

Goffman, I. (1968) *Asylums: Essays on the Social Situation of Mental Patients and Other Inmates*, Penguin, Harmondsworth.

Goldman, H.H., Skodol, A.E. and Lave, T.R. (1992) Revising axis V for DSM-IV: a review of measures of social functioning. *American Journal of Psychiatry*, 149 (9), 1148–1156.

Gray, A.J. (2002) Stigma in psychiatry. *Journal of the Royal Society of Medicine*, 95 (2), 72–76.

Greenblat, L. (2000) First Person Account: Understanding health as a continuum. *Schizophrenia Bulletin*, 26 (1), 243–245.

Gregg, J.A., Callaghan, G.M., Hayes, S.C. and Glenn-Lawson, J.L. (2007) Improving diabetes self-management through acceptance, mindfulness, and values: A randomized controlled trial. *Journal of Consulting and Clinical Psychology*, 75 (2), 336–343.

Happell, B. (2008) Meaningful information or a bureaucratic exercise? Exploring the value of routine outcome measurement in mental health. *Issues in Mental Health Nursing*, 29 (10), 1098–1114.

References

Harding, C.M. (1987) Chronicity in schizophrenia. *Hospital and Community Psychiatry*, 38 (11), 1226–1227.

Harding, C.M. (1994) An examination of the complexities in the measurement of recovery in severe psychiatric disorders, in *Schizophrenia: Exploring the Spectrum of Psychosis* (eds R. Ancill, D. Holliday and G.W. MacEwan), John Wiley & Sons, Ltd, Chichester, pp. 153–169.

Harding, C.M., Zubin, J. and Strauss, J.S. (1987) Chronicity in schizophrenia: Fact, partial fact or artifact? *Hospital and Community Psychiatry*, 38 (5), 477–486.

Harding, C.M., Zubin, J. and Strauss, J.S. (1992) Chronicity in schizophrenia: Revisited. *British Journal of Psychiatry*, 161 (Supplement 18), 27–37.

Harding, C.M., Brooks, G.W., Ashikaga, T., *et al.* (1987a) The Vermont longitudinal study of persons with severe mental illness, I: Methodology, study sample, and overall status 32 years later. *American Journal of Psychiatry*, 144 (6), 718–726.

Harding, C.M., Brooks, G.W., Ashikaga, T., *et al.* (1987b) The Vermont longitudinal study of persons with severe mental illness, II: Long-term outcome of subjects who retrospectively met DSM-III criteria for schizophrenia. *American Journal of Psychiatry*, 144 (6), 727–735.

Harrison, G. and Mason, P. (1993) Schizophrenia – falling incidence and better outcome? *British Journal of Psychiatry*, 163, 535–541.

Harrison, G., Hopper, K., Craig, T., *et al.* (2001) Recovery from psychotic illness: A 15- and 25-year international follow-up study. *British Journal of Clinical Psychiatry*, 178, 506–517.

Harrow, M., Grossman, L.S., Jobe, T.H. and Herbener, E.S. (2005) Do patients with schizophrenia ever show periods of recovery? A 15-year multi-follow-up study. *Schizophrenia Bulletin*, 31 (3), 723–734.

Harvey, J.H. (2000) *Give Sorrow Words: Perspectives on Loss and Trauma*. Brunner/Mazel, Philadelphia, PA.

Hawk, A.B., Carpenter, W.T.J. and Strauss, J.S. (1975) Diagnostic criteria and five-year outcome in schizophrenia. A report from the International Pilot Study of schizophrenia. *Archives of General Psychiatry*, 32 (3), 343–347.

Hayes, S. and Strosahl, K. (eds) (2004) *A Practical Guide to Acceptance and Commitment Therapy*, Springer-Verlag, New York.

Hayward, P. and Bright, J.A. (1997) Stigma and mental illness: A review and critique. *Journal of Mental Health (UK)*, 6 (4), 345–354.

Hegarty, J.D., Baldessarini, R.J., Tohen, M., *et al.* (1994) One hundred years of schizophrenia: A meta-analysis of the outcome literature. *American Journal of Psychiatry*, 151 (10), 1409–1416.

Hemsley, D.R. (1998) The disruption of the 'sense of self' in schizophrenia: Potential links with disturbances of information processing. *British Journal of Medical Psychology*, 7 (2), 115–124.

Henderson, H. (2004) From depths of despair to heights of recovery. *Psychiatric Rehabilitation Journal*, 28 (1), 83–87.

Higgins, E.T., Roney, C.J.R., Crowe, E. and Hymes, C. (1994) Ideal versus ought predilections for approach and avoidance: Distinct self-regulatory systems. *Journal of Personality and Social Psychology*, 66 (2), 276–286.

Hirano, Y., Sakita, M., Yamazaki, Y., *et al.* (2007) The Herth Hope Index (HHI) and related factors in the Japanese general urban population. *Japan Health and Human Ecology*, 73 (1), 31–42.

Hoffmann, H., Kupper, Z. and Kunz, B. (2000) Hopelessness and its impact on rehabilitation outcome in schizophrenia – An exploratory study. *Schizophrenia Research*, 43 (2–3), 147–158.

Hopper, K. (2004) Interrogating the meaning of 'culture' in the WHO international studies of schizophrenia, in *Schizophrenia, Culture, and Subjectivity* (eds J.H. Jenkins & R.J. Barrett), Cambridge University Press, Cambridge, pp. 62–86.

Hopper, K. and Wanderling, J. (2000) Revisiting the developed versus developing country distinction in course and outcome in schizophrenia: Results from ISoS, the WHO collaborative followup project. *Schizophrenia Bulletin*, 26 (4), 835–846.

Huber, G., Gross, G., Schuttler, R. and Linz, M. (1980) Longitudinal studies of schizophrenic patients. *Schizophrenia Bulletin*, 6 (4), 592–605.

Hugo, M. (2001) Mental health professionals' attitudes towards people who have experienced a mental health disorder. *Journal of Psychiatric and Mental Health Nursing*, 8 (5), 419–425.

Jablensky, A., Sartorius, N., Ernberg, G., *et al.* (1992) Schizophrenia: Manifestations, incidence and course in different cultures: A World Health Organization ten-country study. *Psychological Medicine, Supplement*, 20, 97.

Jacobson, N. and Curtis, L. (2000) Recovery as policy in mental health services: Strategies emerging from the States. *Psychiatric Rehabilitation Journal*, 23 (4), 333–341.

Jaffe, D.T. (1985) Self-renewal: Personal transformation following extreme trauma. *Journal of Humanistic Psychology*, 25 (4), 99–124.

Janoff-Bulman, R. (1992) *Shattered Assumptions: Towards a New Psychology of Trauma*, The Free Press, New York.

John (1994) John, in *Altered Lives: Personal Experiences of Schizophrenia*, Schizophrenia Fellowship of Victoria, North Fitzroy, pp. 8–10.

Jorm, A.F., Korten, A.E., Jacomb, P.A., *et al.* (1999) Attitudes towards people with a mental disorder: A survey of the Australian public and health professionals. *Australian and New Zealand Journal of Psychiatry*, 33 (1), 77–83.

Joseph, S. and Linley, A. (2008) Psychological assessment of growth following adversity: A review, in *Trauma, Recovery, and Growth* (eds S. Joseph and A. Linley), John Wiley & Sons, Inc, Hoboken, pp. 21–38.

Kaufmann, C.L. (1999) An introduction to the Mental Health Consumer Movement, in *A Handbook for the Study of Mental Health: Social Contexts, Theories and Systems* (eds A.V. Horwitz and T.L. Scheid), Cambridge University Press, New York, pp. 493–507.

Kelly, M.P. and Millward, L.M. (2004) Identity and Illness, in *Identity and Health* (eds G. Leavey and D. Kelleher), Routledge, London, pp. 1–18.

Keshavan, M.S. (2005) Schizophrenia: First-episode schizophrenia: research perspectives and clinical implications. *Psychiatric Times*, 22 (3), 22–25.

Keyes, C.L. (2002) The mental health continuum: From languishing to flourishing in life. *Journal of Health and Social Behavior*, 43 (2), 207–222.

Keyes, C.L. (2003) Complete mental health: An agenda for the 21st century, in *Flourishing: Positive Psychology and the Life Well-lived* (eds C.L.M. Keyes and J. Haidt), American Psychological Association, Washington, DC, pp. 293–312.

King, L.A. (1998) Personal goals and personal agency: Linking everyday goals to future images of the self, in *Personal Control in Action: Cognitive and Motivational Mechanisms* (eds M. Kofta, G. Weary and G. Sedek), Plenum Press. New York, pp. 109–128.

Kirkpatrick, H., Landeen, J., Woodside, H. and Byrne, C. (2001) How people with schizophrenia build their hope. *Journal of Psychosocial Nursing and Mental Health Services*, 39 (1), 46–53.

Kleinmann, A. (1988) *Rethinking Psychiatry: From Cultural Category to Personal Experience*, The Free Press, New York.

Klinger, E. (1975) Consequences of commitment to and disengagement from incentives. *Psychological Review*, 82 (1), 1–25.

Koehler, M. (1994) My road to recovery, in *The Experience of Recovery* (eds L. Spaniol and M. Koehler), Center for Psychiatric Rehabilitation, Boston, pp. 23–25.

Kohut, H. and Wolf, E.S. (1978) The disorders of the self and their treatment: An outline. *International Journal of Psycho-Analysis*, 59 (4), 413–425.

Kopelowicz, A., Zarate, R., Tripodis, K., *et al.* (2000) Differential efficacy of olanzapine for deficit and nondeficit negative symptoms in schizophrenia. *The American Journal of Psychiatry*, 157 (6), 987–993.

Kruger, A. (2000) Schizophrenia: Recovery and hope. *Psychiatric Rehabilitation Journal*, 24 (1), 29–37.

Lakeman, R. (2004) Standardized routine outcome measurement: Pot holes in the road to recovery. *International Journal of Mental Health Nursing*, 13 (4), 210–215.

Lally, S.J. (1989) Does being in here mean there is something wrong with me? *Schizophrenia Bulletin*, 15 (2), 253–265.

Lapierre, S., Bouffard, L. and Bastin, E. (1997) Personal goals and subjective well-being in later life. International Journal of Aging and Human Development, 45 (4), 287–303.

Lapsley, H., Nikora, L. and Black, R. (2002) *Kia Mauri Tau*. Mental Health Commission, Wellington.

Latham, G.P. and Locke, E.A. (1991) Self-regulation through goal setting. *Organizational Behavior and Human Decision Processes*, 50, 212–247.

Laurenen, E., Koskinen, J., Veijola, J., *et al.* (2005) Recovery from schizophrenic psychoses within the northern Finland 1966 Birth Cohort. *Journal of Clinical Psychiatry*, 66 (3), 375–383.

Leete, E. (1989) How I perceive and manage my illness. *Schizophrenia Bulletin*, 15 (2), 197–200.

Leff, J. (1988) *Psychiatry Around the Globe: A Transcultural View*, Gaskell, London.

Lehman, A.F. (1988) A quality of life interview for the chronically mentally ill. *Evaluation and Program Planning*, 11 (1), 51–62.

Lehman, A.F. (2000) Putting recovery into practice: A commentary on 'What recovery means to us'. *Community Mental Health Journal*, 36 (3), 329–331.

Lehman, A.F., Steinwachs, D.M. and The Survey Co-Investigators of the PORT project (1998) Patterns of usual care for schizophrenia: Initial results from the Schizophrenia Patient Outcomes Research Team (PORT) Client Survey. *Schizophrenia Bulletin*, 24 (1), 11–20.

Leibrich, J. (1997) The doors of perception. *Australian and New Zealand Journal of Psychiatry*, 31, 36–45.

Levenstein, S., Klein, D.F. and Pollack, M. (1966) Follow-up study of formerly hospitalized voluntary psychiatric patients: The first two years. *American Journal of Psychiatry*, 122 (10), 1102–1109.

Liberman, R.P. (1992) *Handbook of Psychiatric Rehabilitation*, Macmillan, New York.

Liberman, R.P. and Kopelowicz, A. (2002) Recovery from schizophrenia: A challenge for the 21st century. *International Review of Psychiatry*, 14 (4), 245–255.

Liberman, R.P. and Kopelowicz, A. (2005) Recovery from schizophrenia: A concept in search of research. *Psychiatric Services*, 56 (6), 735–742.

Liberman, R.P., Kopelowicz, A., Ventura, J. and Gutkind, D. (2002) Operational criteria and factors related to recovery from schizophrenia. *International Review of Psychiatry*, 14, 256–272.

Link, B.G. and Phelan, J.C. (2001) Conceptualizing stigma. *Annual Review of Sociology*, 27, 363–385.

Linley, P.A. (2003) Positive adaptation to trauma: Wisdom as both process and outcome. *Journal of Traumatic Stress*, 16 (6), 601–610.

Linley, P.A (2008) *Average to A+: Realising Strengths in Yourself and Others*, CAPP Press, http://www.suite101.com/content/average-to-a-alex-linley-on-realizing-strength-a60433# ixzz17xCRA4aY (retrieved 05 June 2009).

Linley, P.A. and Harrington, S. (2006) Strengths coaching: A potential-guided approach to coaching psychology. *International Coaching Psychology Review*, 1 (1), 37–46.

Little, B.R. (1998) Personal project pursuit: Dimensions and dynamics of personal meaning, in *The Human Quest for Meaning: A Handbook of Psychological Research and Clinical Applications* (eds P.T.P. Wong and P.S. Fry), Lawrence Erlbaum Associates, Mahwah, NJ, pp. 193–212.

Lukas, E. (1998) The meaning of life and the goals in life for chronically ill people, in *The Human Quest for Meaning: A Handbook of Psychological Research and Clinical Applications* (eds P.T.P. Wong and P.S. Fry), Lawrence Erlbaum Associates, Mahwah, NJ, pp. 307–316.

Lunt, A. (2002) A theory of recovery. *Journal of Psychosocial Nursing and Mental Health Services*, 40 (12), 32–41.

Lynch, K. (2000) The long road back. *Journal of Clinical Psychology, In Session*, 56, 1427–1432.

Lynn, D. (1994) My struggle for freedom, in *The Experience of Recovery* (eds L. Spaniol and M. Koehler), Center for Psychiatric Rehabilitation, Boston, pp. 50–51.

Lysaker, P. and Bell, M. (1995) Work and meaning: Disturbance of volition and vocational dysfunction in schizophrenia. *Psychiatry*, 58 (4), 392–400.

Manschreck, T.C., Redmond, D.A., Candela, S.F. and Maher, B.A. (1999) Effect of clozapine on psychiatric symptoms, cognition and functional outcome in schizophrenia. *The Journal of Neuropsychiatry and Clinical Neurosciences*, 11 (4), 481–489.

Markus, H. and Nurius, P. (1986) Possible selves. *American Psychologist*, 41 (9), 954–969.

Marsh, A., Smith, L., Piek, J. and Saunders, B. (2003) The Purpose in Life Scale: Psychometric properties for social drinkers and drinkers in alcohol treatment. *Educational and Psychological Measurement*, 63, 859.

Marsh, D.T. (2000) Personal accounts of consumer/survivors: Insights and implications. *Journal of Clinical Psychology, In Session*, 56 (11), 1447–1457.

Mary (1994) Mary, in *Altered Lives: Personal Experiences of Schizophrenia*, Schizophrenia Fellowship of Victoria, North Fitzroy, pp. 15–19.

Mason, P., Harrison, G., Glazebrook, C., *et al.* (1995) Characteristics of outcome in schizophrenia at 13 years. *British Journal of Psychiatry*, 167, 596–603.

Massey, S., Cameron, A., Ouellette, S. and Fine, M. (1998) Qualitative approaches to the study of thriving: what can be learned. *Journal of Social Issues*, 54 (2), 337.

McAdams, D.P. (2001) The psychology of life stories. *Review of General Psychology*, 5 (2), 100–122.

McDermott, B.F. (1994) Transforming depression into creative self-expression, in *The Experience of Recovery* (eds L. Spaniol and M. Koehler), Center for Psychiatric Rehabilitation, Boston, pp. 64–67.

McGorry, P.D. (1992) The concept of recovery and secondary prevention in psychotic disorders. *Australian and New Zealand Journal of Psychiatry*, 26 (3), 3–17.

McGregor, I. and Little, B.R. (1998) Personal projects, happiness and meaning: On doing well and being yourself. *Journal of Personality and Social Psychology*, 74 (2), 494–452.

McGurk, S.R. (1999) The effects of clozapine on cognitive functioning in schizophrenia. *Journal of Clinical Psychiatry*, 60 (Supplement 12), 24–29.

McLean, A. (1995) Empowerment and the psychiatric consumer/ex-patient movement in the United States: Contradictions, crisis and change. *Social Science and Medicine*, 40 (8), 1053–1071.

McQuillin, B. (1994) My life with schizophrenia, in *The Experience of Recovery* (eds L. Spaniol and M. Koehler), Center for Psychiatric Rehabilitation, Boston, pp. 7–10.

Mead, S. and Copeland, M.E. (2000) What recovery means to us: Consumers' perspectives. *Community Mental Health Journal*, 36 (3), 315–328.

Meehan, T.J., King, R.J., Beavis, P.H. and Robinson, J.D. (2008) Recovery-based practice: do we know what we mean or mean what we know? *Australian and New Zealand Journal of Psychiatry*, 42, 177–182.

Mental Health Commission of Canada (2009) Towards Recovery and Well-Being: A framework for a Mental Health Strategy for Canada, http://www.mentalhealthcommission.ca (retrieved 13 April 2010).

Mental Health Commission (1998) *Blueprint for Mental Health Services in New Zealand*, Wellington.

Mental Health Commission (2005) *A Recovery Approach within the Irish Mental Health Services: A Framework for Development*, Dublin.

Mental Health Commission (2009) *From Vision to Action? An Analysis of the Implementation of A Vision for Change*, Dublin.

Miller, J.F. (1992) *Coping with chronic illness: Overcoming powerlessness*, 2nd edn, F.A. Davis, Philadelphia.

Minister of Health (2005) Te Tāhuhu – Improving Mental Health 2005-2015: The Second New Zealand Mental Health and Addiction Plan, http://www.moh.govt.nz (retrieved 13 April 2010).

Mould, T.J., Oades, L.G. and Crowe, T.P. (2010) The use of metaphor for understanding and managing psychotic experiences: A systematic review. *Journal of Mental Health*, 19 (3), 282–293.

Murphy, M.A. (1998) Rejection, stigma and hope. *Psychiatric Rehabilitation Journal*, 22 (2), 186–188.

New Freedom Commission on Mental Health (2003a) Achieving the Promise: Transforming Mental Health Care in America. Executive Summary. *DHHS Publication No. SMA-03-3831*, Rockville, MD.

New Freedom Commission on Mental Health (2003b) Achieving the Promise: Transforming Mental Health Care in America. Final Report. *DHHS Publication No. SMA-03-3832*, Rockville, MD.

Noordsy, D.L. and O'Keefe, C. (1999) Effectiveness of combining atypical antipsychotics and psychosocial rehabilitation in a community health centre setting. *The Journal of Clinical Psychiatry*, 60 (Supplement), 47–51.

Noordsy, D.L., Torrey, W., Mead, S., *et al.* (2000) Recovery-oriented psychopharmacology: Redefining goals of antipsychotic treatment. *Journal of Clinical Psychiatry,* 61 (Supplement 3) 22–29.

Noordsy, D.L., Torrey, W., Mueser, K., *et al.* (2002) Recovery from severe mental illness: An intrapersonal and functional outcome definition. *International Review of Psychiatry,* 14 (4), 318–326.

Nunn, K.P. (1996) Personal hopefulness: A conceptual review of the relevance of the perceived future to psychiatry. *British Journal of Medical Psychology,* 69, 227–245.

Oades, L.G. and Crowe, T.P. (2008) *Life Journey Enhancement Tools (LifeJET),* Illawarra Institute for Mental Health, University of Wollongong, ISBN 978-1-74128-156-9.

Oades, L., Crowe, T. and Nguyen, M. (2009) Leadership coaching transforming mental health systems from the inside out: The Collaborative Recovery Model as person-centred strengths based coaching psychology. *International Coaching Psychology Review,* 4 (1), 26–36.

Oades, L.G., Deane, F., Crowe, T.P., *et al.* (2005) Collaborative recovery: An integrative model for working with individuals who experience chronic and recurring mental illness. *Psychiatric Services,* 13 (3), 279–284.

Oades, L.G., Andresen, R., Crowe, T.P., *et al.* (2008) *A Handbook to Flourish: A Recovery-based Self-development Program,* Illawarra Institute for Mental Health, University of Wollongong.

Oades, L.G., Crowe, T.P., Pratt, J., *et al.* (2009) From self-help to self-development. From recovery to flourishing: Evaluation of a positive psychology self-development program for people with enduring mental illness. The Mental Health Services Conference, 1–4 September, Perth, Australia.

O'Hagan, M. (2004) Guest Editorial. Recovery in New Zealand: Lessons for Australia? *Australian e-Journal for the Advancement of Mental Health,* 3 (1), 1–3.

O'Leary, V.E. (1998) Strength in the face of adversity: Individual and social thriving. *Journal of Social Issues,* 54 (2), 425.

Omodei, M.M. and Wearing, A.J. (1990) Need satisfaction and involvement in personal projects: Toward an integrative model of subjective well-being. *Journal of Personality and Social Psychology,* 56 (4), 762–769.

Onken, S.J., Craig, C.M., Ridgway, P., *et al.* (2007) An analysis of the definitions and elements of recovery: A review of the literature. *Psychiatric Rehabilitation Journal,* 31 (1), 9–22.

Oshio, A., Nakaya, M., Kaneko, H. and Nagamine, S. (2002) Negatibu na dekigoto karano tachinaori wo michibiku sinriteki tokusei -Seisinteki kaihukuryoku shakudo no sakusei- [Development and validation of an Adolescent Resilience Scale]. *Japanese Journal of Counseling Science,* 35, 57–65.

Pape, B. and Galipeault, J.-P. (2002) *Mental Health Promotion for People with Mental Illness: A Discussion Paper for the Mental Health Promotion Unit of The Public Health Agency of Canada,* Ontario Public Health Agency of Canada, Ottawa.

Petersen, C. and Seligman, M.E.P. (2004) *Character Strengths and Virtues: A Handbook and Classification.* American Psychological Association and Oxford University Press, New York.

Pettie, D. and Triolo, A.M. (1999) Illness as evolution: The search for identity and meaning in the recovery process. *Psychiatric Rehabilitation Journal,* 22 (3), 255–262.

Pollack, W.S. (1989) Schizophrenia and the self: Contributions of psychoanalytic self-psychology. *Schizophrenia Bulletin*, 15 (2), 311–321.

Priebe, S., McCabe, R., Bullenkamp, J., *et al.* (2007) Structured patient–clinician communication and 1-year outcome in community mental healthcare: Cluster randomised controlled trial. *British Journal of Psychiatry*, 191 (5), 420–426.

Prior, C. (2000) Recovering a meaningful life is possible. *Psychiatric Bulletin*, 24 (1), 30.

Prochaska, J. O. and DiClemente, C. C. (1986) Toward a comprehensive model of change, in *Treating Addictive Behaviors: Processes of Change* (eds W.R. Miller and N. Heather), Plenum Press, New York, pp. 3–27.

Pull, C.B. (2002) Diagnosis of schizophrenia: A review, in *Schizophrenia*, 2nd edn, Vol. 2 (eds M. Maj and N. Sartorius), John Wiley & Sons, Ltd, Chichester, pp. 1–30.

Puschner, B., Steffen, S, Slade, M., *et al.* (2010) Clinical Decision Making and Outcome in Routine Care for People with Severe Mental Illness (CEDAR): Study Protocol. BMC Psychiatry. http://www.biomedcentral.com/1471-244X/10/90 (retrieved 12 November 2010).

Ralph, R.O. (2000a) Recovery. *Psychiatric Rehabilitation Skills*, 4 (3), 480–517.

Ralph, R.O. (2000b) *A Review of the Recovery Literature: A Synthesis of a Sample of Recovery Literature 2000.* National Technical Assistance Center for State Mental Health Planning (NTAC), Alexandria, VA.

Ralph, R.O. and Corrigan, P.W. (eds) (2005) *Recovery in Mental Illness: Broadening Our Understanding of Wellness.* American Psychological Association, Washington, DC.

Ralph, R.O., Kidder, K. and Phillips, D. (2000) Can we Measure Recovery? A Compendium of Recovery and Recovery-related Instruments, *PN–43*, The Evaluation Centre@HSRI, Cambridge, MA.

Ramon, S., Shera, W., Healy, B., Lachman, M. and Renouf, N. (2009) The rediscovered concept of recovery in mental illness: A multicountry comparison of policy and practice. *International Journal of Mental Health*, 38 (2), 106–126.

Read, J., Mosher, L.R. and Bentall, R.P. (eds) (2004) *Models of Madness: Psychological, Social and Biological Approaches to Schizophrenia.* Brunner-Routledge, New York.

Remington, G. and Shammi, C. (2005) Overstating the Case About Recovery? *Psychiatric Services*, 56 (8), 1022.

Resnick, S.G. and Rosenheck, R.A. (2006) Recovery and positive psychology: Parallel themes and potential synergies. *Psychiatric Services*, 57 (1), 120–122.

Resnick, S.G., Rosenheck, R.A. and Lehman, A.F. (2004) An exploratory analysis of the correlates of recovery. *Psychiatric Services*, 55 (5), 540–547.

Resnick, S.G., Fontana, A., Lehman, A.F. and Rosenheck, R.A. (2005) An empirical conceptualization of the recovery orientation. *Schizophrenia Research*, 75, 119–128.

Richardson, G.E. (2002) The metatheory of resilience and resiliency. *Journal of Clinical Psychology*, 58 (3), 307–321.

Rodriguez-Hanley, A. and Snyder, C.R. (2000) The demise of hope, in *Handbook of Hope: Theory, Measures and Applications* (ed. C.R. Snyder), Academic Press, San Diego, CA, pp. 39–54.

Roe, D., Hasson-Ohayon, l., Lachman, M. and Kravetz, S. (2007) Selecting and implementing evidence-based practices in psychiatric rehabilitation services in Israel: A worthy and feasible challenge. *Israel Journal of Psychiatry and Related Sciences*, 44 (1), 47–53.

Roman (1994) Roman, in *Altered Lives: Personal Experiences of Schizophrenia*, Schizophrenia Fellowship of Victoria, North Fitzroy, pp. 41–44.

Rooke, O. and Birchwood, M. (1998) Loss, humiliation and entrapment as appraisals of schizophrenic illness: A prospective study of depressed and non-depressed patients. *British Journal of Clinical Psychology*, 37 (3), 259–268.

Rosen, A., Hadzi-Pavlovic, D. and Parker, G. (1989) The Life Skills Profile: A measure assessing function and disability in schizophrenia. *Schizophrenia Bulletin*, 15 (2), 325–337.

Rosenberg, S. (1993) Social self and the schizophrenic process: Theory and research, in *Schizophrenia: Origins, Processes, Treatment and Outcome* (eds R.L. Cromwell and C.R. Snyder), New York: Oxford University Press, pp. 223–240.

Rutter, M. (2000) Resilience reconsidered: Conceptual considerations, empirical findings and policy implications, in *Handbook of Early Childhood Intervention* (eds J.P. Shonkoff and S.J. Meisels), Cambridge University Press, New York, pp. 651–682.

Rutter, M. (2006) Implications of resilience concepts for scientific understanding. *Annals of the New York Academy of Sciences*, 1094, 1–12.

Ryan, R.M. and Deci, E.L. (2000a) The darker and brighter sides of human existence: Basic psychological needs as a unifying concept. *Psychological Inquiry*, 11 (4), 319–338.

Ryan, R.M. and Deci, E.L. (2000b) Self-determination theory and the facilitation of intrinsic motivation, social development and well-being. *The American Psychologist*, 55 (1), 68–78.

Ryan, R.M. and Deci, E.L. (2002) Overview of self-determination theory: An organismic dialectical perspective, in *Handbook of Self-Determination Research* (eds E.L. Deci and R.M. Ryan), University of Rochester Press, Rochester, NY, pp. 3–33.

Ryan, R.M., Sheldon, K.M., Kasser, T. and Deci, E.L. (1996) All goals are not created equal: an organismic perspective on the nature of goals and their regulation, in *The Psychology of Action: Linking Cognition and Motivation to Behavior* (eds P.M. Gollwitzer & J.A. Bargh), Guildford Press, New York, pp. 7–26.

Ryff, C.D. (1989) Happiness is everything, or is it? Explorations in the meaning of psychological well-being. *Journal of Personality and Social Psychology*, 57 (6), 1069–1081.

Ryff, C.D. and Keyes, C.L.M. (1995) The structure of psychological well-being revisited. *Journal of Personality and Social Psychology*, 69 (4), 719–727.

Sartorius, N. (2002) Iatrogenic stigma of mental illness. *British Medical Journal*, 324 (7352), 1470–1471.

Sartorius, N., Gulbinat, W., Harrison, G., *et al.* (1996) Long-term follow-up of schizophrenia in 16 countries: A description of the international study of schizophrenia conducted by the World Health Organization. *Social Psychiatry and Psychiatric Epidemiology*, 31 (5), 249–258.

Schade, M.L., Corrigan, P.W. and Liberman, R.P. (1990) Prescriptive rehabilitation for severely disabled psychiatric patients, in *New Developments in Psychiatric Rehabilitation*, Vol. 45 (eds A. T. Meyerson and P. Solomon), Jossey-Bass, San Francisco, pp. 3–17.

Schaefer, J.A. and Moos, R.H. (1992) Life crises and personal growth, in *Personal Coping: Theory, Research, and Application* (ed. B.N. Carpenter), Praeger Publishers, Westport, CT, pp. 149–170.

Schiff, A.C. (2004) Recovery and mental illness: Analysis and personal reflections. *Psychiatric Rehabilitation Journal*, 27 (3), 212–218.

Schmook, A. (1994) They said I would never get better, in *The Experience of Recovery* (eds L. Spaniol and M. Koehler), Center for Psychiatric Rehabilitation, Boston, pp. 1–3.

Schmook, A. (1996) Recovery: A consumer/survivor vision of hope. *Psychiatric Rehabilitation Skills*, 1 (1), 12–15.

Schmook, A. (1998) What is recovery? *Recovery Corner,* Alaska Mental Health Consumer Web, Anchorage, http://akmhcweb.org/recovery/whatisrecovery.htm (retrieved 10 December 1999).

Scottish Government. (2009) *Towards a Mentally Flourishing Scotland: Policy and Action Plan 2009-2011,* Edinburgh.

Seligman, M.E.P. and Csikszentmihalyi, M. (2000) Positive psychology: An introduction. *American Psychologist,* 55 (1), 5–14.

Sells, D.J., Stayner, D.A. and Davidson, L. (2004) Recovering the self in schizophrenia: An integrative review of qualitative studies. *Psychiatric Quarterly,* 75 (1), 87–97.

Sheldon, K.M. and Elliot, A.J. (1998) Not all personal goals are personal: Comparing autonomous and controlled reasons for goals as predictors of effort and attainment. *Personality and Social Psychology Bulletin,* 24 (5), 546–557.

Sheldon, K.M. and Kasser, T. (1998) Pursuing personal goals: Skills enable progress, but not all progress is beneficial. *Personality and Social Psychology Bulletin,* 24 (12), 1040–1048.

Sheldon, K.M. and Kasser, T. (2001) Goals, congruence, and positive well-being: New empirical support for humanistic theories. *Journal of Humanistic Psychology,* 41 (1), 30–50.

Sheldon, K. and Lyubomirsky, S. (2006) How to increase and sustain positive emotion: The effects of expressing gratitude and visualizing best possible selves. *Journal of Positive Psychology,* 1 (2): 73–82.

Sheldon, K.M., Williams, G. and Joiner, T. (2003) *Self-Determination Theory in the Clinic: Motivating Physical and Mental Health,* Yale University Press, New Haven.

Shepherd, M., Watt, D., Falloon, I. and Smeeton, N. (1989) The natural history of schizophrenia: A five-year follow-up study of outcome and prediction in a representative sample of schizophrenics. *Psychological Medicine,* 15, 1–46.

Sidell, N.L. (1997) Adult adjustment to chronic illness: A review of the literature. *Health and Social Work,* 22 (1), 5–12.

Siebert, A. (2000) How non-diagnostic listening led to a rapid 'recovery' from paranoid schizophrenia: What is wrong with psychiatry? *Journal of Humanistic Psychology,* 40 (1), 34–58.

Silverstein, S.M. and Bellack, A.S. (2008) A scientific agenda for the concept of recovery as it applies to schizophrenia. *Clinical Psychology Review,* 28 (7), 1108–1124.

Singer, I. (1996) *The Creation of Value,* Vol. 1, Johns Hopkins University Press, Baltimore.

Singer, J.A. (2004) Narrative identity and meaning making across the adult life span: An introduction. *Journal of Personality,* 72 (3), 437–460.

Slade, M. (2002) What outcomes to measure in routine mental health services, and how to assess them: A systematic review. *Australian and New Zealand Journal of Psychiatry,* 36, 743–753.

Slade, M. (2009) *Personal Recovery and Mental Illness: A Guide for Mental Health Professionals.* Cambridge University Press, Cambridge.

Slade, M. and Hayward, M. (2007) Recovery, psychosis and psychiatry: Research is better than rhetoric. *Acta Psychiatrica Scandinavica,* 116 (2), 81–83.

Slade, M., Amering, M. and Oades, L.G. (2008) Recovery: An international perspective. *Epidemiologia e Psichiatria Sociale,* 17 (2), 128–137.

Slade, M., Thornicroft, G. and Glover, G. (1999) The feasibility of routine outcome measures in mental health. *Social Psychiatry and Psychiatric Epidemiology,* 34, 243–249.

Slade, M., Beck, A., Bindman, J., *et al.* (1999) Routine clinical outcome measures for patients with severe mental illness: CANSAS and HoNOS. *British Journal of Psychiatry,* 174, 404–408.

Slade, M., McCrone, P., Kuipers, E., *et al.* (2006) Use of standardised outcome measures in adult mental health services: Randomised controlled trial. *British Journal of Psychiatry* 189 (4), 330–336.

Smedslund, G. (1997) Some psychological theories are not empirical: A conceptual analysis of the 'Stages of Change' Model. *Theory and Psychology*, 7 (4), 529–544.

Snyder, C.R. (1989) Reality negotiation: From excuses to hope and beyond. *Journal of Social and Clinical Psychology*, 8 (2), 130–157.

Snyder, C.R. (1995) Conceptualizing, measuring and nurturing hope. *Journal of Counseling and Development*, 73, 355–359.

Snyder, C.R. (1998) A case for hope in pain, loss and suffering, in *Perspectives on loss: A Sourcebook* (eds J.H. Harvey, J. Omarzu and E. Miller), Taylor & Francis, Washington, DC, pp. 63–79.

Snyder, C.R. (2000a) The past and possible futures of hope. *Journal of Social and Clinical Psychology*, 29 (1), 11–28.

Snyder, C.R. (ed.) (2000b) *Handbook of Hope: Theory, Measures, and Applications*, Academic Press, San Diego, CA.

Snyder, C.R. (2002) Hope theory: Rainbows in the mind. *Psychological Inquiry*, 13 (4), 249–275.

Snyder, C.R., Irving, L. and Anderson, J.R. (1991) Hope and health: Measuring the will and the ways, in *Handbook of Social and Clinical Psychology: The Health Perspective* (eds C.R. Snyder and D.R. Forsyth), Pergamon Press, Elmsford, NY, pp. 285–305.

Snyder, C.R., Harris, C., Anderson, J.R., *et al.* (1991) The will and the ways: Development and validation of an individual-differences measure of hope. *Journal of Personality and Social Psychology*, 60 (4), 570–585.

Snyder, C.R., Sympson, S.C., Ybasco, F.C., *et al.* (1996) Development and validation of the State Hope Scale. *Journal of Personality and Social Psychology*, 70 (2), 321–335.

Snyder, C.R., Feldman, D.B., Taylor, J.D., *et al.* (2000) The roles of hopeful thinking in preventing problems and enhancing strengths. *Applied and Preventive Psychology*, 9 (4), 249–269.

Snyder, C.R., Lehman, K.A., Kluck, B. and Monsson, Y. (2006) Hope for rehabilitation and vice versa. *Rehabilitation Psychology*, 51 (2), 89–112.

Solomon, P. and Stanhope, V. (2004) Recovery: Expanding the vision of evidence-based practice. *Brief Treatment and Crisis Intervention*, 4 (4), 311–321.

Song, L. and Shih, C. (2009) Factors, process and outcomes of recovery from psychiatric disability: The Unity Model. *International Journal of Social Psychiatry*, 55 (4), 348–360.

Spaniol, L. and Gagne, C. (1997) Acceptance: Some reflections. *Psychiatric Rehabilitation Journal*, 20 (3), 75–77.

Spaniol, L., Gagne, C. and Wewiorski, N. (2002) A conceptual model for understanding and researching recovery, *Innovations in Recovery and Rehabilitation: The Decade of the Person*, Boston, Massachusetts.

Spaniol, L., Wewiorski, N., Gagne, C. and Anthony, W.A. (2002) The process of recovery from schizophrenia. *International Review of Psychiatry*, 14 (4), 327–336.

Stedman, T., Yellowlees, P., Mellsop, G., *et al.* (1997) *Measuring Consumer Outcomes in Mental Health: Field Testing of Selected Measures of Consumer Outcome in Mental Health*. Department of Health and Family Services, Canberra, ACT.

Stewart, A.L., Hays, R. and Ware, J.E. (1988) The MOS Short-Form General Health Survey, Reliability and Validity in a Patient Population. *Medical Care*, 26 (7), 724–735.

Strauss, J.S. (1989) Subjective experiences of schizophrenia: Toward a new dynamic psychiatry. II. *Schizophrenia Bulletin*, 15 (2), 179–187.

Strauss, J.S. (2005) What is the reality about severe mental disorder? in *Recovery from Severe Mental Illnesses: Research Evidence and Implications for Practice*, Vol. 1 (eds L. Davidson, C. Harding and L. Spaniol), Center for Psychiatric Rehabilitation, Boston, pp. 49–56.

Strauss, J.S., Rakfeldt, J., Harding, C.M. and Lieberman, P. (1989) Psychological and social aspects of negative symptoms. *British Journal of Psychiatry*, 155 (Supplement 7), 128–132.

Stroebe, W. and Stroebe, M.S. (1993) Determinants of adjustment to bereavement in younger widows and widowers, in *Handbook of Bereavement: Theory, Research and Intervention* (eds W. Stroebe, M.S. Stroebe and R.O. Hansson), Cambridge University Press, Cambridge, pp. 208–267.

Sullivan, H.S. (1953) *The Interpersonal Theory of Psychiatry*, W.W. Norton, New York.

Summerfield, D. (2001) Does psychiatry stigmatize? *Journal of the Royal Society of Medicine*, 94 (3), 148–149.

Tanenbaum, S.J. (2005) Evidence-based practice as mental health policy: Three controversies and a caveat. *Health Affairs*, 24 (1), 163–173.

Tanenbaum, S.J. (2008) Perspectives on evidence-based practice from consumers in the US public mental health system. *Journal of Evaluation in Clinical Practice*, 14 (5), 699–706.

Taylor, S.E. (1983) Adjustment to threatening events: A theory of cognitive adaptation. *American Psychologist*, 38 (11), 1161–1173.

Tedeschi, R.G. and Calhoun, L.G. (1995) *Trauma and Transformation: Growing in the Aftermath of Suffering*, Sage Publications, Thousand Oaks, CA.

Tedeschi, R.G., Park, C.L. and Calhoun, L.G. (1998) Posttraumatic growth: Conceptual issues, in *Posttraumatic Growth: Positive Changes in the Aftermath of Crisis* (eds L.G. Calhoun, C.L. Park and R.G. Tedeschi), Lawrence Erlbaum Associates, Mahwah, NJ, pp. 1–22.

Tenney, L.J. (2000) It has to be about choice. *Journal of Clinical Psychology, In Session*, 56 (11), 1433–1445.

Thornhill, H., Clare, L. and May, R. (2004) Escape, enlightenment and endurance: Narratives of recovery from psychosis. *Anthropology and Medicine*, 11 (2), 181–199.

Tooth, B.A., Kalyanansundaram, V. and Glover, H. (1997) *Recovery from Schizophrenia: A Consumer Perspective*, Final Report to Health and Human Services Research and Development Grants Program, Department of Health and Aged Care, Canberra.

Tooth, B.A., Kalyanasundaram, V., Glover, H. and Momenzadah, S. (2003) Factors consumers identify as important to recovery from schizophrenia. *Australasian Psychiatry*, 11 (Supplement), S70–S77.

Torgalsboen, A.-K. (2001) Consumer satisfaction and attributions of improvement among fully recovered schizophrenics. *Scandinavian Journal of Psychology*, 42 (1), 33–40.

Torrey, W.C., Rapp, C.A., Van Tosh, L., *et al.* (2005) Recovery principles and evidence-based practice: Essential ingredients of service improvement. *Community Mental Health Journal*, 41 (1), 91–100.

Tower, K.D. (1994) Consumer-centered social work practice: Restoring client self-determination. *Social Work*, 39 (2), 191–196.

Trauer, T. (2010) Outcome measurement in chronic mental illness. *International Review of Psychiatry*, 22 (2), 99–113.

Tsuang, M.T., Woolson, R.F. and Fleming, J.A. (1979) Long-term outcome of major psychoses: I. Schizophrenia and affective disorders compared with psychiatrically symptom-free surgical conditions. *Archives of General Psychiatry*, 36 (12), 1295–1301.

Turner, T. (1999) The early 1900s and before. . ., in *A Century of Psychiatry* (ed. H. Freeman), Mosby, London, pp. 2–29.

Turner-Crowson, J. and Wallcraft, J. (2002) The recovery vision for mental health services and research: A British perspective. *Psychiatric Rehabilitation Journal*, 25 (3), 245–254.

Twohig, M.P., Hayes, S.C. and Masuda, A. (2006) A preliminary investigation of acceptance and commitment therapy as a treatment for chronic skin picking. *Behaviour Research and Therapy*, 44, 1513–1522.

Unzicker, R. (1994) On my own: A personal journey through madness and re-emergence. *Psychosocial Rehabilitation Journal*, 13 (1), 71–77.

Valenstein, M.M., Adler, D.M., Berlant, J.M.D.P., *et al.* (2009) Implementing standardized assessments in clinical care: Now's the time. *Psychiatric Services*, 60 (10), 1372.

Veit, C.T. and Ware, J.E. (1983) The structure of psychological distress and well-being in general populations. *Journal of Consulting and Clinical Psychology*, 51 (5), 730–742.

Velligan, D.I. and Miller, A.L. (1999) Cognitive dysfunction in schizophrenia and its importance to outcome: The place of atypical antipsychotics in treatment. *The Journal of Clinical Psychiatry*, 60 (Supplement), 25–29.

Vogeley, K., Kurthen, M., Falkai, P. and Maier, W. (1999) Essential functions of the human self model are implemented in the prefrontal cortex. *Consciousness and Cognition*, 8 (3), 343–363.

Wagnild, G.M. and Young, H.M. (1993) Development and psychometric evaluation of the Resilience Scale. *Journal of Nursing Measurement*, 1 (2), 165–178.

Waller, B.N. (2005) Responsibility and health. *Cambridge Quarterly of Healthcare Ethics*, 14 (2), 177–188.

Warner, R. (2004) *Recovery from Schizophrenia: Psychiatry and Political Economy*, 3rd edn, Brunner-Routledge, New York.

Warner, R. (2009) Recovery from schizophrenia and the recovery model. *Current Opinion in Psychiatry*, 22 (4), 374–380.

Waterman, A.S. (1984) Identity formation: Discovery or creation? *Journal of Early Adolescence*, 4 (4), 329–341.

Waterman, A.S. (1993) Finding something to do or someone to be: A eudaimonist perspective on identity formation, in *Discussions on Ego Identity* (ed. J. Kroger), Lawrence Erlbaum, Hillsdale, NJ, pp. 147–167.

Watson, B.E. (1994) My self story, in *The Experience of Recovery* (eds L. Spaniol and M. Koehler), Center for Psychiatric Rehabilitation, Boston, pp. 68–75.

Weeks, G., Slade, M. and Hayward, M. (2010) A UK validation of the Stages of Recovery Instrument [Electronic Version]. *International Journal of Social Psychiatry*, http://isp.sagepub.com/content/early/2010/04/08/0020764010365414.abstract

Weiner, I.B. (1966/1997) *Psychodiagnosis in Schizophrenia*. Lawrence Erlbaum Associates, Mahwah, NJ.

Weingarten, R. (1994) The risks and rewards of advocacy, in *The Experience of Recovery* (eds L. Spaniol and M. Koehler), Center for Psychiatric Rehabilitation, Boston, pp. 77–78.

Weingarten, R. (2005) Calculated risk-taking and other recovery processes for my psychiatric disability. *Psychiatric Rehabilitation Journal*, 29 (1), 77–80.

Wentworth, V.R. (1994) From both sides: The experience of a psychiatric survivor and psychotherapist, in *The Experience of Recovery* (eds L. Spaniol and M. Koehler), Center for Psychiatric Rehabilitation, Boston, pp. 80–88.

Whitehorn, D., Brown, J., Richard, J., *et al.* (2002) Multiple dimensions of recovery in early psychosis. *International Review of Psychiatry*, 14 (4), 273–283.

Whitwell, D. (1999) The myth of recovery from mental illness. *Psychiatric Bulletin*, 23, 621–622.

Whitwell, D. (2000) Recovery as a medical myth. *Psychiatric Bulletin*, 25 (2), 75.

Wilding, C., May, E. and Muir-Cochrane, E. (2005) Experience of spirituality, mental illness and occupation: A life-sustaining phenomenon. *Australian Occupational Therapy Journal*, 52 (1), 2–9.

Williams, C.C. and Collins, A.A. (1999) Defining new frameworks for psychosocial intervention. *Psychiatry*, 62 (1), 61–78.

Williams, G.C. (2000) Improving patients' health through supporting the autonomy of patients and providers, in *Handbook of Self-Determination Research* (eds E.L. Deci and R.M. Ryan), University of Rochester Press, Rochester, NY, pp. 233–254.

Wing, J.K. (1999) Eugen Bleuler (1857–1939), in *A Century of Psychiatry* (ed. H. Freeman), Mosby, London, pp. 53–54.

Wing, J.K., Cooper, J.E. and Sartorius, N. (1974) *The Measurement and Classification of Psychiatric Symptoms*, Cambridge University Press, Cambridge.

Wing, J., Beevor, A., Curtis, R., *et al.* (1998) Health of the Nation Outcome Scales (HoNOS): Research and development. *British Journal of Psychiatry*, 172, 11–18.

Wolstencroft, K., Oades, L., Caputi, P. and Andresen, R. (2010) Development of a structured interview schedule to assess stage of psychological recovery from enduring mental illness. *International Journal of Psychiatry in Clinical Practice*, 14 (3), 182–189.

World Health Organization (1948) *International Classification of Diseases, Injuries and Causes of Death*, 6th edn, Geneva.

World Health Organization (1973) *The International Pilot Study of Schizophrenia*, Vol. 1, Geneva.

World Health Organization (1979) *Schizophrenia: An International Follow-Up Study*, John Wiley & Sons, Inc, New York.

World Health Organization (1992) *International Classification of Diseases and other Health Related Problems*, 10th Revision, Geneva.

Yamada, S. and Suzuki, K (2007) Application of Empowerment Scale to patients with schizophrenia: Japanese experience. *Psychiatry and Clinical Neurosciences*, 61, 594–601.

Young, S.L. and Ensing, D.S. (1999) Exploring recovery from the perspective of people with psychiatric disabilities. *Psychiatric Rehabilitation Journal*, 22 (3), 219–231.

Young, S.L., Ensing, D.S. and Bullock, W.A. (1999) *The Mental Health Recovery Measure*, Department of Psychology, University of Toledo, OH.

Zautra, A.J. (2009) Resilience: One part recovery, two parts sustainability. *Journal of Personality*, 77 (6), 1935–1943.

Zubin, J., Magaziner, J. and Steinhauer, S.R. (1983) The metamorphosis of schizophrenia: From chronicity to vulnerability. *Psychological Medicine*, 13, 551–571.

Index

acceptance of illness, agentic vs. resigned, 74

'action' stage, 87–101. *see also* Rebuilding stage

activity(ies), in Rebuilding stage, 89–90, 93

adolescence, schizophrenia beginning in, 4

Adult State Hope Scale, 133

age, as factor in cross-cultural differences in schizophrenia, 12

agency
  in hope theory, 140–41
  in Rebuilding stage, 90
  responsibility and, 57

agentic self, 74

aloneness, existential, resilience and, 99

American Psychiatric Association (APA), 6

antipsychotic(s), in schizophrenia recovery, 15

APA. *see* American Psychiatric Association (APA)

apathy, as stage of loss of hope, 55–6

arbitrary grouping, in cross-cultural differences in schizophrenia, 12

attrition pattern, in cross-cultural differences in schizophrenia, 11

authentic self, in Growth stage, 107–109

autointoxication, schizophrenia due to, 4

autonomous goals, in positive psychology relevant to recovery, 141, 144

autonomous steps, in Preparation stage, 79–81

autonomy
  independence vs., 106

in personal treatment and rehabilitation decisions, 59

in recovery from serious mental illness, 71–2

avolition, schizophrenia and, 55

awakening, followed by building healthy interdependence, 43

awareness, as recovery stage, 46, 47

Awareness stage, 67–76
  emotions in, 69–70
  goal in, 69–70
  hope in, 67–70
  identity in, 72–4
  meaning in, 74–6
  overview of, 67
  responsibility in, 70–72

behaviour(s)
  goal-directed, lack of, schizophrenia and, 55
  self-defeating, changing of, 91

benefit-finding, in loss, 84

bias(es)
  methodological sources of, in cross-cultural differences in schizophrenia, 11–12
  sampling, in schizophrenia recovery, 14–17

Bleuler, Eugen, in history of schizophrenia, 4–7

Camberwell Assessment of Need Short Appraisal Schedule (CANSAS), 127

Psychological Recovery: Beyond Mental Illness, First Edition.
Retta Andresen, Lindsay G. Oades and Peter Caputi.
© 2011 John Wiley & Sons, Ltd. Published 2011 by John Wiley & Sons, Ltd.